Preface

Generations of writers have sought creative stimulation by traveling abroad. Before the age of mass communications, the travel book was the principal means through which many would-be travelers endured hardships, sampled the exotic, or vicariously experienced the unknown. Even today, authors such as Bruce Chatwin and Paul Thoreaux search out material for their work in extensive foreign travel to exotic spots. Other writers not only travel abroad but live there as well, becoming, like Gore Vidal or V.S. Naipaul, expatriates for professional or personal reasons. In every generation, too, is a smaller number of literary figures who leave their native lands not to travel or to live, but to become involved in a foreign cause. Lord Byron achieved enduring fame in the early nineteenth century for his participation in the Greek Revolution as did André Malraux a century later for his exploits in the Spanish Civil War. This latter group is, in many ways, the most interesting; for there has always been something both puzzling and alluring about writers as activists, especially when they have directed their efforts toward foreign causes.

This desire to aid others by participating in foreign causes transcends eras and nationalities. In its most universal meaning it is often as much an outgrowth of the emotional and irrational side of the mind as it is a product of reasoning. Some men and women join a foreign cause for well-conceived and clearly defined motives; others do so for reasons far

more difficult to identify. Like Henri Rousseau's "La Bohemienne En-
dormie," they often find themselves in a certain place without quite
knowing how or why. Even Lord Byron did not try to explain his reasons for going to Greece. In a letter to Thomas Moore in 1823 he wrote
simply, "When the proper moment to be of some use arrived, I came
here. . . ."

Although the desire to act abroad extends to all classes and professions, this study is concerned with the activities of one particular group
—modern American writers—who became involved in the turmoil of
foreign causes. In spite of similarities and shared concerns, these American writer activists often differ in motivation and approach from their
counterparts in other countries. Thus while recognizing that the willingness to act abroad in a foreign cause is a universal impulse, as true for
Lord Byron and Malraux as for Hemingway and Pound, this study will
concentrate on the American experience alone. In doing so it will show
how the personalities and interests, as well as the difficulties associated
with being writers in America, shaped the foreign involvements of
eleven modern American writers.

In writing this book I have incurred a number of debts which I wish to
acknowledge. The Marshall University Foundation provided two summer research grants, and the Office of the Provost donated financial
assistance for the final typing of the manuscript. I would also like to
thank the librarians of the University of Tennessee, the Ohio State
University, and Marshall University Libraries as well as the staff, of the
other libraries where I did my research.

Ralph W. Haskins provided both counsel and encouragement during
the early stages of the project, and to him I wish to express my deepest
appreciation. I am also grateful to Joan Adkins, Clay McNearney,
Jeffrey Williams, and Michael Galgano for their critical and insightful
reading of portions of the manuscript, and to Robert Bremner and
Lenny Deutsch for being kind enough to read the entire manuscript.
Further, I owe my thanks to Tony Outhwaite and Leona Capeless of
Oxford University Press for their suggestions and encouragement.

DISTANT OBLIGATIONS

Modern American Writers and Foreign Causes

David C. Duke

New York   Oxford
OXFORD UNIVERSITY PRESS
1983

Copyright © 1983 by David C. Duke

Library of Congress Cataloging in Publication Data

Duke, David C.
Distant obligations.

1. Authors, American—20th century—Political
activity.   2. Americans—Foreign countries.
3. United States—Relations—Foreign countries.
4. Politics and literature.   5. Authors, American
—20th century—Biography.   6. History, Modern—
20th century.   I. Title.
PS129.D84   810'.9'358   82-7866
ISBN 0-19-503221-7   AACR2

Grateful acknowledgment is made to the following individuals, publishers, institutions, and libraries for permission to quote material identified in the text.

The Hoover Institution Archives at Stanford University as the repository of the Charles Beach Boothe Collection and the Joshua B. Powers Collection.

Elizabeth H. Dos Passos for material from the John Dos Passos Archives in the Alderman Library of the University of Virginia at Charlottesville.

The Harvard University Library Archives for material from the reports of the Harvard Class of 1874 concerning Ernest Fenollosa.

George Fischer for material from the Louis Fischer Papers at Princeton University.

Jean Frank for material from the Waldo Frank Collection in the Library of the University of Pennsylvania.

New Directions Publishing Corporation for permission to quote from the following copyrighted material by Ezra Pound: *Selected Prose 1909–1965* (Copyright © 1973 by the Estate of Ezra Pound); *"Ezra Pound Speaking": Radio Speeches of World War II* (Copyright © 1978 by the Trustees of the Ezra Pound Literary Property Trust). Previously unpublished material by Ezra Pound, Copyright © 1983 by the Trustees of the Ezra Pound Literary Property Trust; used by permission of New Directions Publishing Corporation, agent for the Trust.

The University of Chicago for permission to quote from Ezra Pound's letter of November 25, 1934, to Morton D. Zabel in the Morton D. Zabel Papers in the University of Chicago Library.

The Yale University Library for material from Ezra Pound and Edith Wharton in the Collection of American Literature of the Beinecke Rare Book and Manuscript Library at Yale University.

The Houghton Library of Harvard University for material from the Fenollosa, Wharton, Seeger, Reed, Dos Passos, and Pound Collections.

Printing (last digit): 9 8 7 6 5 4 3 2 1
Printed in the United States of America

0195032217

6000503716

Finally, there are two persons without whose assistance the book could not have been completed. My friend and colleague, Donna Spindel, has undoubtedly read through the work more times than she would like to remember, and her criticisms and editing have proven to be indispensable. And lastly and most importantly, my wife, Rainey, has very often taken time from her own busy career to assist me with mine. This book has benefitted enormously from the suggestions and criticisms of the above scholars, but I alone am responsible for its errors.

November 1982 D.C.D.

Contents

DISTANT OBLIGATIONS

1

Motivation and Inspiration

> *Intellectuals do not like one of their number being involved in action; but if he makes a success of it they are more curious about him than about anyone else.*
>
> André Malraux
> *The Walnut Trees of Altenburg*

AMERICA HAS CLEARLY had her writer activists. Like Byron and Malraux they too have longed to be on the spot—to participate in a foreign cause rather than merely share its ideals or try to aid it from a distance. These American writer activists may not be as romantically heralded or universally admired as either the English poet or the French novelist, but they too have devoted a portion of their lives and careers to foreign causes. Their lives span much of the twentieth century, and through their activities abroad they have participated in many of the great events that shape the modern world.

Although acting within an already established historical and literary tradition, none of these American writers saw themselves as latter-day Byrons or self-consciously linked their activities abroad to those of past figures who had joined a foreign cause. But all chose, despite the variety of their motivations and interests, to act rather than to write. Thus the desire to act is the link which holds together the diverse group of eleven writers studied here. Each biography examines the purpose and direction of its subject's activities and the influences which led to his or her participation abroad. Modern writers alone are considered because they seem to be more conscious of belonging to a specific profession than do writers of earlier periods, and they are more uncertain of the relationship between their profession and their society.

The term *writer* is used in the broadest sense to include all who earned or attempted to earn at least a part of their livelihoods with a pen—poets, novelists, journalists, and critics. The literary men and the woman chosen for this study are: Ernest Fenollosa, Homer Lea, Edith Wharton, Alan Seeger, Malcolm Cowley, John Reed, Louis Fischer, John Dos Passos, Ernest Hemingway, Waldo Frank, and Ezra Pound.[1] These individuals were selected because of the unique intertwining of their personal lives and foreign commitments and for the nature and diversity of their acitivities. They were involved in the modernization of Japan, two world wars, the Chinese, Russian, and Fascist Revolutions, the Zionist independence movement, and the Spanish Civil War. While participating in these events, they embraced socialism, fascism, communism, anarchism, militarism, internationalism, social credit, and religious mysticism of both East and West.

Ernest Fenollosa and Homer Lea, for example, were among many Americans interested in the political and cultural affairs of the Far East before World War I. What truly sets them apart from other writers, however, was the way in which their interests led to active involvements abroad. Fenollosa became a Commissioner of Fine Arts in the Imperial Japanese Government and Lea a military adviser to the Chinese revolutionary, Sun Yat-sen. Although the activities and interests of the two differed greatly, they both emerged from their involvements with a world perspective somewhat ahead of its time. Each was impressed, though for different reasons, with modern Japan. More important, however, each was convinced that the Pacific would soon rival the Atlantic in world affairs.

An event that hastened the process anticipated by Lea and Fenollosa was also alluring to dozens of American writers. So many, in fact, participated in World War I in such a variety of ways that it is difficult to generalize. Three such writers—Edith Wharton, Alan Seeger, and Malcolm Cowley—were selected for study because of their different ages, backgrounds, and careers. They were also chosen because their reasons for involvement in the war were as different as their activities. Finally, the three make interesting case studies because of the effect the war had upon their lives—an effect that continued to separate the generations during the postwar period.

An impressive number of American writers also rushed off to Russia after 1917 to see if, in the words of one enthusiastic observer, the future worked. John Reed was among the first to do so. Unlike the majority of those who dutifully made the pilgrimage but did no more than observe, Reed participated. The only writer in this study who joined the Communist party, Reed was active in Russia in a way that was always Janus-faced. Never intending to immerse himself totally in the Russian cause, he hoped instead to rebuild America on the principles of the Russian Revolution.

Recently described as the last great cause of the modern period, the Spanish Civil War attracted a number of writers seeking to give their moral support to the besieged Republic.[2] Louis Fischer was among the first American writers to go. His commitment took a practical turn when he joined the International Brigade and became its quartermaster. Yet Fischer's involvement in the Republican cause marked the last step in a career abroad which began in Palestine, continued briefly in the Soviet Union, and finally ended in Spain. It was this diversity in his activities and the constant tension between his journalistic professionalism and his political commitments that make Fischer a crucial figure in any study of American writer-activists in the modern period.

Two better-known writers who also went to Spain were Ernest Hemingway and John Dos Passos. Both men went to the defense of the Republic in their capacity as writers. They initially planned to use their familiarity with the country, their friendship with one another, and a shared interest in cinematography to produce a film celebrating the Republican cause. The film was eventually completed and shown in both the United States and Spain. But it ended the friendship between Dos Passos and Hemingway, for their shared love of Spain failed to temper the violent disagreements that grew out of their mutual commitments to this foreign cause.

Waldo Frank and Ezra Pound are the final two writers examined in this study, and each suffered greatly for his voluntary involvement in World War II. Frank is an attractive subject in terms of his activities in Latin America, his belief in hemispheric unity, and the symbiotic relationship between his career and his commitment to a foreign cause. Although his activities abroad were among the most intellectually oriented of all the writers examined, the savage beating that he received at the end of a wartime speaking tour in Argentina suggests that ideas, effectively conveyed, are often feared as much as weapons. Ideas were also the hallmark of Ezra Pound's involvement in Fascist Italy, and Pound too paid a heavy price for his activities. He was arrested at the war's end and confined for twelve years in a hospital for the mentally ill. The question of his sanity is inextricably tied to his need to immerse himself in a foreign cause, but so was his belief that his literary talents would equip him well for non-literary activities. In this respect, Pound was much like other writers who felt the same.

In summary, the men and women briefly discussed above were selected for this study because their varying interests involved them in a broad variety of foreign causes, and their involvement, as it developed, drew on an unusually diverse set of backgrounds and beliefs.

Taken together, the lives of eleven American writers studied here represent, in a sense, a paradox. Why would writers, whose very strength is their pen, abandon the world of letters for the world of action? Having made this choice, why would they then leave a familiar homeland and instead participate in the tumultuous events of a foreign nation? Perhaps the answer lies in the need for writers, especially American writers, to shape the world in which they live, a need never satisfied by observation alone. The efforts of writers of the past to impose their will on the world suggests "an organic relation between the writer and his world," and also implies "that if he was to 'regenerate' or 'redeem' this world he must impose upon it his own values."[3] Some writers attempt to mold their world primarily through writing. Others have tried different means.

Why some writers join a foreign cause rather than only write about it is a question which touches on the essence of their motivation. If, as David Potter argues, the individual responds to general ideas in very personal ways, the general and personal influences in the lives of these eleven American writers provided the framework for their action.[4] For these American writers the intertwining threads of disillusionment, guilt, and idealistic commitment became the dominant forces which drew them abroad and led them to act. Yet disillusionment, guilt, and idealism are general ideas which as one writer suggests can be the least compelling on the personal level: "The real events that influence our lives don't announce themselves with brass trumpets but come in softly, on the feet of doves. We don't think in headlines, it's the irrelevant detail that dreams out the plot."[5] The very diversity of the backgrounds, ages, times, and intellectual interests of the writers examined in this study suggests that the "irrelevant detail" which also influenced their commitments abroad may well lie hidden in the complexities of their lives and personalities. Thus, in an effort to understand both the general and personal levels of foreign commitment of these American writers, a biographical approach is used as a method of study.

The mood which captured the minds and hearts of so many American writers and drew them overseas, was as complex as their varying responses to it. These writers were not on a holiday in a foreign country or a walking tour to learn about, sympathize with, or become more inclined toward an alien landscape, people or culture. Tourism, which can be a kind of "moral rest," is the complete antithesis of a mood which demands deep personal involvement.[6] Nor were these writers expatriates. Living in a foreign country, throwing away one's passport, being more French than the French, or expressing a sense of moral indignation by accepting a self-imposed exile from one's native country do not explain the motivations of the subjects of this study. Edith Wharton, Hart Crane, Henry Miller, and Ezra Pound all expatriated themselves for varying periods from their native country while maintaining their American citizenship. All four believed that their literary talents could flourish best outside the United States. But, whereas Crane and Miller remained literary expatriates, content to live and write abroad, not so Wharton and Pound. These two self-exiled writers also actively committed themselves to causes in the countries in which they were living. During the First World War, Wharton believed the needs of

France were her own and actively aided the war effort. Pound likewise donated his services to Italy during World War II, becoming a traitor in the process. The commitments and activities of these two writers set them apart from writers like Crane and Miller, turning them, in the process, from observers into participants, from American expatriates into American activists.

Yet expatriatism and travel abroad did affect the foreign commitments of a number of the writers in this study. Fenollosa, Wharton, Seeger, and Pound, for example, all became involved in the affairs of a foreign country in which they were living. Reed was a journalist in Russia when he became involved in the Revolution, and Fischer was stationed in Palestine as a soldier in the British army when he temporarily walked away from his military duties to support the Zionist cause. Fischer's later presence in Russia at the time of the Purge Trials had much to do with his rushing off to the Spanish Civil War to participate in a cause in which he could still believe. Hemingway and Dos Passos, on the other hand, had traveled extensively in Spain before their commitment there in 1937, and there is no way of separating their activities in Spain from their love of that country and its people. Frank also traveled widely throughout Argentina on a triumphant lecture tour some thirteen years before becoming actively involved there during World War II. By the time of his return in 1942, he no longer viewed Argentina as a foreign country, but as a kind of intellectual second home.

Travel is, in fact, so closely related to the foreign involvement of these writers that only three of the eleven, in part because of their youth, had not previously lived in or at least visited the areas of their commitment. Cowley was barely nineteen when he left Harvard for Europe in 1917; and, like so many of his generation, he was going aboard for the first time. Fischer was only slightly older when he first became involved, but poverty as well as age contributed to his provincialism. His interest in Zionism actually began at home, and he joined the Jewish Legion in 1917 to get to Palestine and to escape the ghetto. Like Fischer, Lea's first foreign commitment also began in the United States when he met and then supported revolutionary exiles from China.

The relationship between travel and involvement in a foreign cause suggests that some of these writers sought adventure and the irresistible enchantment of the distant and exotic. Certainly there is something far more alluring in a cause in China or Russia than in one's own backyard, and the attraction of the unfamiliar—the remote—is a siren song tugging on the imagination of writers of all generations. Closely related to the magnetism of the adventurous and exotic is the writer's unceasing search for copy. The same enthusiasm that brought writers to the Left Bank or Bloomsbury also led them to search for the great work in the turmoil of the great event. Seeger and Cowley were interested in World War I for many reasons, but foremost among their concerns as potential writers was a desire to see firsthand the most cataclysmic event of their young lives. Reed first rushed off to Russia as a journalist to report on the Revolution. The fact that he eventually became involved in foreign revolutionary activities is what sets him apart from other members of his profession, but his initial commitment was merely to see and then report on what was happening in Russia. Hemingway, on the other hand, was always interested in war as a literary subject. Although he eventually went to Spain for political reasons, he never lost sight of the Civil War's literary potential. While there, in fact, he met André Malraux who was also in Spain fighting for the Republic, and, supposedly, they agreed to write about entirely different periods of the conflict in order to avoid competing with one another.

The experience of Waldo Frank suggests still another reason why American writers went abroad. Although a prolific writer, Frank's literary reputation in the United States did not keep pace with his output. Faced with this demoralizing situation, he first went to Latin America because his writing was always more appreciated there.

A comparison between personal commitment to a foreign cause and philanthropy provides a further clarification of the motivation of writer activists. Overseas philanthropy is "private giving for public purposes" which seeks to improve ways of life through social investment.[7] It traditionally involves fund-raising activities or the volunteering of personal services to alleviate problems abroad. Such efforts do not necessarily imply individual commitment to a cause. A philanthropist may have assisted in the great Russian famine of 1919 or raised funds for Spanish

Civil War orphans in the 1930s without sharing the ideals of either the Revolution or the Spanish Republic. Such is not the case for the writers studied here. They are not only involved in causes, but also are committed to them. The philanthropist and the activist may try to accomplish many of the same things, but their motivations and the extent of their personal involvement are fundamentally different. Herbert Hoover, for example, was a humanitarian who hated the suffering that he found in famine-stricken Russia immediately after World War I. Yet he also disliked with equal intensity the ideals of the Bolshevik Government. Not so Reed, who was as strongly committed to helping the Russian people during their time of troubles as to the principles of the Revolution itself.

Another major difference between overseas philanthropy and the writer-activist, is that the former tends to be institutional while the latter is almost always individually oriented. Also, during the last half-century private or voluntary kinds of philanthropy have become so intertwined with government-sponsored efforts that it is difficult to draw sharp distinctions between the two.[8] Certainly the Peace Corps is a recent example of how individual voluntarism has come under government control. Unlike American overseas philanthropists, the subjects of this study engaged in an unofficial kind of commitment—one, in fact, which more often grew from a disillusionment with American life than from a belief in its promise.

American writers who participate in foreign causes are not alone in their disillusionment with life at home, but an exploration of their beliefs can help to define their motivation further. Insofar as there is a human need to believe in myths, many American writers believe in the vast if unfulfilled American dream. Even while satirizing the evangelists of ballyhoo, many still see an America capable of producing the most humane, just, and prosperous society the world has ever known. Yet when the writer looks more closely at his native landscape he all too often discovers that his vision of paradise is tarnished. The faces of Tom Mooney and Leo Frank, Sacco and Vanzetti and the Scottsboro boys, the Okies, the Bonus Marchers, William Dudley Pelley, the Nisei can turn the dream of Eden into "an air-conditioned nightmare."[9] Disillusionment with the unfulfilled potential of one's society is not, of course, a trait peculiar to American writers. Yet, "the cleavage between the artist and capitalist society that runs all through the history of modern Western literature found its first expression in America in people who were themselves, as citizens, stricken by industrial capitalism and frightened by it; citizens who did not so much rebel against the new order as shrink from it."[10] Denis Brogan, an Englishman, claims that America's greatest writers are hostile toward, or at the very best, extremely critical of the quality of American life.[11] Using even stronger language, psychologist Kenneth Kenniston describes the "better" American writers as "alienated men writing about alienated heroes in an alienating society."[12] Indeed, even the most optimistically buoyant American writers have at times gloomily reflected on the ever-widening chasm between what the country is and what it could be. "In vain do we march with unprecedented strides to empire so colossal, outvying the antique, beyond Alexander's, beyond the proudest sway of Rome . . ." laments Walt Whitman in his *Democratic Vistas*. "It is as if we were somehow being endowed with a vast and more thoroughly appointed body, and then left with little or no soul."[13]

Disillusioned by apparent distortions in the American landscape, the writer may also feel a personal sense of isolation from society. Over a century ago the ever observant Alexis de Tocqueville noticed how the nation "often treats its authors as kings usually behave toward their courtiers: it enriches and despises them."[14] Tocqueville possibly overstated the issue, but many perceptive critics from Van Wyck Brooks in the first half of the century to Christopher Lasch in more recent times discuss a personal sense of isolation. If at times America's creative thinkers are treated as a valuable national resource, they are as frequently viewed as "pretentious, conceited, effeminate, and snobbish, and very likely immoral, dangerous, and subversive."[15] While evading overt hostility, the writer can simply be ignored—especially if the public finds his work to be too realistic, too pessimistic, or in conflict with the moral or intellectual consensus of the time. Whereas Melville was generally too gloomy for the opportunistic individualism of his day, Dreiser was too morally devastating for the genteel tradition which pervaded his era.

The penalties meted out in each case were in keeping with the nature of the supposed crime—neglect and censorship. Even if he receives recognition, the writer may learn that his achievements do not guarantee him any real power or influence. If indeed the writer strives to shape the world in which he lives, he will learn that his participation in certain activities such as Presidential dinners and writers' conferences are meaningless gestures without lasting influence. President Lyndon B. Johnson, for example, welcomed the nation's leading writers and intellectuals to the White House Festival of the Arts in 1965, and then lashed out at several who voiced their disapproval of the war in Vietnam. From Johnson's point of view, they had dared to meddle in affairs of state which were beyond their range of expertise.[16] In fact, the American writer is often treated more as an ornament than as a necessary part of the community. Failing to bring about change, the writer, like Ralph Ellison's invisible man, might proclaim his own invisibility.

Ironically, some writers seek invisibility as much as they try to avoid it. Rejecting society and believing that a close association with it might affect the honesty of their imaginative or critical abilities, they seek the isolated security of their own creative world. Once inside this artistic Shangri-La, however, an author may begin to suspect that withdrawal from the world prevents one from experiencing a full life.[17] In other words, the writer has the paradoxical feeling of wanting yet not wanting to be a viable part of his society. He faces the difficulty which may ultimately confront all people: "The individual is not discrete. He cannot find his fulfillment outside of the community; but he also cannot find fulfillment completely within society. In so far as he finds fulfillment within society he must abate his individual ambitions. He must 'die' to 'self' if he would truly live. Insofar as he finds fulfillment beyond every historic community he lives his life in painful tension with even the best community. . . ."[18] Recognizing that withdrawal into self may not lead to a greater sense of life, the isolated writer also discovers that he is even less able to exert any kind of influence on the world around him. Thus, the end result of his escape into self is a greater feeling of powerlessness, sharpened by a society in which the positions of power are commonly conferred upon "tough-minded" problem solvers rather than upon questioning theoreticians. For these reasons social activism rather than criticism appeals to many American writers who believe that their special abilities doom them to the periphery of their world. Max Eastman, for example, expressed his opposition to America's entry into World War I by lecturing rather than by writing newspaper editorials. The fact that he chose to voice his discontent instead of to write it is not in itself surprising, but the manner in which he rationalized his new efforts vividly shows the uneasiness he felt in his role as an American writer. "I have an overriding guilt complex, most unfortunate in a literary man, about being a mere speaker of words. I had to deliver the goods now. I had to go."[19] Such feelings of guilt and a desire to act have influenced other writers and led them to "deliver the goods" by immersing themselves in a cause which lies outside the United States, one to which the writer has shown a commitment by personally acting in its behalf.

Why some writers decide to "deliver the goods" abroad is closely related to their frustration at trying to achieve far-reaching social reform at home. This failure is also a major part of the writer's disillusionment with the promise of American life. Many observers comment on the slow pace of social change in American society, and some, like Daniel Boorstin, praise this characteristic slowness. In *The Genius of American Politics*, he writes, "It is not surprising that we have no enthusiasm for plans to make society over. We have actually made a new society without a plan. Or, more precisely why should we make a five-year plan for ourselves when God seems to have had a thousand-year plan ready-made for us?"[20] Not all interpreters of America—including writers—share Boorstin's optimism or his belief in a Divine national blueprint. Yet even his critics agree with his prediction that it will continue to be difficult to remodel American society in any significant and lasting way.[21] Quite often through experience, observation, or a combination of both, many of our most socially conscious writers discover that meaningful social change in the United States frequently comes in the wake of some national disaster, and then in the most limited ways. Social change which does evolve lacks an ideological foundation which leaves it tentative, sporadic, and without continuity.[22] Even those writers who avoid schemes aimed at social renovation and try instead to organize coal miners or challenge a business-dominated government are often discouraged by the problems they encounter or by the ephemerality of their achievements. When this sense of personal frustration is added to an already acute sense of isolation and powerlessness, it is not surprising that at least some writers question the usefulness of sustained political or social activism. Even the most appealing causes or stirring calls for social involvement can be examined by writers with a devastating skepticism. If familiarity does not necessarily breed contempt, it does, at times, breed a kind of social and political immobility disguised as resignation or cynical pragmatism. Faced with helpless frustration while trying to carry out social or political change at home, some of the writers in this study turned to a foreign cause. Thus, in turning to a form of voluntary exile, they chose to be socially active abroad. From this perspective it is argued that they did not leave their social conscience at home, but rather carried it with them to their foreign destination.

The problems which hampered a writer's efforts at home were, of course, not absent abroad. But lingual and cultural differences, remoteness, censorship, rumor—the swirling mists of turmoil—all hid many of the most glaring realities from sight. Indeed, as one critic suggests, foreigners and exiles in a foreign country are in a sense metaphors, "moving through a world of metaphors."[23] New experiences and activities must, by necessity, undergo a process of perpetual re-evaluation in terms of individual background and culture. Would not this metaphorical experience be even more fitting for many American writers whose backgrounds are often less cosmopolitan than those of writers from other parts of the world? Translation and cultural reinterpretation does not always, therefore, lead to clarity, especially if the writer is more concerned with serving a cause than studying it.

The tendency of some writers to immerse themselves uncritically in an adopted cause is also shared by other groups in American society.[24] Once convinced that their aloofness from society is responsible for their powerless position within it, intellectuals at times suspend their critical abilities. They hurriedly embrace a political party, national cause, or simply the prevailing views of the time without always questioning whether these new-found interests are consistent with earlier held moral, ethical, or social values. Moreover, they are convinced that they are not only going along with historical necessity but also affecting the course of politics. Welcoming public recognition or even power as a reward for orthodoxy, American intellectuals often maneuver themselves into the ironic position of actually justifying the very practices or ideas that they had at one time argued against.[25] Such uncritical commitment is even more likely on the part of activist writers abroad, especially since the causes or events which lead them to action are often so clouded by the dust of tumult that they cannot be clearly understood. Understanding often only comes with actual participation, and by that time criticism is willingly withheld (usually with the belief that such a moratorium is only temporary) because of the "necessities" of war, revolution, or the need for solidarity. Uncritical commitment to a cause, then, revealed in the activities of the subjects of this study, is closely related to the difficulty of being a writer or an intellectual in America.

A personal sense of isolation, disappointment with one's native country, and frustration at achieving social reform are some of the factors that have led American writers to act rather than write. Another vital motivating force is a practical kind of idealism deeply rooted in the country's intellectual tradition.[26] Although this idealistic strain defies precise definition, it is laced with a large dose of realism, more practical than ideological, and more empirical than ethereal. It is also the kind of idealism that embraces unseen goals or principles, and may even be existential in its acknowledgment of the inevitability of human frailty. This idealism is well within the pragmatic tradition. And it is also earthbound in its adherence to William James's belief that the "Knower is an actor, and coefficient of the truth on one side, whilst on the other he registers the truth which he helps create."[27] Not only do American writers then, attempt to deal with feelings of disillusionment, isolation, and powerlessness, but they also try to add meaning to existence by putting their ideas into practice. In doing so they might also be seen as naïve. Confronted by lingual, cultural, and political obstacles, their efforts often seemed futile. As strangers in strange lands, some were mistrusted by the very individuals or groups they were trying to help.

Others, in their initial enthusiasm, planned programs for themselves that went beyond the possible. Most were naïve perhaps in believing that their presence could be felt in an event as monumental as a revolution, civil war, or cultural transformation. Yet, if all of these writers shared a degree of naïveté by merely participating in a foreign cause, for many it was the kind of naïveté from which all idealism springs. It would have been easier to support a cause by joining a committee, writing an article, or signing a petition. Instead, all of these writers, as their actions show, believed that something more was needed; and all left the safety of the sidelines for the uncertainties of the fray.

It is this blend of idealism and disillusionment which makes the commitment of the writers studied here somewhat different from that discussed in Stanley Weintraub's *The Last Great Cause: The Intellectuals and the Spanish Civil War*. Using Ivan Turgenev's romantically disillusioned hero Dmitry Rudin to symbolize the intellectual's frustrated desire for commitment, Weintraub argues that there are certain events or causes (the Civil War in Spain being one) so monumental in scope and so dramatically compelling that they transport the intellectual from the world of thought to the world of action.[28] Along this journey, the intellectual experiences a sense of peace and fulfillment that has otherwise been denied. But why will the intellectual select one foreign cause over another? Weintraub's definition of Rudinism helps explain: "It is not that every foreign barricade exerts the same epic appeal, for it has never been enough that the cause be exotic or international. To hone one's pen on an epical cause—or discard the pen for a sword—requires the magnetic force of the grand, foredoomed tragedy. This is the dilemma—and the glory of Rudinism."[29] Weintraub may overemphasize despair and the lure of tragedy in explaining the magnetic attraction of the creative individual to a foreign cause. Such a one-dimensional view of commitment not only disregards social, ideological, or even moral motivations, but transforms the intellectual into a kind of Hedda Gabler, one whose despair can only be ended by a beautiful tragic gesture. None of the writers in this study were brooding Hamlets. They were as optimistically or pessimistically oriented as is mankind itself. They were moved by the existential need to act within the limitations of all human activity rather than by the need to envelop themselves in the glory of a lost cause.

If there is little of the *Götterdämmerung* mentality in the mood of the American writer activist, his idealistic sense of commitment can be tinged with feelings of guilt. Critics of American thought suggest that while many Americans, particularly writers, often detest what they see as the distortion of the American dream, they also believe themselves to be a part of what they most dislike. That is, they tend to internalize the meaning of America to the extent that they consider the country's failings or guilt to be their own.[30] Such feelings may be tied to the Puritan sense of mission which has pervaded the American experience. Sustaining this mission has been both the goal and the burden of succeeding generations who have, at times, doubted their worthiness.[31] Similar feelings of guilt might also be closely related to a belief in a kind of participatory democracy in which national policy is directly related to national will. In this sense the country's failings are personalized, since national decisions are, theoretically, the responsibility of all. A sense of guilt may likewise arise from a belief that American abundance and general well-being blind the nation to the troubles of the world or to the needs of a particular country. And, finally, guilt-laden support of a foreign cause may be closely related to what one historian describes as a national fondness for the underdog.[32] Support for an underdog can be alluring to the writer who believes that he is confronting an unmitigated evil—an evil that is either ignored or supported by his own country. Going to the aid of the Spanish Republic, for example, was lending aid to the weaker side, but it also showed a willingness to take a stand in the face of international fascism at a time when one's own country remained cautiously inactive.

Whatever the cause, the guilt felt by many American writers is a vital part of their idealistic sense of commitment. Using the terminology of Herbert Marcuse, it compels them to try to change the *is* of their perceptions to the *ought*. In this sense they often act in the same general way as the utopian socialists or the social settlement-house workers of an earlier era. They hope, in essence, that their activities will lead the way to some kind of popular involvement or national change. Even if such national emulation does not develop, the writer activist at least has attempted personally to atone for his country's wrongdoings. In this way he shows the rest of the world that all Americans are not locked into the same apathetic mold. Thus, through his foreign commitment the American writer tries to convince himself and others that there is a time to write and a time to act. While there are some writers who live solely for their work or who see their writing as a form of action, there are others who, like Granville Hicks, believe that "there are causes more important than your work."[33]

Despite the guilt and disillusionment they felt, none of the writers in this study ever completely rejected their native country. Only John Reed joined a foreign party, and only he and Ezra Pound were ever ideologically committed. And, in spite of their commitments, even these two writers were most interested in their new doctrines for future application to America. Furthermore, while several of the writers were living as expatriates before becoming actively involved in a foreign cause, none renounced American citizenship. Paradoxically, it was often their disillusionment which spurred their idealism. By acting on their own in a foreign cause, they were in a sense declaring that they understood America and its needs more clearly than did other Americans. They saw what needed to be done to preserve the American ideal from further harm. What set them even farther apart from their fellow countrymen, however, was the fact that their clarity of vision also demanded action, but action on a personal level. Certain foreign causes had to be supported even if it meant going against national policy or public opinion. In other words, by committing themselves to a foreign cause, these writers were not abandoning the promise of American life, but were hoping to make it a reality. By going to the aid of a foreign country, they hoped that their presence would make a difference. It might awaken their slumbering countrymen, atone for national guilt, or possibly even add a dimension to the meaning of America. In this respect, their involvement in a foreign cause was always Janus-faced.

Thus the participation of the writer in a foreign cause is essentially a non-ideological, voluntary form of personal involvement resulting from both personal and national feelings of disillusionment and guilt. Yet it is a kind of disillusionment and guilt that does not paralyze the writer, but activates him. Idealism rather than despair emerges and encourages the writer to act in a way that turns a foreign cause into one that becomes his own. In the process, the cause also becomes that of America, for none of these writers ever severed all ties with home, and most hoped by example to stir their countrymen to action.

Before turning to an examination of the involvements of these American writers, one additional question is worth considering: why did these writers choose one foreign cause over another? Travel, being in the right place at the right time, the lure of the exotic, a search for copy as well as a personal interest all help to explain why some causes were more alluring than others. Stephen Spender, himself a participant in a foreign cause, offers another possible explanation. He suggests that the choices may be determined by the political tradition and intellectual atmosphere in which the writers work. In attempting to explain why English and American intellectuals respond to particular causes, Spender makes a comparison between France, on the one hand, and Britain and America on the other. French intellectuals and writers, he suggests, are always politically involved in their society. Their British and American counterparts are attracted only to causes offering monumental moral contrasts of "inky black and dazzling white," which Spender believes shows a lack of a sustained political seriousness. "After all," he argues, "the shining emergent causes—Spain, the Bomb, Vietnam—do have chains of further causality stretching before and after. That the intellectuals only have time for them when they have become moral scandals might seem to indicate that they do not have time anyway. . . . The cause evaporates when the crisis in its immediate emanation has passed. The long term causes of the Cause find few among the English and American intellectuals to interest them."[34] In another context, Martin Luther King described this same syndrome when he referred to the United States as "a ten-day nation." American energy, enthusiasm, and willingness to work for lasting change usually evaporate when the glamorous or catastrophic aspects of a chain of events begin to subside. An intellectual tradition which shuns ideology in order to deal pragmatically with immediate issues might well encourage the tendencies that Spender and King describe. Similarly, the distance and obscurity of a foreign cause might also be as attractive as a ten-day cause, especially if viewed by a writer who sees his homeland as an improbable site for meaningful and lasting social change.

Not all of the foreign causes that attracted American writers were of the "shining emergent" variety. Some, like the defense of traditional Japanese art or support for the Bolsheviks were neither popularly acclaimed nor morally scandalous. The foreign involvement of writers like Homer Lea and John Reed was lifelong, and their dedication and personal commitment went far beyond the ephemerality of the ten-day cause. For writers such as Alan Seeger, Edith Wharton, and Ernest Hemingway, activities abroad represent the only sustained social commitment of their lives. Yet they were rare in their ability to combine a productive literary career with participation in the most pressing social and political problems of the day. Few writers have been willing to endure the discomforts, face the dangers, or deal with the uncertainties of participating in a foreign cause.

In attempting to understand the complex and contradictory motivations of the American writer activists, it seems poetically just to conclude with a statement from one of the most heralded modern participants in foreign causes, André Malraux. In Malraux's *The Walnut Trees of Altenburg*, one of the characters proclaims: "The greatest mystery is not that we have been flung at random between the profusion of matter and of the stars, but that within this prison we can draw from ourselves images powerful enough to deny our nothingness. And not only images, but . . . well, just look. . . ."[35] Between the stars of their own creative isolation and the matter of an indifferent society, the subjects of this study tried to define their images in meaningful ways by dedicating a part of their lives to a foreign cause. In doing so they were, in part, responding to a basic element of human nature—the need to go to the aid of one's fellow human beings. They were responding, also, to the difficulties of being writers in America, and without ever losing sight of the American dream, they could be disillusioned by its frailty.

Yet even the shared difficulties of being American writers, the motivating influences of disillusionment, guilt, and idealism, cannot fully explain the nature of their activism. Only by examining the personal needs and ambitions as well as the unique aspects of the lives of these eleven writers can their desire to act rather than write be truly understood.

2

The Chrysanthemum and the Sword

*The Orient, which they fear, is their opportunity;
to embrace that "new."*

William Carlos Williams
Autobiography

IN MARCH 1905 TWO AMERICANS—Ernest Fenollosa and Homer Lea—
were touring the United States for reasons as different as their backgrounds, careers, interests, and ages. At first glance it might appear
that the two had much in common, for each was a self-proclaimed and
self-taught "expert" in his field of interest, each had persistently tried to
direct American eyes toward Japan, and each had devoted a portion of
his life to participating actively in the Far East. Yet the nature of the
tour upon which both men were engaged symbolized just how different
their interests and activities were.

In early March 1905 Ernest Fenollosa, the lecturer, art critic,
philosopher, and former Imperial Commissioner for Fine Arts in
Japan, had just completed a series of lectures in Terre Haute, Indiana,
during which he repeatedly proclaimed the universal splendors of
Oriental and especially Japanese art.[1] Over the years a consuming
interest in the history of Japanese painting had profoundly influenced
Fenollosa. By the time of the Terre Haute lectures he was suggesting
the possibility of an eventual merging of Eastern and Western cultures.
The arts would be in the vanguard of this cultural fusion which, as he
liked to emphasize, would lead to the emergence of a new, excitingly
different, and certainly more dynamic kind of global civilization.[2]

Later that same month General Homer Lea and the exiled Chinese reformer, K'ang Yu-wei, left Los Angeles to inspect a number of Chinese military academies clandestinely established by K'ang's supporters throughout the United States. Soldiers were to be trained in these academies to assist K'ang in restoring the deposed Chinese Emperor, Kuang-hsu. Lea's activities were tied to China but he was anxious about the rapidly increasing military prowess of Japan. Convinced that Japan and the United States were on a collision course which would lead to a gigantic struggle for survival in the Pacific, he regarded a weak, divided China as an American liability and a Japanese asset. Like other nationalistic Social Darwinists such as Josiah Strong, John Fisk and Alfred Thayer Mahan, Lea believed that conflict between nations was an inevitable part of a world-wide struggle for survival. He likewise believed that the United States would have to be militarily as well as psychologically prepared to meet the challenge, and he spent much of his life trying to make sure that the necessary preparations were made.

Like Lea, Fenollosa admired Spencer's cosmic philosophy, but his world view was far more deeply influenced by a life-long infatuation with the dialectical philosophy of Hegel. From the lofty perspective of historical idealism he viewed the convergence of Oriental and Occidental civilizations with more fascination than fear and thus trod the path of cultural pluralism already taken by others such as Emerson, Thoreau, and Whitman. If Lea foresaw the meeting of East and West primarily in terms of conflict, Fenollosa believed that it would be peaceful and would lead to a brilliant new cultural synthesis. Thus, their motivations to act abroad reflected the protean blend of fear and fascination with which so many late nineteenth- and early twentieth-century Americans viewed the "mysterious" Far East.

Fenollosa's father, Francisco Ciriaco Fenollosa, emigrated to the United States from Spain in 1838, settling in Salem, Massachusetts, where he supported himself by teaching music. Thirteen years later he married Mary Silsbee, a daughter of a prominent Salem businessman, and in 1853 their first child, Ernest Francisco, was born, followed by a second son a year later. The two boys attended the Hacker Grammar

School in the city and continued their education at Salem High School, which Ernest entered in 1866. Four years later, after excelling on the qualifying examinations, Ernest entered Harvard as a philosophy major. Among the relatively few students who had entered Harvard via the public schools, Fenollosa found himself outside the university's social whirl; he devoted his time mostly to studies, choral groups, and writing poetry. He graduated Phi Beta Kappa with honors in philosophy, and was awarded a two-year graduate fellowship in his major.[3] After completing his graduate work, including an additional year spent in the Harvard Divinity School, his interests began to shift, and by the spring of 1877 he was studying art history at the Massachusetts Normal School while taking painting classes at the Boston Museum of Fine Arts.[4] Fenollosa was engaged in these new pursuits for a little less than a year when he was offered an academic position that was as exciting as it was unexpected.

The offer came indirectly through another New Englander, Edward Sylvester Morse, who was to become as well known an authority on Japanese pottery as Fenollosa was on Japanese art. A self-educated naturalist, Morse had gone to Japan in the spring of 1877 to further his study of brachipods. Japanese authorities were so impressed by the ability and energy displayed by the New Englander that they asked if he would create a department of zoology at Tokyo's Imperial University and also help establish a national museum of natural history.[5] The University's president asked Morse if he could recommend other American scholars, especially a scientist and a philosopher who would be willing to join the university's faculty. Morse had no difficulty in suggesting the name of several scientists, but sought outside assistance with respect to the philosopher. When he wrote his friend, President Charles Eliot Norton of Harvard, Ernest Fenollosa was recommended as one of the most recently graduated and highly qualified philosophy majors.[6]

When the offer was made to Fenollosa, both his parents had died and he had no other ties binding him to New England. His financial situation was precarious and he had no immediate prospects for employment. To suggest that Fenollosa was disillusioned with the promise of American life as were so many other writers of the time is perhaps overstating the case. Yet Fenollosa had always been an outsider at Harvard, and must have realized that despite his academic qualifications, as a first-generation American he lacked the social mobility of most of his fellow classmates. In addition, some years earlier a high school romance had been broken off, at least in Fenollosa's mind, because of his lack of social position, and now, ten years later, in the best tradition of a Thackerayan character, he was still persistently courting the same girl—Lizze Millett.[7] If the promise of a regular salary in a country having a lower cost of living made marriage to the daughter of a prominent family financially feasible, the fact that his professorship was to be far removed from the scrutiny of Salem and Boston society quite possibly also made the marriage more socially palatable for all concerned. In any case, after signing a two-year contract Fenollosa married his high school sweetheart and the couple sailed for Japan in the spring of 1878. What began as a new career for the young philosopher unexpectedly turned into active involvement in Japanese affairs.

Fenollosa entered Japan during a transitional period in the country's history. Beginning in the early years of the Meiji Restoration and building to a crescendo during the early 1880s, a growing chorus of diverse elements of the population were calling for rapid Westernization of traditional Japanese society. The desire for modernization was so widespread, according to Edwin O. Reischauer, that during this period the Japanese more or less viewed the rest of the world as a gigantic classroom.[8] Accompanying this changing world view was the belief that an effective educational system was one of the most fundamental prerequisites for rapid modernization. As a result, Imperial authorities were anxious for Occidental teachers to share their pedagogical techniques with the newly organized government-sponsored schools.[9] It was to just such a school that Fenollosa came in 1878 when he joined the newly reconstructed Imperial University in Tokyo as a professor of political philosophy.

In spite of vast cultural differences, Fenollosa found his classroom teaching to be exciting. Language was no barrier in that his students were expected to have a proficiency in English before entering his class.[10] The first year he offered courses in political philosophy, the history of philosophy, and political economy; a year later he added two additional philosophy courses which gave him a fifteen-hour teaching load.[11] Delighted by the receptivity of his students, Fenollosa expressed enthusiasm in a letter to the Harvard class secretary: "A finer set of young men, or more earnest workers and keener thinkers, cannot, I venture to say, be found in any university in the world."[12] University officials were equally pleased with the performance of the young New Englander, and renewed his contract in 1880, 1882, and 1884 while allowing him to limit his teaching to courses in philosophy and logic. When not engaged in academic duties, Fenollosa, like other visiting professors, was frequently asked to lecture before equally enthusiastic public audiences. Yet teaching and lecturing were not the only activities in which he was engaged, and what began as a purely casual interest in Japanese art soon developed into a genuine enthusiasm which would ultimately lead to extensive participation in Japanese cultural affairs.

While sightseeing in and around Tokyo, Fenollosa began to collect a variety of *objets d'art* such as *kakemonos*, folding screens, and prints. As his collection grew, so did his interest, but when he showed his acquisitions to a fellow Harvard alumnus and former Japanese noble, Lentaro Kaneko, he was disappointed to learn that practically all of his paintings were pallid imitations of great but forgotten masterpieces.[13] Since there was no museum to which Kaneko could take Fenollosa, he arranged instead a visit to his former lord, Marquis Kuroda, whose ancestral collection contained several originals of the old masters. Unknown to Fenollosa, Kuroda had not wanted to show his collection to a Westerner. In fact, he had been even less willing to show it to an American, believing, as he told Kaneko, "This art is beyond his reach."[14] Kuroda's prediction proved to be wrong, however, for Fenollosa was enthralled by the boldness of line, the subtle use of color, and the beauty he discovered in the works of such traditionalists as Sesshu, Hishikawa Moronobu, Maruyama Okyo, and others. He returned for a second and then a third viewing. By the end of the visits, the young professor was so intellectually stimulated by what he had seen that he was determined to learn as much as possible about the artistic heritage behind the paintings.

Fenollosa's desire to study Japanese painting proved to be far more difficult than he had anticipated. Time-consuming teaching requirements occupied most of the week. When time was available there was no English-language source to which he could turn, and his inability to speak or read Japanese made the task appear impossible. Yet in spite of handicaps, his enthusiasm was so infectious that doors were soon being opened to him that might normally have been closed to most Occidentals. Encouraged by the progress he was making, he began to spend every spare moment visiting shrines, temples, and private collections around Tokyo in order to examine and sketch their hidden treasures. This initial program of study received its most important boost in 1879 when he was introduced by Morse's interpreter to the famous Kano family, whose school of painting dated back to the fifteenth century. Before the year ended, he was being instructed in the development of Oriental art from the family's head, Eitoku Kano, and was also allowed to use rare source materials pertaining to the lives of famous Japanese artists which were in the family's possession.[15] A short time later another unique opportunity arose when the patriarch of the equally famous Tosa family personally introduced him to the exquisitely decorative styles of the Yomato and Tosa schools. Although Fenollosa was devoting more of his energies to these new interests, it was only during vacation periods that he could travel throughout the country in search of new discoveries. The summers of 1880, 1881, and 1882 were devoted, as he later recalled, to touring the interior of Japan "unearthing and identifying in temples treasures of painting and sculpture that had been misnamed by the uncritical historians of the last two centuries and had become forgotten and neglected since the revolution of 1868."[16] Exasperated by the difficulties of systematically examining these masterpieces, Fenollosa decided to begin a collection of his own. He was now collecting with a specific purpose in mind, and explained the pragmatic nature of his new endeavors in a letter to his class secretary at Harvard:

But my chief purpose in collecting had been to illustrate history; and into the collection of materials for a true history of the art of the East I plunged eagerly after 1880. This implied far more than a knowledge of technical details; and I swept into my drag-net varied but classified facts of political history, biography, literature, folklore and traditions, local customs and especially, since it played such a part, in subjects of religion. For many years I had secretaries at work selecting and translating passages from the original books, Chinese and Japanese; and, since they were largely my own graduates in philosophy, they understood well the needs of my historical method.[17]

During the summer of 1882 Fenollosa was joined by Morse and another New Englander, Sturgis Bigelow. Together the three leisurely wandered through many of the southern provinces, with Bigelow searching for sword guards and lacquer, Morse examining the varieties of local pottery, and Fenollosa avidly continuing his study and collection of Japanese painting.[18]

If the summer of 1882 was idyllic in most respects, Fenollosa's growing concern that Japan was losing touch with its ancient artistic tradition had a dampening effect upon many of his activities. Over the years he had become increasingly aware of how the surging tide of Westernization threatened numerous aspects of traditional Japanese civilization. He had likewise observed that often anything tied to either the past or to Eastern cultures was ignored or actively shunned out of a growing national feeling that both somehow symbolized weakness, decadence, and past failures. Such rejection of traditional culture was frequently accompanied by an uncritical imitation of Western tastes and standards which, in Fenollosa's opinion, was no place more blatantly obvious than in the arts:

After the fall of the Shogunate and of native patronage in 1868, the masters starved; only the poorer workman found employment in cheap production for the foreign market. Along with brick and stucco architecture, French clocks, and crimson carpets, it was deemed necessary to import Italian painters and sculptors to educate a new generation of "civilized artists." For nearly a decade large classes of young men trained in crayon drawing from Greek casts, in oil studies of models

with blurry drapery, and in marble madonnas, were turned loose upon
a wondering community to perpetuate travesties of European salons.
It became a disgrace to exhibit a sign of "barbarous" oriental feeling.[19]

The young New Englander's awareness of this disturbing phenomenon
along with his growing appreciation of Japan's cultural heritage—a
heritage that he deemed second to none in the world—so affected him
over the next few years that he became a self-appointed critic attempting to awaken the country to the brilliance of its ancient artistic traditions.

Fenollosa was by no means the first to criticize this widespread
rejection of traditional art and culture. By the late 1870s there were
already a number of groups and individuals calling for the preservation of traditional Japanese civilization. One of the most active of
these organizations was the Ryuehi Society, formed in 1879 to promote and exhibit the traditional schools of Japanese painting.[20]
Important as this society and similar organizations were, it was the
voice of the young American which gradually rose above the others
to become a rallying point for all those who supported Japanese-style
painting. Ironic as it may seem, it was primarily because he was a
Westerner, with all the prestige such a position engendered, that
undoubtedly made many Japanese receptive to his advice even though
he was calling for a thoroughgoing repudiation of Western influences
on Japanese art. Fenollosa launched his defense of traditional Japanese painting in a speech given in May 1882 before a largely aristocratic audience at the Ueno Educational Museum in Tokyo. The
speech, which has been called one of the most significant addresses
by any foreigner during the entire Meiji period, was entitled "Bijutsu
Shinsetsu" or the "True Theory of Japanese Art."[21] More a philippic
than a scholarly presentation, the boldness of the speech must have
astounded this patrician audience, especially when the young American chided them for neglecting one of their most irreplaceable birth-
rights:

> When traditional Japanese painting and Japanese painting in the
> European style are compared on the basis of aesthetic principles,

there is no question about the superiority of the former over the latter. Why do you Japanese people strive to imitate the European-style paintings when you have such excellent paintings of your own? European paintings are becoming more and more realistic and scientific and are declining artistically. The west, in its efforts to find a way to overcome this crisis, is actually turning its eyes to your traditional Japanese art to learn what it can. You Japanese people, therefore, must recognize the virtues of your own painting and do what you can to put new life into it. If only this is done, the value of your traditional Japanese paintings will be universally recognized in the next few years.[22]

The speech almost immediately triggered a response from individuals within government circles who agreed with the critic's brash analysis. That October the Ministry of Agriculture and Commerce held the first National Painting Exhibition at the Ueno Museum and asked Fenollosa to be an adviser to the judges. The purpose of the exhibit was to promote Japanese-style paintings, and all Western-style art was to be excluded.[23] Then, three months later, in January 1883, the Art School of the Imperial Engineering College which had been created in 1878 in order to teach Western art techniques was abolished. Though there is no evidence that Fenollosa had any direct influence on this decision, there can be no doubt that he heartily approved of it. Early in 1884 his reputation as a critic was given a prestigious lift when his knowledge of Japanese art was recognized by the Kano family and he was authorized to use their name when certifying the authenticity of Japanese paintings.[24] During this same period he also helped form the Kangwakai or Painting Appreciation Society whose primary functions concerned reviving interest in traditional Japanese art and also authenticating the work of the ancient masters. In a letter to Morse in 1884, Fenollosa boasted about the increasingly active role that he was playing in the club's undertakings: "Three artists, including the present head of the Kano and Tosa Schools and myself, compose the criticising committee of four. We hold meetings in which we exhibit old paintings, I lecture on art, and we undertake to criticize any paintings brought, and give certificates, if desired."[25] Each month the club featured in its exhibits a different school of traditional Japanese artists; frequently Fenollosa provided an accompanying lecture dealing with the school's distinguishing characteristics.[26] Some years later Sturgis Bigelow recalled that the most salient feature of these lectures was the logical clarity with which Fenollosa constructed his arguments. Yet even more vivid in Bigelow's memory was what he considered to be the utter "strangeness of the situation—that a young American should be lecturing to Japanese in praise of their own art to which they showed indifference or hostility."[27] In addition to its other activities, the Kangwakai hoped to encourage and educate contemporary Japanese artists to paint in a traditional medium, and special meetings were held to display, compare, and criticize original contemporary works.[28] In April 1884 a second National Painting Exhibition was held and Fenollosa again served in an advisory capacity. It was at this second exhibition that he met the painter Kano Hogai. From this meeting a friendship eventually developed which, according to Fenollosa's Japanese biographer, is comparable to such famous artist-critic relationships as Turner and Ruskin, or Picasso and Apollinaire.[29]

Always fearful that irreplaceable art objects were being lost through natural deterioration and neglect, Fenollosa had a sense of urgency in his activities. Anxious whenever possible to travel, he spent the summer of 1884 in the central portion of the country feverishly discovering, studying, and authenticating long-forgotten art treasures. Accompanied by Bigelow and an official from the Ministry of Education, whose presence ensured cooperation from local authorities, the party visited scores of temples and palaces to examine their contents. By late September Fenollosa could barely contain his excitement concerning the summer's activities, and his enthusiasm spilled over into a letter to Morse:

> We may say in brief that we have made the first accurate list of the great art treasures kept in the central temples of Japan, we have overturned the traditional criticism attached to these individual specimens for ages, the Dr. has taken 200 photographs and I innumerable

sketches of art objects (paintings and statues); and, more than all, I have recovered the history of Japanese art from the 6th to the 9th centuries A.D. which has been completely lost.[30]

In spite of the range of activities during the vacation period, Fenollosa also found time to write a lengthy review of the French critic Louis Gonse's chapter on Japanese painting in *L'Art japonais*. The review was first published in the Japanese *Weekly Mail* and later sent to friends in a pamphlet. The review was Fenollosa's first critical writing on Japanese art, and in it he lamented Gonse's propensity to admire "as typical in Eastern art, that painter whose qualities are the farthest removed from the genius of that art, being the nearest approximation to the qualities of European, is to confess one's self to have no taste for the special flavor of the former."[31] Fenollosa's criticism of Gonse went beyond mere scholarly disagreement in that he had been campaigning for some time against the practice in Japanese elementary schools of teaching art by using Western techniques and instruments. He had grown particularly incensed upon learning that at the beginning of the "Westernization craze" in the early 1870s, instruction in pencil and crayon sketching had replaced traditional tutelage in soft brush and ink in Japanese elementary schools.[32] His opposition to this change was culturally as well as technically oriented, for, as he argued, "That the development of Fine Art in a nation is an important requisite of its spiritual improvement is the prime fact to be kept in mind. Spiritual excellence includes all kinds of refinement which raise man above the condition of a mere economical machine. Fine Art here stands side by side in importance with literature and good manners. It softens and purifies man's heart."[33] The teaching of Western techniques to school children would soon blind them to what was unique in their own culture, and, even worse, would eventually lead to the separation of Japanese art from Japanese life. From Fenollosa's perspective, such a break would be both spiritually and socially tragic.

Efforts at changing this policy began to achieve results in November 1884. At this time the Ministry of Education established a Painting Education Study Group to evaluate art instruction at the elementary level. A month after its creation Fenollosa was asked to join. The following year the Educational Department accepted the group's suggestion that instruction in Japanese-style painting, including use of the traditional ink and soft brush, should be re-established on the elementary level. Obviously impressed with Fenollosa's abilities, the Educational Ministry in December 1885 asked him, his friend, Hogai Kano, and a former student, Kakuzo Okakura, to serve on a committee which was to investigate the possibility of establishing a national school of art. After several months of deliberation, the committee suggested that final administrative and curricular decisions be postponed until art programs and schools in other countries could be examined.[34] By the time the committee submitted the report, Fenollosa's fame as critic and defender of traditional Japanese art was nearing its peak. His prestige was enhanced even more when in the summer of 1886 the Department of the Imperial Household commissioned him to prepare a list of all valuable art objects in the Kyoto and Osaka districts.[35] Several weeks later while in the midst of his surveying activities, the government, in an unprecedented move, asked Fenollosa to resign from Tokyo University in order to accept appointment as an Imperial Commissioner. Aware of the honor that such an invitation carried and delighted in being able to set aside time-consuming academic duties, he accepted immediately.

The appointment was to be for four years and Fenollosa would be jointly employed by the Ministries of the Imperial Household and Education. His first assignment as Commissioner was to continue investigating the steps necessary for the creation of a national school of art. Convinced that a fact-finding trip was necessary before anything else could be done, he and two other commissioners began making preparations to go to Europe and America that fall. Although the purpose of the trip was to be educational, Fenollosa also believed that it symbolized a new interest in the arts on the part of the Japanese government. In an address delivered shortly before departing, he suggested that the sending of the commissioners to Europe meant "the inevitable triumph of the cause of progress in art, because it shows that the authorities of this country have at last taken the matter to heart."[36]

The tour lasted from late September 1886 until October 1887 with the commissioners visiting the United States, England, France, Germany, Holland, Belgium, Austria, and Spain. Since the first leg of the journey was to the United States, Fenollosa deposited his family with relatives in Salem, where he also discussed the purposes of the tour with a local reporter. In the course of the interview, he explained to the local journalist his belief that contemporary Japanese artists should immerse themselves in their own artistic heritage before undertaking a study of the European tradition. Even then study should not lead to blind imitation. "Japanese art ought not to be a copy of the European," he emphasized, "for this would destroy it altogether."[37] The commissioners visited art establishments in Boston and New York before concluding the American portion of their journey in the nation's capital. In Europe their program continued to be a varied one. They examined the organization as well as the teaching methods of art schools, the arrangement and management of art societies, the administrative and display techniques of art museums, differing methods of reproduction, preservation, and restoration. They were also extremely interested in the way the arts were promoted in the West, in the nature of government sponsored and administrated fine arts programs, and, of course, in the historical development of Western art.[38] The trip also provided Fenollosa with a unique opportunity to familiarize himself with the direction of modern European painting. Yet he appears to have given the matter little attention, and although he was in France when Neo-Impressionism was predominant it made no lasting impact on him.[39] In fact the trip strengthened views he already held, and he returned to Tokyo more convinced than ever "that Japan's unquestioned supremacy in artistic capacity for design, makes it certain that she can become the focus of the world's art life and education, and permanently control the world's market for art production of the highest grade."[40]

Fenollosa's interest in the exportation of Japanese art products for commercial gain was by no means a passing fancy. He had, in fact, been convinced for some time that practical economic arguments as well as artistic ones were necessary in order to gain lasting support for such programs as a national museum and a government-sponsored school of art. To emphasize the commercial potential of Japanese art, he maintained in a specially written report that all great painters were equally great designers. Thus, a creative genius like a Raphael "could sit down to design a beautiful table or lamp, or a piece of gold jewelry, as easily as he could plan a picture or design a house. The same qualities of his mind were employed in each."[41] By encouraging traditional Japanese painting the government would also be encouraging the development of such art industries as the production of silk goods, tapestries, rugs, porcelain, metal work, furnitures, and lacquers. All of these items would be readily marketable because of the superior nature of Japanese design. Fenollosa concluded the report by suggesting that if the projected art school were organized according to his plans, not only would the economy be stimulated, but also traditional artistic excellence would be maintained.

The commissioners were back in Japan by the fall of 1887. Okakura and Fenollosa spent most of the next year making what they hoped were final preparations for the opening of the Tokyo Imperial Art School. Still concerned about how the Imperial cabinet would react to the proposed program, Fenollosa believed that the economic arguments would be a deciding factor. On the other hand, he had no doubts whatsoever about the basic soundness of the overall proposal, and in a letter to a friend displayed a self-confidence that bordered on the arrogant: "we represent the most advanced, sound, and liberal opinions on art in the world today, I can guarantee; and they would soon be followed by foreign nations. I can prove my position in the face of the world. If the cabinet throw us away, they are throwing away their greatest possible advantage, they are ignoring a remarkable opportunity which can never occur again."[42]

Fears that the cabinet would reject the commission's proposals were unfounded, and classes began in the new school in February 1889. Initially there were sixty-five pupils taking a varied curriculum including courses on aesthetics and art history taught by Fenollosa. Classes in painting emphasized the traditional techniques suggested by the American commissioner who, soon after the school's opening, emphatically predicted: "A new art is going to grow in this school and it will dominate all Japan in the near future and will have a good influence over the world."[43] During this period Fenollosa's energies were not directed solely toward the new school's activities. Shortly after returning from abroad he had been asked to serve on the administrative committee of the newly established Bureau of National Treasures. Then, in May 1889, when the section devoted to art in the Imperial Museum was opened, he was also asked to be on its board of advisers. He was particularly interested in serving on this board because of the views that he held concerning the role of a museum in a nation's cultural activities. In a manuscript entitled "The Prospect of Japanese Art," he argued that traditionally Japanese museums had served merely as storehouses rather than educational institutions. From his perspective the museum had just as important an educational role to play as a national school of art:

> The special value of such a museum for educating Japanese artists and public taste can be seen at a glance. The future art movement in Japan is not to copy blindly the styles of the West; neither is it to work out into something absolutely new and strange cut off from all past tradition. It is to have its roots in the best Eastern work of the past, and to develop from what is vital in their law. In the museum arranged as above suggested, the artists would study as an essential part of their course, the great models of antiquity. How rich Japan is in these, is not generally suspected. In the course of a few years, we might have 10,000 workers of art of first class quality, work from which the best art schools in the West would find something to learn.[44]

By the time of his appointment to the Imperial Museum's board of advisers, Fenollosa believed that all programs pertaining to the arts in Japan should be under the supervision of a single individual. And there was no doubt in his mind that he was best qualified to fulfill the duties of such a position.[45] Whether or not this ambition could ever have become reality is uncertain, but in mid-1889 he received an unexpected offer of a totally different nature. The Boston Museum of

Fine Arts asked if he would organize and direct a new department of Japanese art. The offer was particularly attractive to Fenollosa in that he would be working with his own collection of Japanese paintings, which he had sold in 1886 to a wealthy Boston surgeon, Dr. Charles Goddard Weld. The sale was concluded only after it was agreed that the collection would be permanently housed in the Boston museum and be known as the Fenollosa-Weld Collection.

Fenollosa put off making a decision for almost a year. The offer itself was attractive and most certainly influenced his thinking, but there were changes that were already taking place within Japan which were perhaps even more influential in persuading him to make the decision. By the late 1880s there was a growing resentment throughout the country over the condescending way in which the major Western powers continued to treat Orientals. There was also a growing national revulsion against two decades of the most uncritical kind of imitation of Western civilization, and this revulsion had already begun to push the pendulum in the opposite direction toward traditional Japanese institutions, traditions, and ideals. Mirroring this nationalistic impulse, many Japanese universities were beginning to refuse to renew the contracts of their foreign teachers. It was, in fact, becoming clear that the day of the Western adviser was rapidly nearing an end.[46] Although Fenollosa had risen to prominence through his defense of traditional Japanese art, there is no way of knowing just how much if at all his position as commissioner or his influence in general would have been affected by this new attitude. It is quite possible, however, that since most of his proposals concerning the preservation of Japan's traditional artistic heritage were in the process of being implemented, he realized that as a Westerner there was little else that he could hope to accomplish. Thus, in view of the changes taking place in Japan and the attractiveness of the offer from Boston, it is not surprising that he decided to return to the United States.[47] Shortly before sailing with his family in the summer of 1890, Fenollosa was once again honored by the government. After decorating the American for services rendered to Japan, the Emperor asked that Fenollosa continue his activities: "We request you now to teach the significance of Japanese art to the West as you have already taught it to the Japanese."[48]

Although Fenollosa visited Japan several times in later years, he was never again directly involved in Japanese affairs. He worked as curator of the Boston museum until a divorce scandal and his remarriage to Mary McNeil forced his resignation in 1896. From that point until his death he pursued a career of lecturing and writing. He completed a draft of *Epochs of Chinese and Japanese Art* in the summer of 1906, but planned to revise the manuscript after a final research trip to Japan. This last visit to Japan never took place, for Fenollosa suddenly died of a heart attack in London on September 21, 1908, while vacationing there with his wife and step-daughter. Twelve years later a number of his former students dedicated a stone memorial on the grounds of the Tokyo Art School to honor Fenollosa's contributions to Japan and her artistic heritage.

In 1912, the year Mary McNeil Fenollosa finally published *Epochs of Chinese and Japanese Art*, another book about the Far East also appeared on the American market. Unlike Fenollosa's magnum opus, *The Day of the Saxon* received neither public nor critical acclaim. Before the year ended, its author, General Homer Lea, was dead. His death like his book passed virtually unnoticed. Yet Homer Lea had a remarkable career. Enigmatic, deformed, five feet two inches tall, he had been active for years in Chinese revolutionary affairs and had been an adviser to Sun Yat-sen.

Born on November 17, 1876, in Denver, Colorado, Homer Lea was dropped while an infant and suffered a permanent curvature of the spine which stunted his growth and left him a hunchback. The same accident caused him to suffer severe headaches and occasional periods of blindness throughout his life.[49] Lea's youth was further traumatized by his mother's early death, although his father soon married again and moved the family to Los Angeles. While attending Los Angeles High School, Lea became infatuated with military science and began to read everything on the subject that he could find. He also built in his backyard a miniature battlefield to re-create many of the great campaigns from the past.[50] In 1896 Lea entered Occidental College in Los Angeles. A year later he transferred to Stanford University which he attended for two years although he never graduated. At Stanford he took the usual courses for the liberal arts requirement, gained a reputation as a masterful poker player, and displayed his martial interests by decorating the walls of his room with military maps. Also known for his enjoyment of debates on military or political issues, Lea attracted the attention of the reform-minded president of the University, David Starr Jordan. In his autobiography Jordan remembered Lea as a "youth of extraordinary parts—ready memory, very vivid imagination, imperturbable coolness, and an obsession for militarism and war." It was possibly this last quality which rankled Jordan's own pacifistic views, for he patronizingly concluded: "One could hardly help a kindly feeling for the ambitious little romancier trying to make the most of his short life, limited physique, and boundless imagination."[51] The only other collegiate activity that rivaled his interests in military affairs and poker was Lea's curiosity about the Chinese community in San Francisco. He often wandered the city's Chinese sections fascinated by the cultural differences he observed. Certainly none of his fellow classmates who occasionally accompanied him on these excursions could have guessed that this youthful interest in Chinese-Americans would lead to later involvement in the Chinese Revolution.

Lea left Stanford before graduating for both physical and financial reasons and returned to Los Angeles. Although no longer a part of the academic world, his interests remained the same and he began to make frequent visits to that city's Chinese community. During one of these excursions in 1899 he met Tom Tsai Hin, one of the local leaders of the Pao-huang-hui (Chinese Imperial Reform Association).[52] The Pao-huang-hui was formed by the classical Chinese scholar and reformer K'ang Yu-wei after he fell from power in the Imperial government in 1898. During the mid-1890s K'ang became convinced that China's defeat by Japan in 1895 and her weakness in the face of Western imperialism tragically showed the need for modernization along the lines already carried out by the Meiji reformers in Japan. In

1898 he persuaded the young Emperor Kuang-hsu to sponsor such reforms aimed at modernizing the entire governmental structure. The resulting Hundred Days of Reform, however, ingloriously ended when the Empress Dowager Tz'u-hsi forced her nephew into seclusion and arrested and executed all reformers not fortunate enough to escape. K'ang was among those able to flee China. He went to Japan and there organized the Pao-huang-hui, which he hoped would help restore the young emperor to the Manchu throne and the reforming impulse to his country.

Why Lea became involved with the Pao-huang-hui at this particular time is difficult to explain. Even were he aware of events in China, there is nothing to suggest that he felt any special commitment toward the deposed emperor or any opposition to the Dowager Empress. In fact, it appears likely that he first became interested in the society for personal rather than political reasons. Having been forced to drop out of college and going through a period of personal ennui, Lea may initially have seen the society as an interesting form of diversion whose secrecy appealed to his imagination. His interests in military affairs, perhaps even in a military career, and the realities of his physical deformity quite possibly played an equally important part in his involvement: the society was the closest thing to a military organization in which he could ever hope to play a role. By joining it as he did in 1900 he was creating a career for himself that would otherwise have been impossible.

What the society saw in Lea is also uncertain. He was enthusiastic, claimed to be a military genius, and, as an American citizen, could prove to be useful should the society's activities come under official scrutiny. In any case, by March 1900 he was on his way to join the San Francisco branch of the Pao-huang-hui with glowing letters of recommendation from Tom Tsai Hin in his pocket. Although a banquet was held by the San Francisco branch in mid-March to welcome its newest recruit, little is known of Lea's activities until late April. On April 22 the San Francisco *Call* carried a picture of him flanked by Tom Tsai Hin and another Pao-huang-hui member.[53] The accompanying article claimed that the society recognized Lea's military abilities, and that Tom Tsai Hin outlined these abilities in a letter of introduction to K'ang Yu-wei. In the letter to the society's founder, he described Lea as a sympathetic American who "feels greatly for China on account of her weakness and does not like to see things unequal. He wants to teach Chinese to become soldiers, so as to become free. He is willing to go to the interior of China to get up a school to teach 2000 soldiers."[54] As improbable as this offer must have seemed to those who knew about Lea's handicaps, even more astonishing was the fact that shortly after the article appeared, Lea was indeed on his way to China.

It was a June telegram from K'ang Yu-wei asking the San Francisco branch of the Pao-huang-hui to send funds to his supporters in China that made the extraordinary journey possible.[55] With China in turmoil over the Boxer Rebellion, K'ang was actively financing the efforts of Hunanese reformer T'ang Ts-ai-ch'ang to ferment an anti-government uprising in Hankow. It was hoped that such a revolt would spread throughout all of south China and would eventually lead to the fall of the Empress. The time to act had come. K'ang's plea for assistance caused a flurry of activity in the headquarters of the Pao-huang-hui in San Francisco. Within a week after the arrival of the telegram, it was decided that Homer Lea would carry to China $60,000 of the society's funds.[56] The selection of Lea for this important mission undoubtedly suggests the confidence local authorities had in him. Yet his nationality also enhanced his value to the society. During this period Westerners could move in and out of treaty ports with far greater ease than could the Chinese themselves, and it was perhaps such practical considerations that led the society to choose Lea as its financial courier.[57]

Although an aura of mystery surrounds Lea's trip, it appears likely that he disembarked in either the British colony of Hong Kong or in Portuguese Macao, and that he spent most of his stay in the latter. According to a report received by Sir Henry Black, the governor of Hong Kong, Lea tried unsuccessfully in Macao to organize a coolie army of 25,000 to attack Canton. He also tried to bribe Portuguese officials and even promised territorial compensation to the Colony's

governor should the attack succeed.[58] As might be expected this bizarre scheme was never carried out and nothing else is known of Lea's
activities in these colonies. Some years later, however, he claimed to
have attempted much more and to have organized troops in the interior of China in an unsuccessful attempt to link up with the forces of
T'ang Ts-ai-ch'ang.[59] Though it is remotely possible that Lea might
have traveled in southern China during this period, neither his military
claims nor his presence have ever been verified by either Chinese or
Japanese sources.[60] On the other hand, Lea did not confine his activities solely to China. At some point during the ten months spent in
the Orient he visited Japan, where he chanced to meet David Starr
Jordan in the city of Nagasaki. While chatting with the touring aca-
demician, Lea announced that he was on his way to Tokyo where he
hoped to persuade the American minister there, Alfred M. Burke, to
influence the world powers to restore the Chinese emperor.[61] Once
again there is no evidence that Lea carried through on this project and
ever met with Burke. Yet he was more successful in another area and
did obtain an interview with the ex-prime minister and head of the
Japanese Liberal party, Shigenobu Okuma. For years Okuma had
been advocating Japanese assistance to China in her continuing struggle against Western imperialism, and, for this reason, was undoubtedly
interested in the goals of the Pao-huang-hui.[62] Whether or not this
meeting led to anything more than a sharing of views is unknown. In
any case, by April 1901 Lea was back in the United States proudly
bearing the title of "General," which he claimed to have received
while commanding troops in the service of the deposed Emperor.[63]

For the next two years Lea's activities are unknown. It was not
until 1903 that he publicly re-emerged at the head of a number of
secretly organized Chinese military academies supported by Pao-
huang-hui funds.[64] The primary function of these academies was the
training of Chinese officers who were to be slipped into China in order
to organize a resistance movement against the Dowager Empress.
Eventually twenty such academies were established throughout the
United States with a general headquarters located in a large brick
building in the Chinese section of Los Angeles. Lea played an instru-

mental role in shaping the Los Angeles academy. He was joined by a retired sergeant of the U.S. Fourth Cavalry, Ansel E. O'Banion, who took over most of the actual training activities. According to O'Banion, the true purpose of the academies was veiled from the public by disguising them with appropriate pedagogical apparel—books, desks, and course listings. The activities of the would-be officers, however, were far more martially oriented, with marching, drilling, and similar pursuits occupying most of their time.[65] Apparently the military focus of the academies was never intended to be kept completely secret. In December 1904 the adjutant-general of the State of California granted permission for the cadets in the academy to march with arms in the Tournament of Roses Parade in Pasadena.[66]

Over the next two years Lea's activities were devoted almost entirely to the academies. Since he had no visible means of support during this period, it is possible that he received funds from the Pao-huang-hui treasury. Lea kept K'ang Yu-wei fully informed about his activities, and in the fall of 1904 received a long-awaited letter from the Pao-huang-hui leader. After apologizing for his tardiness in replying to earlier letters, K'ang acknowledged Lea's accomplishments by writing: "How thankful I am to hear that you are so kind as to render your assistance to our cause. I shall leave here to go to America in a very short time. I hope that I may soon have the pleasure of meeting you. I shall let you know when I arrive in America."[67] Lea had been awaiting such a meeting for some time with the hope that it would lead to his playing a more important role in the organization's activities.

When K'ang stepped from the train in Los Angeles on March 16, 1905, he received full military honors. First Lea greeted him, wearing a blue officer's uniform adorned with epaulettes and two rows of brass buttons down the front. Then followed a review of a company of the academy's cadets who were also dressed in the blue uniforms of the reform army. K'ang's stay in Los Angeles was brief, and he and Lea left the city in mid-March to begin an inspection tour of the society's military academies. The trip was extensive, including visits to cities in the Pacific Northwest, the Middle West, and along the Eastern seaboard. They reached the East Coast by mid-June and were able to obtain an interview with President Roosevelt on June 24, 1905. Lea's presence during this interview suggests his growing importance in K'ang's eyes. The meeting itself was brief, with K'ang and the President doing most of the talking. They discussed the treatment of the Chinese in the United States and K'ang described for the President the nature of the military academies.[68] Several days later Lea and K'ang were in New York, drawing even more attention to themselves by marching in a parade which included a number of uniformed cadets from the local Pao-huang-hui academy. While the press expressed interest in the spectacle, a number of by-standers were totally perplexed by what they saw. "Them's the Japs," exclaimed one knowledgeable longshoreman to another. "Who'd think to look at 'em that they could fight that way," chimed in a third.[69] It was also while in New York that Lea tried to explain the purpose of his activities in the Pao-huang-hui to an inquiring reporter. Since he represented no political party, Lea claimed that his activities had always been misunderstood. They had been most misunderstood, he explained, by the Dowager Empress who "has felt that I was acting against the wishes of the government, which is not true. I believe, however, that the restoration of the young Emperor would bring about the appointment of ministers better able to maintain a strong government, but if China under its present government should ask for help these men at my command would respond. Their wishes are my wishes." Though sounding like a modern-day condottiere, Lea also suggested that China's regionalism and lack of a unifying nationalism had perpetuated her weakness. The only thing that could correct this weakness would be the emergence of a cohesive Chinese nationalism which would have to be supported by a well-trained national army.[70] The creation of such an army had become Homer Lea's self-appointed mission. It also enabled him to fulfill a dream that would have been possible in no other way.

By the end of the summer of 1905 Lea enjoyed tremendous prestige in the Pao-huang-hui. He had been at K'ang Yu-wei's side over the past five months while inspecting the military academies, and had, in the process, met most of the society's important local officials. But during the next three years his enthusiasm for the Pao-huang-hui's objectives and his trust in its leadership began to decline. Even before leaving on their tour in the spring of 1905, K'ang and Lea had an unpleasant misunderstanding concerning whether or not Lea was to be the acting head of the military academies in the United States. Although K'ang ultimately chose Lea over another claimant, a degree of mistrust continued to plague their relationship.[71] At the same time, K'ang gave no indication that he had any immediate plan for using the troops in China. To a romantic like Lea in search of a military career, such inactivity must have been disillusioning. Then, in 1908, K'ang's revolutionary fervor, if not his honesty, was brought into question when it was learned that he had invested substantial sums of Pao-huang-hui funds in a Vera Cruz streetcar company. It was open to debate whether the investment was made for personal or revolutionary reasons.[72] And finally, the *raison d'être* of the entire society was dealt a staggering blow that same year when both the Dowager Empress and the imprisoned Emperor died within a few days of each other. At the same time these events were occurring, Lea's interests were developing in a new direction. In 1908 he contacted a group far more revolutionary than the Pao-huang-hui with which it had been competing for the support of the overseas Chinese.

In the spring of 1908 Lea met Charles E. Boothe, a retired businessman living in Pasadena. Before his retirement Boothe had gained a solid business reputation as an investment counselor and a leaser of machinery. The monotony of retirement had apparently led Boothe to consider an elaborately devised scheme of Lea's which was of dubious legality. Lea argued that a privately financed uprising against the Manchus in south China could ultimately lead to a fortune in economic concessions. For the scheme to work, Boothe and other businessmen would have to raise the capital. They would then have to gain the support of several secret anti-Manchu societies in south China, and financially back these societies in a revolt against the Imperial authorities. Once the uprising was completed, negotiations for economic concessions would then be initiated with the new government as a form of repayment for the money lent by the American backers. Apart from capital, the most important requirement for a successful uprising would be capable leadership. Above all, the leader would need a thorough understanding of Chinese affairs, and there was no doubt in Lea's mind who this person should be. "My knowledge of the Chinese people," he boasted in a letter to Boothe in the fall of 1908, "is probably equal in all respects to any American who has had long and varied experience in the Orient, while politically and racially, in a personal and sociological sense I do not think it possible to find any one in this nation who understands more thoroughly the Chinese. You are fully cognizant of this fact from personal knowledge."[73]

Boothe was initially so impressed by the scheme that he persuaded a boyhood friend, W. W. Allen, a consulting engineer in New York, to participate. A short time later the inner circle was expanded to include a fourth associate, Yung Wing, who had been the first Chinese student to be educated in the United States. Living at the time in Connecticut, he and Lea may have met years earlier in China when Lea was acting as courier for the Pao-huang-hui. In any case, it was Lea who introduced Yung to Boothe.[74] As might be expected, this fantastic scheme for insurrection never got beyond the planning stage. To begin with it was totally unrealistic. In addition, the schemers themselves included such a bizarre mixture of military and political intriguers and business-minded capitalists that any operational consensus would have been unlikely. Boothe, for example, was fascinated by the possibility of excitement and profit; Allen, the practical, hard-boiled businessman, was interested in gaining valuable railroad, banking, coinage, and mining concessions.[75] Yung Wing, on the other hand, attracted by political and financial dreams, hoped that once the Manchus had departed southern China he would be able to fill the political void. Lea, who was more interested in the political and military aspects of the scheme, usually emphasized the economic concessions since he realized the need for attracting capital.

From the very beginning the four conspirators also disagreed over whether or not K'ang Yu-wei should be included in the inner circle. When he had first met Boothe, Lea was still a member of the Pao-huang-hui, and it was initially agreed that K'ang should be included.[76]

Once Allen and Yung joined the group, they began to oppose such a collaboration. Allen was convinced that K'ang had misappropriated Pao-huang-hui funds and would be a liability when contacts were made with potential revolutionaries in south China. Yung Wing's dissent was more personal. He saw K'ang as a potential political rival.[77]

Although the conspirators had corresponded for almost a year, by the middle of 1909 they had done little more than disagree among themselves. They had raised no capital and made no efforts to contact any anti-Manchu elements in China. Yet in the same letter in which he had announced his opposition to K'ang Yu-wei, Allen had mentioned a revolutionary leader who he believed should be considered for future consultation. "Sun Yat-sen of Canton," he wrote "is considered the most reliable of all. Twice he has nearly taken Canton in his attempts to organize a rebellion. He is considered a tower of strength in the Canton province and a man that can be relied upon, although probably somewhat too mercurial and liable to act in advance of the right moment."[78] With the exception of this brief reference, it was not until late December 1909 that Sun's name again appears in the correspondence of the conspirators. At this time Yung Wing, who had met Sun years earlier in China, telegraphed Boothe urging him and Lea to come to the East Coast to meet with the recently arrived revolutionary. Lea was ill at the time and Boothe was unable to accept because of previous commitments.[79] But a meeting did take place three months later when Sun Yat-sen came to California.

The very fact that Sun Yat-sen was willing to meet with the conspirators is not in itself surprising. As his most recent biographer has shown, Sun was constantly plagued by a multitude of financial problems and would usually consider any fund-raising scheme.[80] At the same time, although Sun's primary objective was the overthrow of the Manchus, he realized that if this were to be accomplished without the further dismemberment of China by Western powers, the revolution would have to appear respectable in Western eyes. What better way of achieving respectability and much-needed financial assistance than by cooperating with a group of American businessmen? In any case it seems likely that during their initial meeting Sun promised that if his revolutionary activities were financially supported by Boothe and his associates, at least some of the desired economic concessions would be provided once his government was in power. And finally, before leaving California, the revolutionary leader commissioned Boothe as his special American financial agent in charge of securing loans and "receiving monies."[81]

Even though the meeting between Boothe and Sun Yat-sen suggested that at long last the plan would be launched, just the opposite proved to be true. Well before the California meeting, W. W. Allen had begun to voice his skepticism about finding any willing investors.[82] Another question that continued to plague him was the nature of the government to be created in south China once the Manchus had been removed. Although never mentioning the kind of government he preferred, Allen was adamant in his belief that the creation of a republic would be catastrophic. Convinced that the Chinese were unfit for republicanism, he also believed that such a government would immediately invite foreign intervention. Such intervention would, of course, threaten the financial dreams around which the plan was built. Allen had earlier raised yet another concern which, among other things, convinced him to drop out of the scheme a few months later:

> I do not believe this man is recognized as The Leader; he probably is a Leader but until they agree upon one who shall be The Leader, every effort will fail and every dollar put into it is worse than lost, because it puts the other fellow on his guard and makes the second attempt twice as difficult as the first would have been, and so on in GEOMETRIC progression. Until a definite organization and disciplin [sic] is established and in full operation, it would be an insult to the intelligence of any capitalist to ask him to risk his money in the project, and the man who would propose it would be damned for all time.[83]

Allen was not the only conspirator whose enthusiasm began to cool. Yung Wing, who undoubtedly saw Sun Yat-sen as yet another political rival, seems also to have lost interest in the scheme as evidenced by the decreasing volume of his correspondence.[84]

Disillusionment with the plan was not a one-way process. By the early summer of 1910 Sun Yat-sen was repeatedly inquiring about the long-overdue financial aid that had been promised him. Even though Lea had estimated that about four and a half million dollars would be needed by Sun Yat-sen to conduct a successful uprising, no funds had been forthcoming. Tired of waiting, Sun wrote to Boothe, in September 1910, asking for an advance on the required sum: "If you think that our project of raising the funds will be surely succeeded and final settlement is only a question of time; I should like you would advance me a sum of $50,000 American dollars from your own account for the preparatory work. . . ."[85] By early November Sun was hoping for even half a loaf when he again wrote to Boothe: "We are not in need of so large a sum as we first proposed in your house, for many of the preparatory works have been done since my returning here."[86] Although Sun continued to keep in contact with Boothe for several months longer, he had apparently decided by the fall of 1910 that his best hope for financial aid in America was not Charles B. Boothe, but instead the originator of the plan, General Homer Lea.

There is no clear documentation of the first meeting between Sun and Lea, or, even more important, of their collaboration. It appears likely, however, that their initial meeting did not occur until late 1909.[87] Sun later recorded in an autobiographical article his reaction upon first meeting Lea although there is no mention of exactly when or where this encounter took place:

> I was speaking to a company of my followers when my eye fell on a young man of slight physique. He was under five feet high; he was about my age; his face was pale, and he looked delicate. Afterwards he came to me and said:—"I should like to throw in my lot with you. I should like to help you. I believe your propaganda will succeed."
>
> His accent told me he was an American. He held out his hand. I took it and thanked him, wondering who he was. I thought he was a missionary or a student. I was right. After he had gone I said to a friend:—"Who was that little hunchback?" "Oh, that," said he, "is Colonel Homer Lea, one of the most brilliant military geniuses now alive. He is a perfect master of modern warfare." The next morning

I called on Homer Lea, now General, and the famous author of the "Valor of Ignorance." I told him that in case I should succeed and my countrymen gave me the power to do so, I would make him my chief military adviser.

"Do not wait until you are President of China," he said. "You may want me before then."[88]

That Sun Yat-sen was more familiar with Lea's writing than with his rank was indicative of a direction that the little Californian's career had been heading for some time. Interested since college in publicizing his military theories, he had temporarily postponed such an undertaking and first tested his writing abilities in the realm of fiction. In 1908, with the aid of a secretary-typist, Ethel Powers, a divorcee whom he married in 1911, Lea published a sweeping melodramatic novel, *The Vermilion Pencil: A Romance of China*. The next year he turned to what fascinated him most and completed the first of a projected trilogy on political and military affairs, *The Valor of Ignorance*. Writing from a Social Darwinistic viewpoint, Lea argued that the "expansion of a nation's boundaries is indicative, not only of its external growth, but of the virility of its internal constitution; the shrinkage of its boundaries, the external ex-emplification of its internal decay."[89] Like other imperialists of the day, Lea believed that national survival depended upon continuing expansion. Conflict between nations was to be anticipated since no two nations could hope to expand continually along parallel lines. National interests were bound to collide when their "lines of convergence" met at some point in the world. From Lea's perspective the "lines of convergence" of the United States and Japan had been on a collision course in the Pacific for over two decades. Such a collision worried Lea since he believed that Japan's military potential was increasing with each year as demonstrated by her victories in the Sino-Japanese and Russo-Japanese wars. Lea interpreted these victories as vigorous manifestations of a superior civilization based on the martial strengths of Bushido and, unlike the United States government, he was convinced that the Japanese recognized the immediacy of the conflict and were making the preparations necessary for survival.[90] The same could not be said of his own country. A growing acceptance of pacifism, the ineptness of democratic rule, widespread public apathy, and, most important of all, a national propensity to worship at the shrine of Mammon instead of Mars were all weakening the United States' chances for victory.[91] As the day of reckoning drew closer, Lea's self-appointed mission became all the more clear. His writing, and perhaps more significantly, his actions would somehow have to remedy the national myopia and awaken the country to the inevitable confrontation. His China activities, then, were not only a means of pursuing an otherwise unachievable military career, but were also intended to head off a national catastrophe.

Lea saw his most immediate task to be the preservation of China's independence for economic and military reasons which were important to the United States. As early as 1905 he had justified his activities in the Pao-huang-hui to a New York reporter in the most nationalistic of terms: "All efforts of mine for the benefit of China have been misinterpreted by the American people and the Chinese government. But also I have been working for the good of this my own country. America should not allow China to be cut up and its trade destroyed, because in one year China brings America more trade than the Philippine Islands."[92] Yet Lea's concerns went far beyond the economic premises of the Open Door, for he believed that a militarily strong China was a necessary counterweight in the Pacific to a rapidly expanding Japan. Until 1905 he was convinced that his participation in the Pao-huang-hui would help create an independent China which would ultimately be closely tied to the United States.

Lea switched his support from the Pao-huang-hui to Sun Yat-sen's revolutionary T'ung-meng-hui by 1908 with all the nonchalance of a businessman changing civic clubs. Yet the change was consistent with his ambitions and beliefs. Certainly his mistrust of K'ang Yu-wei made the decision easier. Perhaps even more important, however, was Lea's view of himself as a man of action. Undoubtedly he must have compared K'ang's policy of cautious inaction to the eight uprisings—even though unsuccessful—that Sun's revolutionary alliances had sponsored in China from 1907 to 1908. The chance for an active career seemed far more likely with the T'ung-meng-hui. And finally, even though Sun apparently hoped to get financial help from Lea, he was also willing to accept Lea's assistance on its own terms—as a military professional. Although Sun's letters to Lea were often filled with financial requests, he also wrote to the little Californian as a comrade-in-arms.[93] By September 1910 Sun was writing to Lea as a fellow revolutionary, suggesting that "before starting the movement from Canton it is of vital importance for us to secure a perfect understanding of the English Government. To do this you and I must go to London and work together."[94]

Although Lea's role in T'ung-meng-hui activities was obviously increasing, very little is known about his activities during the early part of 1911. A possible explanation may be that he was living the secluded life of a semi-invalid. In early 1910 his eyesight became so poor that he found it difficult to work on the second volume in the projected trilogy, *The Day of the Saxon*. And when his vision continued to deteriorate, he decided to see a specialist in Wiesbaden, Germany. He sailed for Europe in June 1911, accompanied by his wife of only a few days, Ethel Powers. Lea was apparently still resting in Germany when news of the outbreak of revolutionary activity in the city of Wuchang reached Europe early in October 1911. Whether or not he was fully recovered by this time is unknown, but by the end of the month he was in London at Sun's request frantically attempting to negotiate loans for the revolutionary cause.[95] Sun Yat-sen joined Lea in England in early November, and together the two spent the next few weeks unsuccessfully soliciting loans from the London banking community.[96] They were somewhat more successful in another area and obtained the promise of the foreign secretary, Sir Edward Grey, to use his influence in persuading a four-power consortium of British, American, French, and German bankers to stop payment on a loan made earlier that spring to the Manchus.[97] Such a policy, they hoped, would weaken the ruling dynasty. The revolution had been in progress for well over a month before Sun Yat-sen finally decided to leave for China. In addition to a small retinue of supporters, he was also joined by Lea—reported to be the "chief military adviser for the revolutionaries"—and his wife.[98] After a brief stopover in Paris, the party traveled to Marseilles, from whence it sailed on November 24 for Colombo, Ceylon, aboard the liner *Marta*. After reaching Colombo the party transferred to the *Devanha*, whose ultimate destination was China.

As the *Devanha* inched slowly toward Shanghai stopping at Penang, Singapore, and Hong Kong, Lea made what was to be his only significant contribution to the Revolution. When the vessel docked at Penang in mid-December, Sun Yat-sen went ashore briefly but refused to be interviewed. Lea, on the other hand, was not so reticent and acted more like an advance man for a public relations firm than a military adviser. In an obvious bid to win British sympathy for the T'ung-meng-hui, he told a reporter from the Penang *Gazette* that a weak China would represent a continuing threat to British interests in the Pacific by inviting Japanese and Russian expansion. He reiterated his conviction that the emergence of Japan as a major power had upset the "political equilibrium in the Orient" and that in the future it would be necessary either to "break down Japan, or strengthen and consolidate China, so that the latter became a great military power. . . ." A strong China would not only be a counter-balance to Japan, but also would serve as a deterrent to Russian expansion. Lea also emphasized that Sun's activities were bound to be beneficial to the United States as well. It was simply a question of who was to control the Pacific; if Japan remained supreme and China divided and weak, American economic interests were bound to suffer.[99]

The *Devanha* arrived in Singapore on December 15 and meetings were held with local T'ung-meng-hui supporters. Later that day good news arrived from the mainland. As Lea recalled:

> . . . word was received that 16 out of 18 provinces of China had been enrolled as revolutionary, asking instructions, and, in the picturesque language in the east, telling how anxiously they awaited the arrival of their beloved leader. There was great rejoicing and when once more on the last long lap of the journey Dr. Sun turned to his friends and with that smile that all who know him love lighting his face

said: "We can't fail now [,] the whole country is like an over ripe
plum. It could remain on no longer. The Tching Dynasty is doomed";
all doubt vanished.[100]

While the revolutionary entourage lingered in Singapore, some who
had come to the port to get a glimpse of Sun Yat-sen were apparently
more intrigued by his military adviser. A reporter for the Singapore
Free Press, for example, in a burst of journalistic hyperbole described
Lea as the "Von Moltke" of the revolution and then warned: "It will
not encourage Peking to know that they have only YUAN SHIH-KAI
to pit against the brain of Homer Lea."[101]

In spite of the general optimism aboard ship, there was still the
possibility of foreign intervention should the revolution appear to be
too radical in Western eyes.[102] As a result Sun Yat-sen was eager for
any opportunity in which to publicize, preferably through official
channels, the respectability of his intentions. Such an opportunity
arose when the vessel reached Hong Kong a few days before Christmas, and when Lea called for his mail at the office of the American
Consul-General, George E. Anderson. While there, he and Anderson
discussed the present activities and future plans of the T'ung-meng-
hui. Undoubtedly Lea did all that he could to allay any American
fears. When the Consul-General asked if Sun Yat-sen would officially
confirm his intentions in writing, Lea arranged that same day a meeting with the revolutionary leader aboard the *Devanha*. Afterwards he
and Anderson drew up a policy statement of the T'ung-meng-hui's
intentions which was then cleared with Sun and other party members.[103] The statement was then cabled to the State Department.
Among other things the T'ung-meng-hui promised to call for the creation of a provisional government with Sun as president and with
Lea serving as chief of staff. Although the revolutionaries demanded a
total surrender of power by the Manchus, they left open the possibility
of outside mediation:

> We propose if necessary to request the President of the United States
> mediate with Manchus but offer no compromise or conditions but the
> above mentioned. We propose select the best provisional administra-

tors independent present officials. Provisional Government military; permanent Government strongly centralized Republican Government modified American plan. We propose employ eminent American jurists to assist framing constitution.[104]

The degree of Lea's influence in drafting the cablegram is unknown, although he most certainly agreed with its philosophy. There was to be the creation of a unified government with a military orientation, and it was implied that this government would be closely tied to the United States. Lea's military dreams were to be fulfilled, for he obviously believed that he was to play a significant role once the Republic was established. Actually, his involvement was nearing an end, and by arranging the meeting between Anderson and Sun Yat-sen he had already played his most significant role in the Chinese Revolution.

Nonetheless, when the revolutionary party finally reached Shanghai toward the end of 1911, Lea was as buoyant as ever about his prospects in China. He informed reporters that before leaving Europe he had talked with enough diplomats to feel assured that there would be no foreign intervention in the revolution.[105] He also answered questions about his background and what his role with Sun Yat-sen might be:

"How long have you been connected with the revolutionary movement in China" he was asked.

"For about twelve years."

"What is your official capacity?"

"I am chief of the General Staff."

"What will be your duties in that capacity?"

"The usual duties of a chief of staff."

"Then you will direct all the military operations of the Revolutionary Army, including those of General Li Yuan Hung?" was suggested.

"No, I don't expect to interfere with General Li's operations. Of course a chief of staff is simply the means of transmitting orders from the president to the army."[106]

Whether or not Sun ever offered Lea a position in his cabinet is unknown. Mrs. Lea later claimed that he did, but allegedly her husband turned it down for fear that a foreigner in an official position would create tensions among the revolutionists.[107] Yet even if Sun Yat-sen had continued as president of the republic and if Lea had remained healthy, it is highly unlikely that he would have held any position other than that of an unofficial adviser. In any case, little is known about his activities in Shanghai, and he apparently remained discreetly in the background during the short time that Sun remained in power. Selected as provisional president of the Chinese Republic on January 1, 1912, Sun held the position for only six weeks. Hoping to avoid civil war, foreign intervention, and further chaos, he stepped down on February 12 in favor of the former premier under the Manchus, Yuan Shi-kai. Lea's activities in the revolution had already come to an end when he suffered a stroke which caused partial paralysis. Although he remained in China for two months longer, his illness effectively severed him from the political events of the time. Finally, in early May 1912, the Leas returned to the United States where he hoped to recover fully from the stroke.

Although still partially paralyzed, Lea never lost his interest in China. He wrote Sun Yat-sen in midsummer offering advice and continuing service to the cause. "I am improved so far that I am quite confident," he announced in late July, "as are my doctors, that I will be able to return to China about the middle of September and will again devote myself to whatever tasks you have for me there."[108] Lea was unable to keep this promise, but he continued to send Sun memoranda which the revolutionary leader promised to discuss when the two were reunited. Such a meeting never occurred. Lea died from a second stroke on November 1, 1912. His death came only six months after he returned from the revolution in which he had so much wanted to play a role. Like that of Fenollosa, Lea's ultimate burial was to be in the country with which he had been actively involved. On April 20, 1969, through arrangements made by his stepson with the Nationalist government on Taiwan, Lea's ashes were placed in a tomb at Yang-mirashan in suburban Taipei. Yet even this grave was regarded as temporary. It was announced at the burial ceremony that the ashes of General Homer Lea would accompany Chiang Kai-shek in his long-prophesied return to the mainland.[109]

Involved as they were in the same general area of the world, the foreign activism of Ernest Fenollosa and Homer Lea was inspired by outlooks as different as were their Hegelian and Social Darwinistic world views. Fenollosa saw the meeting of East and West primarily in cultural terms with the result being a brilliantly new global synthesis. Lea also envisioned such a meeting, but was convinced that it could only end in conflict as part of the worldwide struggle for survival. There were also similarities in the motivations and activities of these two Americans. Both were disillusioned with aspects of American society, and both imaginatively created careers for themselves in spite of either social or physical handicaps. And finally, both were deeply committed to a cause in a part of the world still relatively unknown to most of their fellow countrymen.

Fenollosa, clearly, went to Japan for personal reasons. Sensing the handicaps that he would face as a first-generation American, yet wanting to marry into one of Salem's prominent families, he accepted the teaching post at Tokyo University as a means of advancing his career and as a way of escaping the rigidity of a staid and traditional society. In Japan he enjoyed the status and economic security that had been unattainable in New England, and the necessary free time to turn a hobby into an obsession. At first Fenollosa's activism in Japan was that of a sensitive, culturally eclectic outsider who simply wanted to save something beautiful from extinction. But as his interest in traditional Japanese art grew, so too did his immersion into traditional Japanese society. He ultimately came to realize that the two could not be separated. In an address probably given after his return to the United States in 1890, Fenollosa emphasized the connection between Japanese art and life. Western observers of Eastern art must always remember that "it is not a craze, or a style; it is a life. With us art is little more than an affection, though admittedly a thoroughly wrought one. With Asiatics it is a necessity like language and food. Apart from

Eastern life it is nothing."[110] In keeping with his belief in the relation between Japanese art and life Fenollosa tied himself even more closely to traditional Japan by formally converting to Buddhism. If at first his activism was a response to modern trends threatening to destroy an ancient artistic tradition, it gradually became a defense of his newly embraced lifestyle. A devotee of traditional painting techniques, an adopted member of the Kano family, a Tendai Buddhist, and eventually an official member of the Imperial bureaucracy, Fenollosa had made himself an intrinsic part of all that he was defending. Uprooted from his own society, he tenaciously held to what seemed most meaningful in his adopted one.

But no matter how strong was his identification with traditional Japanese civilization, Fenollosa never rejected his own cultural heritage. Throughout his life he maintained an enthusiasm for the eclectic philosophies of Emerson and Whitman as well as a deep personal commitment to the comprehensive teleology of Hegelianism. Committed as he was, therefore, to two cultural traditions and steeped in the dialectical process, it is not surprising that he came to view the eventual merging of these two cultures in the most positive terms. Still, the idea grew slowly and the concept of a worldwide cultural synthesis was probably not completely worked out in his own mind until well after he had returned to the United States in 1890. There had been times, in fact, during his twelve-year stay in Japan when he appeared to be moving in the opposite direction and was guilty of a kind of inverted parochialism. All too often, for example, he had condemned Western-style paintings by Japanese artists for no other reason than because they were Western-style and did not follow the techniques of traditional Japanese schools.[111] By the time of his return to the United States in 1890 the conflict had been resolved and an endangered birthright preserved. In the tranquility of the Museum of Fine Arts in Boston, he advocated a universal cultural synthesis. Fenollosa discussed many of his ideas in a long poem, "East and West," completed in 1893, but presented a more concise statement of these beliefs several years later in a rough draft of *Epochs of Chinese and Japanese Art*:

"East is East and West is West, and never the two shall meet," so runs Kipling's specious dictum; and American orators use it to-day to affect our treaty legislation. But the truth is that they have met, and they are meeting again now; and history is a thousand times richer for the contact. They have contributed a great deal to each other, and must contribute still more; they interchange views from the basis of a common humanity; and humanity is thus enabled to perceive what is stupid in its insularity. I saw firmly, that in Art, as in Civilization generally, the best in both East and West is that which is common to the two, and eloquent of universal social construction. Translate China into terms of man's experience, and it becomes only an extension of the *Iliad*.[112]

Through his activities in Japan, Fenollosa had tried to ensure that this cultural meeting would not be one-sided, dominated by Western values, but would be truly a symbiosis.

Like Fenollosa, Homer Lea would have found Kipling's dictum to be specious, but from his Social Darwinistic perspective, Lea could only view an East-West meeting in terms of conflict. If Fenollosa saw culture as a cohesive force capable of uniting mankind, Lea was convinced that war, as a symbol for the continuing struggle for survival, was an inevitable part of the human condition. And finally, whereas Fenollosa saw the universal elements in American and Japanese civilizations as part of an overall cultural synthesis drawing East and West together, Lea believed that national self-interest and conflicting ambitions must draw the two countries into an unavoidable confrontation.

If miles apart philosophically, the involvement abroad of Lea and Fenollosa was similar in that both men had initially become involved in a foreign cause as a result of personal needs and ambitions. With normal channels for a military career closed because of his physical defects, Lea simply created his own career. He did this by becoming a self-styled military "expert" and adviser to any and all who accepted his services. Whatever the Chinese Imperial Reform Association and the T'ung-meng-hui may have represented in his later geopolitical theories, initially they were simply the most convenient vehicles for achieving his military ambitions. It is unlikely that Lea was ever formally commissioned as a general, but, like the general in Genet's *The Balcony*, he came to feel and thus act as though he were one. The imaginary thus became the real. In this process, Lea was able to fulfill deep personal needs which were at the heart of his China activities.

Associated as he was with the Pao-huang-hui and the T'ung-meng-hui, Lea was never as totally immersed in Chinese life and culture as Fenollosa was in Japanese civilization. Lea's knowledge of China was limited, for with the exception of two brief trips there, most of his activities took place in the United States. Even more important, however, is the fact that Lea's involvement in Chinese affairs was always related to his own brand of American or perhaps Anglo-Saxon nationalism. Convinced that his own commercially oriented country was militarily unprepared to confront Japan, he hoped personally to help turn the tide in the Pacific. Believing that a militarily strong China closely linked to the United States was necessary for national survival, Lea devoted most of his energies to achieving this end. In his eyes the issues were strikingly clear. He predicted in a posthumously published article: "Whatever nation secures the dominion of the Pacific and maintains it has reached the sphere and possibility of world empire. No nation that does not first possess this sovereignty can aspire to the hope of greatness; and unless the Republic secures that dominion now, it is lost to it forever."[113] To stand still in geopolitical affairs was actually to go backward, and this is what Lea through his China activities hoped to keep the United States from doing. Thus as personal ambitions and national needs merged together in Lea's mind, his involvement in Chinese affairs became a protean blend of the two.

Although a fervent nationalist, a militarist, and a propagator of the need for Anglo-Saxon unity, Lea, unlike many of his fellow countrymen, was not racially biased against Orientals. Measuring the value of everything from a military perspective, he praised the Chinese by claiming that they were potentially good soldiers who simply had had the wrong kind of leadership. On the other hand, his fear of Japan was mixed with an admiration for the militant, non-commercial spirit of self-sacrifice which he believed permeated that entire country. And even when he clambered onto his nationalistic soap-box to warn his slumbering countrymen of the dangers of a "yellow peril," he was thinking purely in military terms. Associated as he was with Chinese-Americans throughout his entire life, he never participated in any nativistic organization or expressed sympathy for the racial abuses being heaped upon Orientals by so many of his fellow Americans.[114]

In the final analysis, despite the tremendous differences between the activities abroad of Fenollosa and Lea, their activism separated them from a narrow kind of parochialism that so characterized the Western world view during much of the nineteenth and twentieth centuries.[115] Certainly both men recognized long before most of their countrymen the increasing significance of China and Japan in world affairs. Even more important they also realized that in the years to come East and West were bound to meet and interreact with increasing frequency. Both Fenollosa and Lea were far ahead of their time. As historian Geoffrey Barraclough suggests, the period from 1890 to 1961 separates the contemporary from the modern era of the Renaissance—the Enlightenment and the French Revolution.[116] During these years the Pacific began to replace the Atlantic as the economic, political and cultural locus of world civilization. As their involvement in the affairs of China and Japan suggest, Lea and Fenollosa were keenly aware of this phenomenon.

3

The Maelstrom of War:
Wharton, Seeger, and Cowley

> *Every human generation has its own illusions
> with regard to civilization; some believe that they
> are taking part in its upsurge, other that they are
> witnesses of its extinction. In fact, it always both
> flames up and smoulders and is extinguished, ac-
> cording to the place and the angle of view.*
>
> Ivo Andric'
> *The Bridge on the Drina*

DURING THE EARLY SUMMER OF 1914 while the clouds of war hovered
over Europe, Henry James, the elder statesman of American belles-
lettres, was immersed in writing *The Ivory Tower*, a rather ambitious
novel with an American setting. Once the storm began, however, and
inundated the Continent, James quickly discovered that he was unable
to concentrate upon his writing. Instead he began to devote more and
more of his energies to the Allied war effort, although age and poor
health limited his activities. He visited hospitals, wrote an occasional
patriotic tract, and incessantly fretted to friends about his inability to
play a more active role. This feeling of personal inadequacy was sharpened by a gnawing sense of frustration at the continuing neutrality of
his own country. In an attempt to awaken his countrymen to the need
for involvement, he published a small pamphlet calling for American
volunteers to serve in the Ambulance Corps in France. "We Americans
are as little neutrals as possible where any aptitude for any action, of

whatever kind, that affirms life and freshly and inventively exemplifies it, instead of overwhelming and undermining it, is concerned. Great is the chance in fact for exhibiting this as our entirely elastic, our supremely characteristic, social aptitude."[1] Yet as the summer of 1915 approached and America's "social aptitude" continued to be "neutral" rather than participatory, James was more determined than ever to do something to dramatize his commitment to England and the war effort. If America would not act, he must act for her, and in what he considered to be an appropriate symbolic gesture gave up his American citizenship and became a citizen of Great Britain on July 16. A few days earlier he had explained his decision to a nephew:

> It will probably interest you to know that the indispensability of my step to myself has done nothing but grow since I made my application; like Martin Luther at Wittenberg "I could do no other". . . . I have testified to my long attachment here in the only way I could— though I certainly shouldn't have done it, under the inspiration of our cause, if the U.S.A. had done it a little more for me. Then I should have thrown myself back on that and been content with it; but as this, at the end of a year, hasn't taken place, I have had to act for myself, and I go so far as quite to think, I hope not fatuously, that I shall have set an example and shown a little something of the way.[2]

Seven months later Henry James was dead, *The Ivory Tower* still not completed; the artist had made the supreme sacrifice—he had neglected his work for the war. Well before the United States finally fulfilled James's desires by entering the conflict, other American writers, many of them considerably younger, had also become actively involved in the struggle on the side of the Allies.[3] For some, at least, the cost was to be far greater than that of an unfinished manuscript.

Unquestionably James's thirty-nine years' residence in England, his basic enthusiasm for British social institutions, and his closeness to the battlefield all help to explain his commitment to the Allied war effort. Yet, as had so often been the case during a long and brilliant career, James was out of step with the opinion of many of his fellow countrymen. While most Americans would not have agreed in 1914 that the war in Europe was in any way their personal concern, few would have viewed it by 1915 with the cynical detachment of F. Scott Fitzgerald's Amory Blaine who proclaimed that beyond "a sporting interest in the German dash for Paris the whole affair failed either to thrill or interest" him.[4] At the time of James's death the battle was still remote to most Americans who were too absorbed with their own problems to be tied emotionally to those of Europe. The country's political and creative energies were focused on the revolution in Mexico, the reforms of the New Freedom, attempts to limit immigration, continuing adjustment to the automobile, and what one historian has labeled the "Rebellion" in the arts.[5] Change and revolt, prosperity and excitement were in the air—so much so that Europe seemed much farther than three thousand miles away, and the President's admonition to remain neutral in thought as well as in action seemed perfectly appropriate.

Yet, in spite of distance, neutrality proclamations, and the pressing realities of day-to-day existence, there were some Americans, who, like Henry James, found it impossible to ignore the Great War. In fact, by the time the United States entered the war in April 1917 the number of American writers actively engaged in some facet of the conflict was large. These American writers were to be found in practically every kind of wartime activity from fighting in the front lines, to driving ambulances and munition trucks, or helping with hospital and refugee problems in Paris. By April 1917 some had been killed, some wounded, some imprisoned, and, particularly among the young participants, almost all had seen far too much violence and death too soon in their lives. During the period before America's entry into the conflict, Louis Bromfield, John Dos Passos, Ernest Hemingway, E. E. Cummings, Harry Crosby, Slater Brown, Dashiell Hammett, Sidney Howard, Robert Hillyer, John Howard Lawson, and William Seabrook were either ambulance or munitions drivers. William Faulkner was a cadet in the Royal Canadian Air Force, and Victor Chapman was flying with the Lafayette Escadrille. In addition Dorothy Canfield Fisher followed her husband to France and worked with Belgian and French refugees and the war blind, while Gertrude Stein and Alice Toklas drove their own Ford through the narrow streets of Paris delivering hospital supplies. Included in this list should be three other writers—Edith Wharton, Alan Seeger, and Malcolm Cowley—whose wartime activities were as different as their personalities. The fact that their voluntary pursuits span the entire period from early 1914 to the fall of 1917 as well as their differences in age, background, and motivation make these three writers excellent case studies for writer activism during the wartime period. In like manner, the ultimate impact that the war had upon these three lives also suggests the way in which different generations responded to this cataclysmic event.

Edith Wharton was the first of the three writers to become personally involved in the war. The fact that she was residing in Paris when the hostilities began helps to explain her early commitment. Yet apart from being close to the fighting, there was nothing in the background of this fifty-two-year-old woman to have suggested personal participation in the war. Edith Wharton was born in 1862 into the socially well-ordered world of aristocratic New York society. She spent much of her childhood traveling and living abroad since her family's fortune, based upon real estate holdings, enabled her parents to pursue the diversions of the leisure class. With the spread of industrialism and the rising influence of the *nouveaux riches* the family found it to be both financially and socially advantageous to alternate their time between fashionable Newport and various Continental cities where living expenses were low. Such continuous movement and prevailing attitudes concerning the education of women meant that her education was a combination of carefully chosen tutors and constant, if undisciplined, reading in her father's "gentleman's library." Her childhood was not a happy one. Because of a basic shyness and, at times, a social awkwardness, she never felt that she was meeting the expectations of a rigid and dominating mother.[6] Her intellectual precocity was tolerated, occasionally encouraged, but never to the extent of allowing deviation from the prescribed ritual that all young women of her background were expected to follow. Thus, at the age of seventeen she was dutifully presented to New York society, and six years later she married Teddy Wharton, a Harvard graduate twelve years her senior.

From the beginning the marriage appears to have been held to gether by little more than its social respectability. Over the next few years Edith Wharton's life remained the same, resembling that of a Jamesian heroine, her outward decorum giving little hint of any inner discontent. But discontent there was. As her biographers suggest, from the beginning Wharton was unable to find either sexual or intellectual fulfillment in her marriage with the result that she and Teddy lived together more as amicable companions than as husband and wife. As part of a social milieu in which careers or serious intellectual interests among women were discouraged, Wharton, since early childhood, had sought escape by making up stories and then gradually writing them down.[7] When she was sixteen, her mother had encouraged the publication of a private edition of her poems, and Wharton had continued to publish an occasional poem during the first years of her marriage. It was not until 1890, however, that her first piece of fiction appeared in *Scribner's*, with several other stories being published over the next few years. If her writing helped her deal psychologically with the tedium of a deteriorating marriage and a measured existence, it did not represent a rebellion against her environment; for as Alfred Kazin has observed, she became a writer "not because she revolted against her native society, but because she was bored with it."[8] In the late 1890s she suffered an emotional breakdown caused in part by sexual frustration, the continuing tensions of her marriage, and her fears about committing herself to a literary career. With recovery came a new enthusiasm for writing, and she began to pursue the kind of creative existence she would follow for the rest of her life. Her first collection of short stories, *The Greater Inclination*, appeared in 1899, followed the next year by a novelette, *The Touchstone*. Finally in 1905 she completed *The House of Mirth*, which firmly established her reputation in the literary world.

Accustomed since childhood to traveling in Europe, and increasingly affronted by the rawness of industrial society, Edith and Teddy began spending longer periods living in Paris in the fashionable Faubourg Saint-Germain. By the end of the first decade of the new century, she had long since outgrown the narrowly constructed caste of her earlier environment and now included among her intellectual coterie such diverse personalities as Charles Eliot Norton, Paul Bourget, Jean Cocteau, Bernard Berenson, and a friend whom many have called her literary mentor, Henry James. In 1911 while living in Paris she completed *Ethan Frome*—still her best-known and most widely read work.

The following year brought about a drastic change in her life. Because of her husband's worsening mental disorders and a total lack of conjugal compatibility, Wharton ended her marriage in the spring of 1913. Financially secure through a substantial inheritance and rapidly increasing royalties, she decided to remain in Paris. Surrounded by a bevy of dogs, servants, friends, and luxury she continued to live the sedate but stimulating life of a socially prominent middle-aged woman of recognized literary talents. There was nothing in her background to suggest that the events of August 1914 would in any way alter this routine.

When the war began Wharton was about to leave Paris for England, where she had rented a country home for the summer social season. Her departure was delayed, and while she waited for transportation across the Channel, the Comtesse d'Haussonville, a friend who was president of one of the bureaus of the French Red Cross, asked her to help organize a workroom for the wives of soldiers who had been recently mobilized. In addition Wharton learned that with the departure of men to the front, a number of hotels, restaurants, and shops had been forced to close resulting in even more widespread unemployment. Although lacking organizational experience, Wharton agreed to establish a workshop for seamstresses to provide employment not only for wives and mothers of soldiers, but also for other needy women who had no relatives in the army. As originally planned, the workshop was to be only for women in Wharton's arrondissement, but because of her effective solicitation among wealthy Paris friends she was able to raise two thousand dollars and thus employ women from other parts of the city as well. A large flat in the Faubourg Saint-Germain was selected as the site for the workshop, and by late August some ninety seamstresses were at work.[9]

Only women not already receiving a military allowance were

eligible to sew in the shop. For six hours' work a seamstress received about twenty cents a day, a noon meal, medical attention, and free coal in the winter. Soon after the workshop opened, a plan of rotation was adopted since there was a long waiting list of women who wanted jobs. After two months of work in the shop a seamstress had to leave, but could do piece work at home for an additional month if she so desired. At the end of that month, if a position was available, she could return for another two months and continue this rotation indefinitely. Initially, Wharton had hoped to provide for the workshops solely through donations and to give away all of the garments that were made. But as it became obvious that the war was going to last more than a matter of weeks, she decided that the workshops must be made as self-sufficient as possible, and this could only be done by selling the finished products. From the very first she had persuaded the seamstresses to specialize in "fashionable lingerie" as well as in the usual hospital supplies with the intention of selling some of the items to friends in America.[10] It was also decided that material donated to the workshop was to be used to make items that would be given to hospitals or refugee organizations whereas materials bought with workshop funds were to be sold.

Besides coordinating the operation of the workshop, Wharton devoted countless hours to soliciting orders and donations from friends in France and the United States. Never having had to worry about earning a living, she showed a surprising degree of Yankee ingenuity when selling the products of the workshop. Realizing that humanitarian appeals would only go so far, she added the lure of a bargain when writing an American friend and potential customer: "if you want any [blouses] later you need only tell me your price and you will get about one third more for the money than in any shop."[11] Bad news from the front and the mounting casualty lists at times engulfed the workshop in gloom, but Wharton recorded how everything would temporarily brighten when a new order was received. "Often, when I come into the work-room, I am met by an excited cry: 'A new order! A big order!' and there is not one of our staff who does not often work over-time to get these coveted orders 'rushed through. . . .' "[12] Such *esprit de corps* enabled the workshop to thrive, and on the first anniversary of the undertaking Wharton announced to her seamstresses that an average of sixty "work-women" had been employed during the previous year working the equivalent of 14,733 days while producing $17,000 worth of garments which had either been sold or given to charities.[13]

Wharton had another reason for insisting that the workshops be self-sufficient. By the fall of 1914 she was deeply involved in another war charity, which by its very nature would have to depend solely on contributions from America. This new effort was aimed at bringing relief to thousands of French and Belgium war refugees who began to wander into Paris. To meet this new emergency a group of French and Belgians had improvised a relief organization—Le Foyer Franco-Belge—which was soon inundated by requests for help. Impressed by the success of Wharton's workshop, the organization asked her to create an American committee to aid with the refugee problem. Working at first through the French and Belgium group and then branching off on her own, she began to establish several refugee centers that collectively would be known as L'Accueil Franco-Américain. Within a month's time she had obtained from friends the use of three large houses: two were furnished with approximately a hundred beds and the third was used for a restaurant and a medical center. When refugees entered the city, they were processed through the French-Belgium center and some were then sent to be housed and fed by the L'Accueil Franco-Américain. Food and shelter were but a part of refugee needs and, exhibiting what one biographer calls a genius for organization and administration,[14] Wharton set up centers which provided so many other services that the L'Accueil Franco-Américain began to resemble a wartime Hull House. Since many of the refugees entered the city with little more than the clothes on their backs and these often in rags, a Clothing Depot was established and appeals for boots and other apparel were made throughout France and the United States. Wharton applied the format used in the sewing workshops to the refugee situation; she established a work-room in one of the houses and shortly thereafter fifty women were busily making garments for the needy. No sooner was the workshop operating than it became obvious that some form of child care was needed, and within a few days a nursery was opened. The children were given organized singing and sewing classes while adult refugees were encouraged to take classes in English. Wharton was also concerned about the psychological well-being of the refugees. Believing that some kind of employment would fill time and boost morale, she helped establish an agency which by the war's end had assisted more than 3400 refugees in finding various kinds of work. As the scope of L'Accueil Franco-Américain expanded, Wharton did less administrating and more fund-raising. With the assistance of her former sister-in-law in the United States, Wharton was able to raise enough funds to meet the needs of L'Accueil. Yet to accomplish this she carried on a correspondence which would have overwhelmed a less active person.[15]

In early 1915 heavy fighting in western Belgium led thousands more refugees to flee to Paris. Among the most helpless and needy were the hundreds of orphaned or abandoned children. In April 1915 these Belgium children became the next to benefit from Wharton's boundless energies. This third of her wartime activities actually began when she was asked by the Belgium government to provide care for sixty children along with their Flemish nuns. Once again through the assistance of wealthy friends she obtained the use of a vacant house to the west of Paris in Sévres. Seven months later the Children of Flanders Rescue Committee was in full operation maintaining five houses, caring for almost nine hundred persons including the children, their wards, and almost two hundred elderly refugees who, like the children, had been abandoned. The Belgium government shared the expense of furnishing and heating the houses while the French government allowed the organization a ten cents per diem for each child. This governmental assistance scarcely covered the operating costs of the committee. In addition to food and clothing, funds were needed to provide medical supplies, the salaries for attendant doctors and various educational services such as sewing and vocational training classes. What this meant for Edith Wharton is that, like a mendicant friar, she was forced to beg even farther afield as her wartime involvement continued to expand.[16]

During the remainder of 1915 the range of Wharton's activities was indeed staggering as she divided her time and energies between the workshops, L'Accueil Franco-Américain, and the Children of Flanders Rescue Committee. There was no slackening in her duties. During the spring of 1916 the tempo increased when she became involved in a fourth and final major wartime activity. Once again the French government had turned to her, and Wharton had agreed to help create a cure program (Tuberculeux de la Guerre) for French soldiers suffering from tuberculosis. Her involvement with this program also increased her concern for the spread of the disease among the refugees with whom she was working. As she wrote to her sister-in-law, "All such sanatoria in France are closed at present except for soldiers, and there is no place to which we can send the women and children among our refugees who are spreading contagion in their families."[17] With assistance from the Paris municipal government and donations from American friends, she opened convalescent homes at Groslay, located near Paris, and at Arromanches in Normandy. By November 1917 she could report to a prospective contributor that the homes were caring for approximately one hundred and forty women and children from the various refugee hostels and an additional fifty children suffering from tuberculosis of the bone who had been sent by the Assistance Publique.[18] Wharton believed that her work with the tuberculosis victims was her most important contribution to the war effort and her most enduring legacy to the postwar period.[19]

With so much of her energy consumed by wartime activities, it is remarkable that Wharton found the time to do anything else. Yet even though her creative production diminished somewhat during this period, she still managed to work on a major novel (*Summer*) and several other shorter pieces of fiction. Since writing by this time was such an intrinsic and necessary part of her personality, it is not surprising that she would use it to contribute to the war effort. Early in 1915, in response to a request by the French Red Cross, she made a tour of military hospitals located near the front to evaluate and send back lists of their most pressing medical needs. Several weeks later she was granted permission to visit the lines from Dunkerque to Belfort. Wharton undertook the trip with an express purpose in mind: she planned to gather material for a series of articles which "might bring home to American readers some of the dreadful realities of war."[20] The articles began to appear in *Scribner's* that spring and were a blend of descriptive and propagandistic writing. While describing the destructiveness of the war, Wharton also wrote about the enduring courage of the French people and what she felt to be the unprincipled brutalities of the "German beast."[21] She hoped that the articles would lead American public opinion toward direct intervention, and would create a more sympathetic atmosphere in which to solicit wartime contributions. Toward the end of 1915 she donated her literary talents to still another fund raising activity by agreeing to edit *The Book of the Homeless*. This was a collection of original contributions by Sarah Bernhart, Rupert Brooke, Jean Cocteau, Joseph Conrad, Thomas Hardy, Henry James, W. B. Yeats, and others, the proceeds from which were given to Wharton's various charities.[22]

Wharton's constantly multiplying organizational, administrative, and fund-raising activities exacted so heavy a physical toll that in November 1916 she collapsed from total exhaustion. After a few weeks' rest, however, she resumed her activities following the same frantic pace of previous years. Yet as America's entry into the conflict drew near, Wharton's activities were actually nearing an end, for the Red Cross had gradually been taking over a number of her charities. The others were running so smoothly and self-sufficiently that during the spring of 1917 she had begun to devote additional time to writing and living as she had during the prewar years. The French government had already expressed its appreciation by awarding her the Legion of Honor in 1916, and, at the war's end, she was also decorated by the King of the Belgians. Still, her work did not completely end, for as late as 1919 she continued to correspond with friends and contributors concerning the fate of various relief agencies. She was particularly pleased in November 1919 to announce to a friend that the tubercular convalescent homes had sufficient funds to continue operating until the French Ministry of Interior and the Department of the Seine could take over and "run them as a permanent memorial to American work for the tuberculous in France."[23] Several weeks earlier she had spoken to another friend about establishing a scholarship in France to honor a young American who, like herself, had participated in the war.[24] This young man, a poet Alan Seeger, was an American expatriate living in Paris when the war began. Seeger had immediately volunteered his services, but unlike Edith Wharton, he did not live to receive the gratitude of the French government, for he was killed in action in 1916.

Whereas Edith Wharton was middle-aged and an established writer at the war's beginning, Seeger was twenty-six years old and virtually unknown. He was born in 1888 and spent his early childhood in a large, rambling Victorian house on Staten Island, suggesting the protective atmosphere of a suburban existence. Seeger attended the private Staten Island Academy and then the Horace Mann School after the family moved into the city. Several years later the family moved to Mexico City where Charles Seeger had established a business. There the education of the Seeger children was entrusted to tutors, who introduced then to the enchantment of such classics as the *Iliad* and *Odyssey, The Faerie Queen, Don Quixote,* and many others. As Seeger and his older brother approached college age, their father desired a more traditional pedagogical atmosphere, and the boys were sent in 1902 to the Hackley School in Tarrytown, New York. Seeger's stay there differed little from that of most of his middle-class classmates.[25]

Alan Seeger's future continued to follow well-established guidelines, and he entered Harvard in the fall of 1906. At Harvard, Seeger's shyness led him to shun most social activities. He totally immersed himself in his academic work, and except for his brother and a few other acquaintances, one of whom was John Reed, he was content to remain by himself much of the time during his first two years. It was easy to stay in the shadows in the Harvard of this period; the famous class of 1910 included such future illuminati as Reed,

Walter Lippman, T. S. Eliot, Heywood Broun, and the minnesinger to the Nazi court, Ernst (Putzi) Hanfstaengl. Seeger remembered that during his first two years at Harvard his life "was intellectual to the exclusion of almost everything else. The events of that life were positive adventures to me. Few, I am sure have known more than I did then the employ of intellect as an instrument of pleasure."[26] At the beginning of his junior year, however, his interests and lifestyle began to change radically. Perhaps it was a reaction against two years of intensive study and self-imposed loneliness. His change in attitude might also have developed from a course that he was taking on the Romantic Movement. Enthusiastic about the entire course, he was particularly excited when he began to read Jean Jacques Rousseau. It was not the theoretical Rousseau of the *Social Contract* that he found to be most appealing, but the romantic Rousseau, the lonely wanderer of the *Reveries of a Solitary Walker*. Specifically, it was the personality of the man rather than the ideas of the social critic that totally enthralled Seeger. "It is Rousseau the romantic solitary," he excitedly wrote to a friend that fall, "the misanthrope, the dreamer apart, the hyper-aesthetic of the exquisite sensibilities and the extraordinary emotions, and to many other qualities to which I avow passionate sympathy."[27] Rousseau was not alone in this newly constructed Pantheon. Shelley and Byron were also included since they too exuded a spirit of "eternal youthfulness" which Seeger believed was needed to cut through the cant of outworn tradition.[28] The Romantics were to be admired, in fact to be emulated, because they had dared to throw restraint to the winds. By so doing they had been able to write greatly and to live greatly as well. The idea of living well had become clear to Seeger in another course, during a lecture on Goethe. The professor, as Seeger recounted to a friend, alluded to the "old Mediaeval notion that if Restraint were removed from the individual, three passions or lusts, would be discovered,—the lust of power, the lust of feeling, and lust of knowing. . . ."[29] Seeger felt that the lust of feeling was most lacking in his own life and he began remedying the deficiency with a vengeance. Affecting the bohemian—long hair, baggy trousers, and bulky sweaters—he self-consciously neglected his studies for the less structured and hopefully more passionate life of an artist. During his senior year the ideal day, as described to his father, included a morning of tennis and writing poetry, an afternoon of writing prose with an hour set aside for German, and an evening of reading or conversations with friends.[30] By this time his poetry was being recognized in the university's literary circles, and he was rewarded with an editorial position on the *Harvard Monthly*. Despite his newly adopted lifestyle, Seeger must have kept up with more conventional academic courses, for he graduated, in June 1910, with honors and a major in Celtic literature.

Seeger left Harvard with dreams of becoming a poet. That fall he rented a furnished room in Greenwich Village at Washington Square, and then set about making an entry into New York's literary circles. His plans were as grandiose as his failures. He had little success in getting his poetry published, and was barely able to live on the pittances he earned from tutoring or the selling of an occasional article. Literary recognition may have been slow in coming, but he was determined to live as passionately as the Romantics. At all hours of day and night he could be seen stalking the Village streets wearing a flowing black cape with a guitar slung across his back. Fellow Harvard classmate and friend John Reed frequently encountered and later gently satirized Seeger during his New York period:

> A timid footstep,—enter then the eager
> Keats—Shelley—Swinburne—Mediaeval—Seeger;
> Poe's raven bang above Byronic brow,
> And Dante's beak,—you have his picture now;
> In fact he is, though feigning not to know it,
> The popular conception of a Poet.
> Dreaming, his eyes are steadily alight
> With splendors of a world beyond our sight;
> He nothing knows of the material sphere,—
> Unwilling seems, at times, to linger here;
> Beauty is all his breath, his blood, he says,—
> Beauty his shrine, and Love its priestesses.
> Wildly he talks, with solemn, bell-like voice

> In words that might have been old Malory's choice,—
> Proclaiming, in the manner of ascetics,
> "For ethics we must substitute aesthetics!"[31]

For two years Seeger continued to live passionately, but in the process discovered that such an existence did not compensate for a literary career. As he grew frustrated by personal failure and the lack of recognition, he became disenchanted with New York and then the entire American environment. He began to see it not as spontaneous and creative, but as a crass society devoted to material comfort and intellectual convenience. Even more important, he believed it was an environment that deadened the sensibilities of a dedicated writer, and, like another young poet, Ezra Pound, who permanently left the United States in 1908, Seeger also felt that his own creative survival demanded departure. It was not just a change of scenery he wanted, but an entirely different cultural ethos which he believed could only be found in Europe: "it seems to me that Europe will continue for some time yet to sing the world's great songs and make the world's great poems. For she has known great élans, and from the pinnacles of enthusiasm vision will have been revealed to her more wonderful than have yet been dreamed of."[32] Feeling as he did, to remain in the United States was out of the question, and Seeger left for Paris in the spring of 1912.

As exciting as a change of scenery was for Seeger, it did not appreciably alter the routine that he had followed in New York. When not writing he was either roaming the city or busy sampling the pleasures of café life. By the fall of 1912 he was as passionately committed to Paris as had been the young romantics of an earlier era, and in a letter home he happily announced that he was quickly purging himself of the "spirit of America." Although plans for the future were still unclear, he was at least certain that he had found the best possible place in which to write. "I am in the Old World for good I hope, and do not care if I never see the other side of the Atlantic again. In fact I pray that I may not."[33] The joy of living abroad spilled over into his work, and during the little more than two years that he spent in Paris, Seeger wrote most of the poems that became part of his only collection, *Juvenilia*. He was in the process of trying to get the collection published when the war began.

The excitement that engulfed the city when war was declared was enough to make Seeger forget his poetry temporarily. To the young expatriate, the war represented the opportunity to achieve what he had been striving for since leaving Harvard. The war was the most important thing that was happening in the world, and by participating in it he would, at long last, have the opportunity to live greatly. In his mind this was the substance out of which great poets are made. At the same time, his presence in France when the fighting began made him, like Edith Wharton, feel as though he too were a part of that endangered nation. A sense of guilt also touched his feelings and in an article written for the *New Republic*, he explained why he felt the need to play a combat role. "In every case the answer was the same. That memorable day in August came. Suddenly the old haunts were desolate, the boon companions had gone. It was unthinkable to leave the danger to them and accept only the pleasures oneself, to go on enjoying the sweet things of life in defense of which they were perhaps even then shedding their blood in the north."[34] The opportunity to participate directly in the conflict was made possible when the French War Ministry decided that aliens could enlist in the Foreign Legion for the duration of the war instead of for the usual five-year period. Since a recruit had simply to swear an oath to uphold the rules and discipline of the Legion, which technically was only a fighting force and not a government, he would not run the risk of loss of American citizenship by participating in the affairs of another country. Thus on August 4, while the German armies were preparing to cross the frontier into Belgium, Seeger enlisted in the Legion. After a brief but exhilarating parade in Paris, with Seeger proudly carrying the American flag, he and the Legion's other recruits traveled by rail to Toulouse, where they began the initial phases of their training.

The beauty of southern France as well as the joy of drilling in the crisp autumn air within sight of the Pyrenees excited Seeger and awakened his poetic instincts, but he never doubted his decision to postpone a literary career for the life of a soldier. Convincing himself

of this was easier than convincing a worried mother. Hoping to comfort her, he tried to explain his decision by placing it in a larger
perspective: "Nature to me is not only hills and blue skies and flowers,
but the Universe, the totality of things, reality as it most obviously
presents itself to us, and in this universe strife and sternness play as
big a part as love and tenderness, and cannot be shirked by one whose
will it is to rule his life in accordance with the cosmic forces he sees
in play about him."[35] Whether his philosophizing comforted a distressed parent is unknown, but shortly after writing the letter Seeger's
desire to participate directly in the conflict came a step closer to being
realized. He and his fellow recruits departed their idyllic setting for a
new training site at Camp de Nailly in Aube, where they would put
the finishing touches on their combat readiness. Finally, near the end
of October, Seeger's battalion began to march toward the front. By
November 4 they were in the trenches at Cuiry-les-Chaudardes
(Aisne), located near the center of the gigantic battle line that, like an
earthquake shaken structure, was in the process of settling into what
would soon be called the Western Front. Before the year's end Seeger
had become accustomed to the monotonous routine he was to follow
for the duration of his service at the front: six days in the first line
trenches, six days' rest usually several kilometers behind the line, six
days in ready reserve, six more days of rest and then back to the first
line trenches again.[36] Like countless other soldiers, Seeger discovered
that the danger of battle was muted and often forgotten in the face of
the sheer discomfort of trench life. When not fighting fatigue, mud,
wet clothing, and lice, there was always the problem of how to deal
with the soldier's most constant companion—boredom. Furthermore,
with week after week of bombardment and enemy sniping, the nature
of combat was proving to be quite different from what Seeger had
envisioned. Particularly unpleasant to the young romantic was the
possibility of being killed by an unseen enemy in a prosaic way. "This
is what is distressing about the kind of warfare we are up against—
being harried like this by an invisible enemy and standing up against
all the dangers of battle without any of its exhilarations or enthusiasm—."[37] The élan of a bayonet charge was the cure that he felt was

needed to transform his wartime experiences into the passionate expectations of his dreams. Yet physical misery, the humdrum of routine, and unfulfilled expectations failed to daunt his enthusiasm, and in a late December (1914) entry in his diary he could still write: "This life agrees with me; there will be war for many years to come in Europe and I shall continue to be a soldier as long as there is war."[38]

Seeger had begun to realize what political and military leaders all over Europe were also learning—that the war would not be over as rapidly as everyone had thought. As Seeger became more accustomed to a soldier's life and the routine of the trenches, he had more time to reflect on his poetry. In the spring of 1915 he was particularly disturbed by an article he read about another poet-soldier, Rupert Brooke. In the article Seeger was compared to Brooke, but what troubled the young American was that unlike his British counterpart, he had no published works.[39] Shortly before joining the Legion he had been trying to negotiate the publication of *Juvenilia*, but it was not in print by 1915 and Seeger was concerned that something might happen to him before his poems would appear. It may well have been this concern that encouraged him to continue writing during the war and to publish in 1916 what became one of the most widely read wartime poems, "I Have a Rendezvous with Death."

In spite of his literary concerns and the miserably cold winter of 1914–15, Seeger never wavered in his commitment to a military existence. Hardships aside, he felt that he was experiencing life as never before. A June 1915 entry in his diary records: "I pity the poor civilians who shall never have seen or known the things that we have seen and known. Great as are the pleasures that they are continuing to enjoy and that we have renounced, the sense of being the instrument of Destiny is to me a source of greater satisfaction."[40] In spite of his continuing enthusiasm, Seeger was disappointed that he still had not gone over the top in an offensive charge. Months spent in the trenches had failed to dispel this romantic illusion of glory, and he was finally able to experience the long-awaited maneuver in late September 1915. His battalion was in the second line of attack in the Battle of Champagne which, after an initial success, failed to dislodge the Germans from their second line of defense. Military failure did not daunt Seeger's thrill of at last being out of the trenches on the attack. Fortunate enough to have escaped injury, he jauntily informed his mother later: "We knew many splendid moments, worth having endured many trials for. But in our larger aim, of piercing their line, of breaking the long deadlock, of entering Vouziers in triumph, of course we failed."[41] After this brief encounter with glory, his regiment spent almost the entire winter of 1915–16 in reserve and did not return to the trenches until the early spring of 1916. Seeger's absence from the front was even more prolonged because of illness. In early March he suffered a severe attack of bronchitis and spent the next three months recovering in Biarritz. Although the comforts of civilian life were welcome, he was anxious to rejoin his regiment. After a month in Paris, he was back at the front by May 1916.

By early 1916 the war in the West was nearing the peak of its absurd brutality. Determined to break the deadlock, commanders on both sides were displaying the same restlessness and unimaginative persistence that would lead to even greater carnage in the coming months. In late February the Germans had begun their massive attack on the Verdun salient. Although the French had held and had begun to counterattack in May, the battle would drag on until December without major military consequences, but with a staggering loss of life on both sides. To relieve the pressure on their French allies, the British General-Staff decided on the same murderous strategy of a frontal attack along the Somme which was proving to be so costly at Verdun. Alan Seeger was to be a part of this most costly of military blunders, for when he returned to the front that spring he learned that his regiment was to take part in the great offensive. Participation in such a massive attack was what Seeger had been hoping for. He proudly wrote to a friend a few days before the battle began: "I am glad to be going in the first wave. If you are in this thing at all it is best to be in to the limit. And this is the supreme experience."[42] Tradition has it that Seeger was killed in an attack on Belloy-en-Santerre on July 4, although a more recent scholar claims that his death did not occur until almost three weeks later on July 23.[43] Thus Seeger, like so many others, met his "rendezvous" during the brutal insanity of the Somme offensive.

Alan Seeger was already a romantic legend when nineteen-year-old Malcolm Cowley—the youngest of the three Americans—arrived in Europe in May 1917. By this time Edith Wharton had also engaged in her wartime activities and was eagerly anticipating rest and a change of scenery in a trip to Morocco. Cowley had come to France not to serve his country, which had declared war on Germany a month earlier, but instead, like so many other writers of his generation, he had rushed from a college campus to Europe to see something of the war before it ended. His involvement would be measured in months instead of years, and would be much safer than Seeger's, but more dangerous than Wharton's. It was also a kind of involvement that was far more detached and "spectatorial" than that of the two older Americans. Cowley's activism abroad seemed to symbolize a whole generation of young writers, such as E. E. Cummings, John Dos Passos, Ernest Hemingway, and Slater Brown, who volunteered their services to a number of noncombatant organizations in order to get to Europe to see the war firsthand.

If Cowley's attitude towards participating in the war was markedly different from that of Wharton and Seeger, so too was his background. He was born on a farm near the small town of Belsano, Pennsylvania, in the foothills of the western Alleghenies. His father was a physician with a practice in a working-class district in Pittsburgh where, according to a friend of the family, he often donated his time to impoverished patients.[44] Due to his father's practice, Cowley's youth was pleasantly divided between summers on the farm and living in the more exciting urban atmosphere. There was little that was truly unique about these formative years except that Cowley and several of his high school classmates, the best known of whom was the future critic Kenneth Burke, rather self-consciously intended to pursue careers in the arts. "We were like others," Cowley wrote some years later, "we were normal—yet we clung to the feeling that as apprentice writers we were abnormal and secretly distinguished: we lived in the special world of art; we belonged to the freemasonry of those who had read modern authors and admired a paradox."[45] The beginning of the war in Europe had little or no effect upon the carefree high school atmosphere: unlike thousands of European youths already on their way to the front, Cowley and his circle passed an uneventful senior year eagerly awaiting each issue of *The Smart Set*, taking college entrance examinations, and deciding which university they would attend in the fall.

In 1915 Cowley entered Harvard with a scholarship, still planning to become a writer. Cowley was somewhat disillusioned by his college experience. Another Harvard graduate, Henry Adams, had discovered years earlier that his nineteenth-century education was almost totally unsuited for preparing him to live in an era that was increasingly dominated by the dynamo. In a similar way Cowley and many of his generation were finding their own educational experiences to be equally inappropriate. What they learned in the classroom seemed in no way related to the perplexities of a rapidly changing urbanized-industrialized society, or, for that matter, to the intellectual ferment that engulfed the country during the prewar period.[46] Too often learning seemed to be artificially separated from life, and to an aspiring writer there was no greater disservice that a classroom could provide. "What we were seeking, as sophomores and juniors, was something vastly more general, a key to unlock the world, a picture to guide us in fitting its jigsaw parts together." It was not as though his professors were unable or unwilling to provide such a guide, but, as he remembered: "The trouble was that the world they pictured for our benefit was the special world of scholarship—timeless, placeless, elaborate, incomplete and bearing only the vaguest relationship to that other world in which fortunes were made, universities endowed and city governments run by muckers."[47]

In a personal history of his generation written some years earlier, Cowley suggested that another vexing and more lasting effect of his educational experience was the way in which it had led to a continuing process of deracination. At Harvard, regional and ethnic differences had been subtly bleached to meet the requirements of new, "unspoken standards." These standards were usually not so much provided by the faculty as by fellow classmates who had followed a socially traditional, clearly demarcated path from Eastern prep-schools to membership in prestigious dining clubs at the university. The accepted virtues that dominated the campus thus had a recognizable Victorian aura about them, but might also have been lifted from Veblen's description of the leisure class. In recalling them Cowley stressed that the most important were "good taste, good manners, cleanliness, chastity, gentlemanliness (or niceness), reticence and the spirit of competition in sports. . . ."[48] Bedazzled by the burden of tradition that they found at Harvard, and perhaps somewhat unnerved by their public school backgrounds, Cowley and others like him often felt their own cultural heritage was in a state of siege. Most certainly no generation has ever found its educational experiences completely suitable to its social needs, but Cowley believed that his tended to destroy any sense of belonging to a city, a region, a country, or, for that matter, even a cultural tradition. Instead it had provided him with a classic and scholarly universalism which he found instructive, but which left him without a tangible sense of identity. "Whatever the doctrines we adopted during our college years, whatever the illusions we had of growing toward culture and self-sufficiency, the same process of deracination was continuing for all of us. We were like so many tumbleweeds sprouting in the rich summer soil, our leaves spreading while our roots slowly died and became brittle."[49]

The educational dissatisfaction that so many of this younger generation of writers felt helps explain why they so eagerly rushed from the halls of academe to what they believed was a truer kind of classroom.[50] Cowley and his generation of writers, like Alan Seeger, also viewed the war as the most important event of their lives, and therefore believed that it had to be experienced firsthand. Perhaps they went to Europe at this time, too, because they feared the war might end while they were still on the sidelines. Thus by the winter of 1916–17 Malcolm Cowley was determined to go to France and drive an ambulance. He arrived in Paris in May 1917 with every intention of joining the American Field Service, but discovered that there was no need at the time for ambulance drivers. Instead, the French military transport was desperately short of personnel and welcomed anyone who could drive a truck. Arrangements allowing American volunteers to serve with the French military transport had been worked out that April by A. Pratt Andrew, Inspector General of the American Field Service. Shortly after the United States entered the war, he had telephoned the head of the French Automobile Service to inquire if there was anything that members of the Field Service could do now that many of its duties would be taken over by the American army. Andrew learned that there was great need for several thousand truck drivers who could serve in the *Réserve Mallet* under the same conditions governing the ambulance sections of the American Field Service.[51] It was because of these arrangements that Malcolm Cowley was able to serve voluntarily in the conflict even though the United States had officially entered the war.

Soon after joining the *Réserve Mallet*, Cowley was assigned to T. M. U. 526 (*Transport de Matériel Etats-Unis*—the *U* was an arbitrary abbreviation for Etats-Unis—United States) and sent to a newly opened training camp at Chavigny, which was located near Longpont in the northeast of France. After a quick course in which the recruits were taught how to operate, service, and drive in convoy the five-ton Pierce-Arrow transport trucks, they were bustled off to various sectors of the front. Cowley and most of the American volunteers transported materials in an area roughly from Soissons to a few kilometers west of Rheims. They would load their trucks at various railheads on the Soissons-Fismes road and then carry the materials to some point usually near the Chemin des Dames sector. Practically all of the loading was done during the day, the cargo consisting mostly of shells for the famous French Soixante-quinze, but the driving was done at night without headlights in order to minimize the risk of attracting fire from artillery or patrolling airplanes.[52]

During the massive French attack in late October and early November 1917 along the Chemin des Dames sector, which ultimately caused the German armies to fall back to the Oise-Aisne Canal, T. M.

U. 526 played an important role. Often suffering from lack of sleep because of loading activities during the day, the American drivers night after night eased their trucks along the deeply rutted, dust-clogged roads which were lined on each side with burlap camouflage. Occasionally the artillery parks where they loaded the trucks came under fire, but, for the most part, exhaustion rather than bombardment was their most persistent enemy during that entire fall. If not particularly glamorous, the role that they played was a vital one as they provided a continuous flow of ammunition for the French artillery. In fact, from the spring through the fall of 1917 the American contingent of the *Réserve Mallet* hauled more ammunition than the American army fired during its part of the war.[53]

After only five months the American sections of the *Réserve Mallet* began to break up. This occurred in the fall of 1917 when the United States Army tried to enlist as many as possible of its eight hundred American volunteers. Cowley left the T.M.U. that fall and returned to the United States, enlisting in the Field Artillery a week before the war ended. Like Cowley, most Americans who enlisted in the *Réserve Mallet* remained in it briefly. But in evaluating their activities, A. Pratt Andrew claimed that their driving was one of the most important contributions made by any group of volunteers during the war. In addition, he added, "These men and boys were giving the most gruelling service that any American volunteers were giving to France."[54] Cowley's recollections of his service with the *Réserve Mallet* were far more lighthearted. In fact, he remembered his role in the war as being almost ideal: "It provided us with fairly good food, a congenial occupation, furloughs to Paris and uniforms that admitted us to the best hotels." More important yet, at least from the perspective of a young, aspiring writer, "It permitted us to enjoy the once-in-a-lifetime spectacle of the Western Front."[55] Still, in spite of the carnival-like atmosphere in which they viewed it, the war had its costs for Cowley and his generation of writers. If it continued the deracination process begun some years earlier, it also encouraged amongst them a spectatorial attitude toward society and life itself.

By the time the war was over, the voluntary activities of Wharton,

Seeger, and Cowley had been completed for several months. While pursuing their diverse activities they had traveled over much of the Western Front and had seen the war from a perspective unknown to most of their fellow countrymen. At times they had also been close to or even part of some of the war's most important engagements. While their participation had been motivated by reasons as different as their personalities, backgrounds, and ages, they also held enough attitudes in common to lend a degree of similarity to their commitment.

All three writers could not ignore the war, for it represented something larger than their work or education, and thus had to be dealt with in a personal way. Seeger, for example, repeatedly stressed in letters to family and friends the enormity of the event in which he was participating. To his mother in particular he tried to explain that there was simply nowhere else in the world he preferred to be. "Success in life means doing that thing than which nothing else conceivable seems more noble or satisfying or remunerative," he wrote after a year already spent in the trenches, "and this enviable state I can truly say that I enjoy, for had I the chance, I would be nowhere else in the world than where I am."[56] Almost ten years younger than Seeger, and in high school rather than France in 1914, Cowley was at first unaffected by the onset of the fighting. It was not until he reached Harvard that the war electrified him, and, like a child forced to practice piano while a treasure hunt is taking place outside within clear view, he felt that he had to get to Europe before it was too late. In short, the Western Front and not the streets of Cambridge was the only proper classroom for a young, aspiring writer who felt as though he were missing the most significant event of his life. On the other hand, neither Cowley nor Seeger had firmly settled into a career or lifestyle at the time of their involvement in the war, and their participation was not as personally disruptive as was that of Edith Wharton. Literarily and socially established, accustomed to a patterned, somewhat luxurious existence, Wharton's participation in the conflict is even more amazing. Until World War I she had never shown more than a cursory interest in international affairs of any kind. Except for a friendship with Teddy Roosevelt which was more social and literary than anything else, she had lived a life detached from the most important social and political events of her day. In fact, almost exactly a year before the war began, Wharton, Bernard Berenson, a maid, and a pet dog made a trip through Germany during which she was so totally absorbed by a dislike of the countryside, boredom with museums, and concern about inadequate hotels that she was oblivious to the militaristic nationalism engulfing the country. If war in Europe was becoming more likely in the near future, Wharton and her entourage failed to notice it.[57] Yet routine, social obligations, and writing were all put aside after the invasion of France, and Edith Wharton committed herself to a cause for the first time in her life. But even this commitment was temporarily put aside when shortly after the fighting began she made a brief trip to England to cancel arrangements for a summer house she had rented for the coming social season. Although she planned to return immediately to begin organizing the workshops about which she had already been approached, her stay in England was prolonged since the Battle of the Marne was underway and transportation across the Channel was impossible to obtain. Already fired with the same enthusiasm that would help her through an exhausting variety of wartime activities, she complained to a friend about her forced inactivity: "I have just come from Paris, & of course all my heart is there where the whole nation is rising to face this Black Death, & not playing cricket and philandering like the British fritter— and I find apathy here very trying."[58] Similar to Seeger and Cowley, she too felt that her place was in France in the midst of things, and she constantly fretted until she could cross the Channel again.

Although their reasons were different, Wharton, Seeger, and Cowley all felt compelled to be in France close to the war, but all three had a naïve idea of just what it was they were rushing toward. In the not so distant past the glory of the Civil War hung like a consuming mist over the American landscape; the gala reunions of the Grand Old Army and the tragic grandeur of the Lost Cause had long since romanticized the agonies of that conflict. Closer to the present, remembrances of that splendid little excursion into Cuba continued to thrill the hearts of young and old while the more glaring postwar

residue of an extended guerilla conflict in the Philippines was con-
veniently forgotten. The pre-1914 glorification of war is difficult to
understand for Americans still cringing from a Vietnamese debacle so
vividly brought into their homes by television. But, according to one
observer, Americans of the early twentieth century were almost totally
lacking in any understanding of the nature of warfare, and still credu-
lously held to what he terms the "Winchester-on-the-wall frontier
tradition, or with the military romanticism personified by Teddy
Roosevelt. . . ."[59] War, then, was something to be savored, fully
experienced, even enjoyed—a proving ground on which to test one's
courage or manhood by living in constant danger and with the persistent threat of death. "You went to war," Malcolm Cowley later wrote,
"and it was like going to a theatre that advertised the greatest spectacle in history."[60] To a nineteen-year-old the process of getting to the
war probably seemed more important than understanding the war itself, and Cowley left for France as though going toward a grand
adventure. Alan Seeger might well have done the same. But the longer
he remained in the trenches the more he believed that the conflict was
to be understood not in theatrical but in cosmological terms. In this
respect he was something like Homer Lea in that Seeger also thought
that warfare was less an aberration than a natural part of human
existence. War, he felt, was beyond good and evil, and should not be
viewed in terms of traditional morality. Instead it should be seen as
part of a continuing evolutionary process since "evolution proceeds
quite as much through destruction as through creation." At the same
time, as Seeger explained in a letter to his mother, those participating
in the conflict should be neither praised nor pitied: "If I want any
credit for being here it is not for trying to right a wrong or any such
naivetes, but for being willing to make myself one of the instruments
through which a greater force works out its inscrutable ends."[61] Re-
flection had thus not bred regret. Seeger embraced the conflict as
ardently in 1915 as he had on that August day when he had led the
other recruits in their buoyant march through the streets of Paris.

Without the need to find new material to write about, or the desire
to experience personally the realities of war, Edith Wharton might

have viewed the war in a different light than did Seeger and Cowley. In some respects she did, and her work with abandoned children, the aged, the ill, and destitute were somber backdrops to any romantic illusions that she might have had. Yet when she returned from a visit to the Argonne sector in 1915, where she witnessed suffering and endless slaughter, she still described war as "the stimulant of qualities of soul which in every race, can seemingly find no other means of renewal."[62] But Wharton was not describing just any war. She could not totally separate the events of World War I from her love of France. In her mind the conflict at hand should be viewed through a moralistic lens as a kind of crusade in which the sacredness of the cause far overshadowed the dangers endured and the sacrifices made. This attitude colored practically everything connected with the conflict including the way in which she viewed the soldiers at the front. True they had been uprooted from families and jobs, and faced the possibility of death, but they were not to be pitied; the slipper had fit and like Cinderella they were in the process of moving on to far greater things. "More than half of these men were probably doing dull or useless or unimportant things till the first of last August; now each of them, however small his job, is sharing in a great task, and knows it, and has been made over by knowing it."[63] Wharton thus viewed the war with much of the same enthusiasm as Seeger and Cowley. However, what most influenced her were not personal concerns, but rather the greatness of the task at hand. In this respect, when she described France's commitment to the struggle, she was also describing her own: "If France perishes as an intellectual light and as a moral force every Frenchman perishes with her; and the only death that Frenchmen fear is not death in the trenches but death that the whole nation is fighting; and it is the reasoned recognition of their peril which, at this moment, is making the most intelligent people in the world the most sublime."[64]

Postwar writers have ignored the intense idealism and personal sense of commitment to the war that Wharton and others like her shared. Like many of the war participants themselves, these writers have focused on the brutalities of the trenches and the disillusionment which accompanied the peace. The participants, however, did not view the war solely with bitterness and cynicism. For some it was always seen in a most idealistic way. As historian Charles A. Fenton has warned, the intellectual historian must be extremely careful in using such books as *A Farewell to Arms, The Enormous Room,* and *Three Soldiers* as reflections of the wartime attitude. All three works were reactions to unpleasant wartime experiences of their young authors who had volunteered their services, all three were written after 1918, and, to a degree, all three were reactions to the failure of Wilsonian idealism in the postwar period. Thus Frederick Henry's statement in *A Farewell to Arms* that he was "always embarrassed by the words sacred, glorious, and sacrifice" must be juxtaposed against the words of a character in Wharton's own postwar novel, *The Marne,* who observed: "There had never been anything worth-while in the world that had not had to be died for, and it was as clear as day that that world which no one would die for could never be a world worth being alive in."[66] Perhaps the difference in attitudes was primarily generational, but perhaps it was also a fundamental difference in beliefs concerning why the war was being fought in the first place. And it is this difference in the way in which the conflict was viewed that most differentiates the motivations of these three American writers.

Edith Wharton always viewed World War I from a moral perspective. She accepted the total righteousness of the French in the defense of their homeland and the total culpability and brutality of the Teutonic invader. Atrocity stories of the diabolical German Red Cross, mutilated French soldiers, defiled Belgium women, and assassinated priests were all accepted at face value and often related to friends across the Atlantic.[67] It was not stories of German atrocities, however, that most concerned her, but rather the conviction that the defeat of France would deal an immeasurable blow to civilization itself. As her latest biographer suggests, Wharton, like most of her generation, rejected the newly emerging idea of total war.[68] In her trips to the front she viewed the destruction of French farms and villages as a process that went beyond military necessity. In her eyes it was an attempt by the Germans to destroy the very tradition upon which French civilization rested.[69] While traveling in the north of France she had visited an abandoned classroom where the nuns and children, in fleeing German bombardment, had left their belongings scattered about the floor. The feeling that this scene evoked in her was similar to that which she experienced while viewing the ruined cathedral at Rheims. The destruction represented more than merely a disruption of school or religious services: "It symbolized the senseless paralysis of a whole nation's activities. Here were a houseful of women and children yesterday engaged in a useful task and now aimlessly astray over the earth. And in hundreds of such houses, in dozens, in hundreds of open towns, the hand of time had been stopped, the heart of life had ceased to beat, all the currents of hope and happiness and industry had been choked—not that some great military end might be gained, or the length of the war curtailed, but that, wherever the shadow of Germany falls, all things should wither at the root."[70] She felt the destruction personally, for over the years France had come to symbolize for Wharton all that she found to be best in human existence. In a wartime article she summarized what she most admired in France: the eloquence of the language, the intelligence of the French people, their aesthetic sensibility as well as their commitment to the process of living, a national dislike of militarism, and, of course, an overwhelming sense of courage in the face of adversity.[71] It was this last trait that she came to admire greatly as she saw an entire nation working together in defense of its way of life:

> In great trials a race is tested by its values; and the war has shown the world what are the real values of France. Never for an instant has this people, so expert in the great art of living, imagined that life consisted in being alive. Enamoured of pleasure and beauty, dwelling freely in the present, they have yet kept their sense of larger meanings, have understood life to be made up of many things past and to come, of renunciation as well as satisfaction, of traditions as well as experiments, of dying as much as of living. Never have they considered life as a thing to be cherished in itself, apart from its reactions and its relations.[72]

It was this ability for national sacrifice and willingness to see beyond the immediate present that made France seem so attractive to

Wharton, especially when compared with the policy of neutrality of her own country. The inability of Americans to appreciate the magnitude of the conflict and the incalculable loss to world civilization should France be defeated grew on Wharton with each passing month. She was both embarrassed and ashamed of her country's attitude. In 1914 in a letter to an old American friend she revealed just how deeply she feared a German victory: "For heaven's sake, when you get home, proclaim every where, & as publicly as possible . . . what it will mean to all that we Americans cherish if England & France go under, & Prussianism becomes the law of life. So take up the gospel, & spread it about, & insist on it. . . ."[73] Spreading the gospel, however, was not enough for Wharton, and from the very beginning of the war she was committed to France. Even if the American government would not act, at least individual Americans could do so, and she organized her charities with the help of contributions of friends in the United States. To a degree these contributions helped alleviate some of the guilt that she felt as an American living in France. The donations enabled her to blame the country's leaders rather than the American people for the policy of neutrality, and she lamented the fact that her old friend Teddy Roosevelt was no longer President. As the war worsened her anger grew. In September 1915, while describing to a friend General Joffre's inscription in *The Book of the Homeless* in which he praised American voluntary contributions, Wharton expressed her disgust: "General Joffre's few lines are splendid; more than our country deserves just now. I can't tell you with what a contraction of the heart we Americans over here read of Newport balls & tennis tournaments, & of President Wilson's meditations. . . ."[74] Over the next year and a half, like a long-suffering missionary awaiting the conversion of recalcitrant souls, she continued to fret about America's failure to accept a role in the great conflict. It was only after Congress finally committed the country to the war that she felt that the burden of national humiliation was lifted. The mood she expressed to a fellow American in May 1917 was one of relief more than anything else: "First of all, let us embrace on the glorious fact that we can hold up our heads with the civilized nations of the world. If you could hear the note of genuine enthusiasm in every French voice when our country is spoken of it would do you good."[75] For almost three years Edith Wharton had felt that her own country was not part of the civilized world, and this belief had been extremely disillusioning to her. This disillusionment mixed with a passionate dedication to France led to a wartime involvement that was totally unlike anything that she had ever done or would do in the future. In this respect it was a commitment arising partly from a personal sense of love for an adopted country and partly from disillusionment with the failure of her own country to act.

Fellow expatriate Alan Seeger was an equally fervent admirer of French civilization, and this admiration also formed an important element in his involvement. It was an admiration, however, that was less morally oriented and more personally romantic than that of Wharton. In a letter to his sister written some four months after the war's outbreak, Seeger explained that he was on the French rather than German side of the trenches primarily because of his own temperament. Since he believed that the victor's life and world view would predominate in the postwar world, Seeger claimed that he was fighting on the side of France simply because intellectually he was inclined more toward Latin than Teutonic culture.[76] Even then his commitment to France did not signify his hatred of Germany; while facing the enemy across the wastes of no man's land, he refused to give in to Germanophobia. "But let it always be understood that I never took arms out of any hatred against Germany or the Germans," he wrote in his diary during the summer of 1915, "but purely out of love for France. The German contribution to civilization is too large, and German ideals too generally in accord with my own, to allow me to join in the chorus of hate against a people whom I frankly admire. It was only that France, and especially the Paris, that I love should not cease to be the glory and beauty that they are that I engaged."[77] Seeger's attitude was similar to that of another young American, E. E. Cummings, who was imprisoned in a French military camp because a friend's letters (including one to Emma Goldman) describing the war weariness of the French *poilu* were viewed as seditious by an overzealous censor. Cummings could have avoided punishment simply by expressing hatred for the enemy. But when his French interrogators asked "Est-ce-que vous détestez les boches?" Cummings would reply only, "Non, j'aime beaucoup les français."[78]

When Seeger's *Letters and Diary* was published only a month after the United States entered the war, *Scribner's* through a selective process of editing portrayed him as a young romantic who had courageously died while fighting for a cherished ideal. Missing from the book was much of Seeger's apolitical philosophizing, especially those portions of his letters which expressed his thoughts on the overall meaning of the conflict. As an idealist Seeger most certainly would have preferred a French victory, but he was also philosophically willing to contemplate defeat. In Seeger's eyes the war had little to do with right or wrong since both sides had legitimate reasons for fighting. If the French were fighting for a way of life, "high-minded" Germans were merely trying to accomplish what Napoleon had failed to do—to re-create the order and unity of the Roman Empire. Such unity could only be achieved when the balance of power in Europe had been completely broken and when one country dominated all the rest. At such a time, and only then, would lasting peace be achieved. Thus, while Seeger believed that Germany was the aggressor in the war, at the same time he felt that there was a more important question to be asked than simply who started the conflict. He posed it in a letter to his mother: "If Germany could attain a supremacy which would put in her hands the policing of Europe, thus ensuring a lasting peace with all its benefits, would not all the calamities she has precipitated really have served a good purpose? Would not the end more than justify the means?"[79] Like the young romantic Goethe watching the Battle of Valmy and wondering if the spread of the Revolution's ideas was not, in the long run, essential to the health of Europe, Seeger enjoyed toying with the idea that World War I was somehow beyond good and evil and simply a working out of a larger cosmic process. After almost a year in the Legion this idea had, if anything, been strengthened. In another letter home he repeated his view: "It may be that historic fatality will bring about Germany's triumph in this war and her supremacy during the 20th century. . . . Whether I am on the winning or losing side is not the point with me, it is being on the side where my sympathies lie that matters, and I am ready to see it through to the end."[80]

Because Seeger's views were hardly the kind to have boosted the morale of new recruits being carried to training camps all across the country, *Scribner's* probably felt it necessary to delete them from his *Letters and Diary*. But if his opinions were out of step with the patriotic temper of the time, they were very closely attuned to the ethos of an earlier period. Like the Romantic poets he so greatly admired, Seeger believed that to achieve a creative existence one had to choose a course of action and be totally committed to it. It was only by honestly following the dictates of one's imagination and emotions that the poet could live greatly and rise above the petty artificialities of life. Seeger tried to pursue this course at Harvard, in the Village, and in Paris. And he was convinced that by joining the Legion he was continuing this process. Once involved in the war, Seeger was determined to see it through to its conclusion. He felt that he and his comrades were experiencing sensations that went far beyond the parochial grasp of his fellow countrymen who continued to be yoked to what he labeled "foolish American ideas of 'success'."[81] Success from Seeger's perspective could only be measured in terms of living as fully as possible, and he believed that he had discovered the ultimate experience by becoming a soldier in the Great War. Repeatedly in letters to parents and friends he cheerfully announced that there had been relatively little choice involved in his joining the Foreign Legion, especially in view of his ambitions. In the spring of 1916 he re-emphasized the inevitability of his actions in a letter to his sister: "My interest in life was passion, my object to experience it in all rare and refined, in all intense and violent forms. The war having broken out, then, it was natural that I should have staked my life on learning what it alone could teach me. How could I have let millions of other men know an emotion that I remained ignorant of?"[82] World War I was an event that he believed was reshaping the course of civilization, and, quite simply, he had to be a part of it.

Like the young British poet, Rupert Brooke, Seeger contemplated his own death. During the war his poem, "I Have a Rendezvous with Death," became a romantic symbol for what all soldiers faced:

> God knows 'twere better to be deep
> Pillowed in silk and scented down,
> Where Love throbs out in blissful sleep,
> Pulse nigh to pulse, and breath to breath
> Where hushed awakenings are dear. . . .
> But I've a rendezvous with Death
> At midnight in some flaming town,
> When Spring trips north again this year;
> And I to my pledged word am true
> I shall not fail that rendezvous.

Death, then, as Seeger romanticized it, was merely one of the risks involved in the course of action that he had taken, and time and again he asked no more of himself than that he meet it with courage and enthusiasm. In 1915 he wrote to his mother that were he killed his death should not be viewed as tragic, since it would have occurred during a peak in his life. "I have always had the passion to play the biggest part within my reach and it is really in a sense a supreme success to be allowed to play this. If I do not come out, I will share the good fortune of those who disappear at the pinnacle of their careers."[83] At this point in his life Seeger had yet to prove that he could write great poetry, but he believed that by participating in the war he was laying the foundation for greatness by living life to its fullest.

Although considerably less fatalistic than Seeger, Cowley was equally fascinated by death. It was a fascination, however, that had more to do with how the closeness of death worked on his senses than with an acceptance of his own demise. Cowley's view of death symbolized his wartime activities in that it was always somewhat detached and spectatorial in nature. "The war created in young men a thirst for abstract danger," he later wrote in *Exile's Return*, "not suffered for a cause but courted for itself; if later they believed in the cause, it was partly in recognition of the danger it conferred on them. Danger was a relief from boredom, a stimulus to the emotions, a color mixed with all others to make them brighter." At times in France, therefore, the possibility of dying did not frighten Cowley so much as it stimulated his senses in a way never before experienced. "The trees were green, not like ordinary trees, but like trees in the still moment before a hurricane; the sky was a special and ineffable blue; the grass smelled of life itself; the image of death at twenty, the image of love, mingled together into a keen, precarious delight."[84] On one occasion when his convoy had come under fire, Cowley recalls how at first everyone had scrambled for cover. As the shelling continued, however, someone discovered that as soon as one shell exploded, there was just enough time to rush into the road and gather the still warm fragments before the next shell arrived. Of course, any change in timing or elevation would have meant death, but the participants continued their game. "Spectators, we were collecting souvenirs of death," he remembered, "like guests bringing back a piece of wedding cake or a crushed flower from the bride's bouquet."[85]

Cowley and other young writers like him had indeed rushed off to Europe as nonchalantly and perhaps as naïvely as though they were attending a wedding celebration rather than a war. They had, in fact, turned from their peacetime occupations to the war with as much ease as present-day students might transfer from one university to another. Once in Europe most of these younger writers were not directly involved in the fighting, but instead joined noncombatant and relatively safe services like the ambulance corps or the French military transport. The lessons learned in Europe were far more exciting and perhaps more enduring, at least for potential writers, than those to be gained from the classroom. Still, as valuable as these lessons might have been, they exacted a price because they continued the process of rootlessness that had already begun for many while in college and they encouraged a personal detachment toward existence that would have ramifications after the war.

In an article for the American Field Service written shortly after the war's conclusion, Cowley suggested that he and others like him had come to France in order to help in whatever way they could.[86] Such an admission would suggest that he and his generation were not totally immune to all feelings of idealism concerning their voluntary activities. This was certainly true, but in spite of the degree of idealistic commitment that accompanied them to Europe, they were never dedicated to any country in the way that Wharton and Seeger were dedicated to France. For the most part, Cowley and other young writers had rushed off to Italy or France hoping to see something of the war before it ended, yet more than willing to do something useful in the process. But the war was never their war, and they never really felt a part of it. During his service with T.M.U. 526, Cowley spent almost two weeks with a battalion that had participated in the 1917 mutinies which eventually touched some sixteen corps in the French armies. He recalled that in three years of fighting, 15,000 men had either been wounded or killed in this single battalion. The life expectancy for a battalion member averaged about four months. Choice no longer seemed to be an option for them as human beings, but it was always their fate and not his own that Cowley remembered contemplating.[87] On one occasion he and his fellow drivers watched what seemed like an endless line of soldiers from all parts of the French empire marching through the village where he was quartered. The multiplicity of nationalities, the supply trains and rolling kitchens, and the airplanes keeping watch overhead would have suggested a carnival-like atmosphere had it not been for the sullen faces of the passing soldiers. Cowley was a detached observer: "The long parade of races was a spectacle which it was our privilege to survey, a special circus like the exhibition of Moroccan horsemen given for our benefit on the Fourth of July, before we all sat down at a long table to toast *la France héroique* and *nos américains* in warm champagne. In the morning we should continue our work of carrying trench-mortar bombs from the railhead to the munition dumps just back of the Chemin des Dames—that too would be a spectacle."[88]

This spectatorial attitude that distinguished Cowley's wartime involvement from that of Wharton's and Seeger's was related to the deracination process that had begun earlier while he was in college. Had the normal pattern of life been allowed to reassert itself, perhaps his lack of a sense of belonging might have disappeared after college. Instead, it was the abnormal that shaped Cowley's world and as he and other young writers scurried off to see a war their sense of root-lessness was exacerbated. They could not believe in the war as did Edith Wharton or see it as part of the natural order of things as did Alan Seeger; rather they viewed it as something apart from themselves and adopted the noncommittal role of spectator at someone else's conflict. Moreover, how better could these young writers deal with the violence and death they saw in Europe than by psychologically remov-ing themselves as far away from it as possible? Finally, when the war ended, the failures of the peace added to their sense of disillusionment, and, as Floyd Dell, a somewhat older writer has suggested, they were as unprepared for the postwar period as they had been for the war itself.[89] They had not always been as cynical and detached as they were at the war's end, but, like Frederick Henry, their wounds encour-aged them to make a separate peace. As a result this disengaged attitude and feeling of displacement which so characterized Cowley's kind of involvement, was one of the conflict's most tragic legacies to an entire generation of young writers. They had indeed seen a war at first hand, but in doing so had become even more detached from the society in which they lived. "School and college had uprooted us in spirit," Cowley writes,

> now we were physically uprooted, hundreds of us, millions, plucked from our own soil as if by a clamshell bucket and dumped, scattered among strange people. All our roots were dead now . . . even the habits of slow thrift that characterized our social class. We were fed, lodged, clothed by strangers, commanded by strangers, infected with the poison of irresponsibility—the poison of travel, too, for we had learned that problems could be left behind us merely by moving elsewhere—the poison of danger, excitement that made our old life seem intolerable.[90]

It was a most paradoxical turn of events that activism abroad ulti-mately led to social detachment rather than commitment. But indeed it had, for over the course of the next decade many of these same young writers became so self-consciously absorbed in their own art, their personal problems, or simply in the details of daily existence that they could find no time whatsoever for any kind of social concern or commitment. Their participation in the First World War had thus speeded up a process of deracination already begun.

By the early fall of 1917, even though the war continued, the war-related activities of the three writers had ended. Seeger was dead, Wharton working on another novel, and Cowley about to begin the rootless wandering that would continue over most of the next decade. Of the three Wharton had always been the most dedicated Francophile and most determined foe of the Germans. Seeger had viewed the war in the most Romantic terms, believing that regardless of the outcome it was shaping the course of history. Cowley remained the most detached and ultimately disillusioned. Whereas both Wharton and Seeger were convinced that their war efforts were in defense of some of the most enduring aspects of modern civilization, Cowley by the war's end felt that the conflict showed little else than the madness of Western civilization. What contributed to the foreign involvement of these three writers was their disillusionment with various aspects of American society. Wharton's and Seeger's presence in France in August 1914 helps explain their early commitment to the war, and Cowley's dissatisfaction with his education helps, to some degree, to explain his. Finally, as different as the three writers were in backgrounds, motivations, and wartime activities, they did share one trait which makes them worthy symbols of American writer activists. All three viewed the war as something that could not be ignored and something that demanded their personal involvement.

4

John Reed:
Sometimes the Hare and Sometimes the Hound

> *We were carrying realism so far in those days that it walked us right out of our books. We wanted to live our poetry.*
>
> Max Eastman
> *Heroes I Have Known*

EVEN ON THE MOST FESTIVE OCCASIONS Moscow never fully sheds its somber, dignified appearance. On a cold Sunday in late October, 1920, heavy overcast skies, rain, snow, and a biting wind lent an added touch of gloom to the city's already uninviting countenance. The unaccustomed visitor could not but feel depressed by the bleak monotony of the weather, the gray buildings, and the undeviatingly dark, wintry dress of the Muscovites. Inside the Trades-Union Hall, however, the atmosphere was quite different if only because of the shelter it offered and the warmth of the gaily colored revolutionary posters which decorated its walls. The large crowd that filled the hall on this October Sunday was attending the funeral of an American poet, journalist, and revolutionary, John Reed.[1] His coffin rested on a dais, covered with flowers whose tin leaves and petals had probably adorned the casket of more than one revolutionary hero. Leaving the hall, the crowd marched slowly to the newly dug grave under the

Kremlin wall where a large red banner bore the collective inscription for all buried there: "The leaders die, but the cause lives on."[2] John Reed had died on October 17, three days before his thirty-third birthday; his passing brought a talented career to a startlingly abrupt end, but, at the same time, ensured Reed a significant place in the folklore of the Russian Revolution.

Twelve years after Reed's death, Lincoln Steffens, who had been something of a spiritual father to him, found himself in the awkward position of having to answer the impassioned pleas of Reed's disturbed mother to remove all mention of her son from the heading of the American Communist literary organization named in his honor. Steffens was unable to give her legal advice or consolation. He did, however, try to persuade Mrs. Reed that her son had deeply believed in what he was doing at the time of his death and would have been nowhere else in the world than but in revolutionary Russia. "He became a hero in Russia; he will be for ages a Soviet Russian hero. And, Mrs. Reed, I'm afraid that you are wrong about him not standing for the use of his name by the clubs. My impression is that Jack would approve of that, or if he objected, he would have complained only that the Reed Clubs do not go far enough. He might say to them what he said to me that night on a street corner in New York: 'Go on—the limit.'"[3] With his reporter's eye, Steffens captured the essence of this poet turned revolutionary. Over the years there would be others, who like Reed's mother, would try to disassociate his name from the cause in which he so much believed. But John Reed died still committed to the movement in which he had dared to go the limit.

Reed was born October 20, 1887, in his maternal grandmother's mansion, Cedar Hill, on the western edge of the still raw, but fast growing city of Portland, Oregon. His father, Charles Jerome Reed, was by birth an upstate New Yorker who later made a political name for himself in the Pacific West as a United States marshal. Appointed during Theodore Roosevelt's administration, he had joined with Francis J. Henry and Lincoln Steffens in helping to smash an Oregon land fraud ring in 1905. Though by no means a wealthy man, Charles Reed sent both John and his younger brother Harry to Portland Academy, a good private school in the city. Small for his age, John developed a kidney ailment when he was eleven which, though supposedly cured some six years later, continued to bother him through much of his life. In an autobiographical essay he recalled that "a great deal of my boyhood was illness and physical weakness, and I was never really well until my sixteenth year."[4] Graduating in 1904 from Portland Academy, Reed entered an eastern preparatory school, Morristown, in New Jersey. A gangling six-foot, one hundred and thirty-four pound youth, he divided his interests between football, track, and writing for the school's monthly magazine, the *Morristonian*. Since early youth he had shown an interest in writing creatively and now began to channel more of his energies in a literary direction. Literary enthusiasm, however, rarely spilled over into his other academic endeavors, and during his two years at Morristown he was, at best, a mediocre student. Some years later he looked back on this period of his life and remembered it as being almost idyllic: "Boarding school, I think, meant more to me than anything in my boyhood. Among these strange boys I came as a stranger, and I soon found out that they were willing to accept me; I was impressed by its traditional customs and dignities, school patriotism, and the sense of a long settled and established civilization, so different from the raw, pretentious West."[5] These carefree years abruptly ended in the fall of 1906, when after barely passing the entrance examinations, Reed entered the more intellectually and socially demanding atmosphere of Harvard.

Whereas his classmate and friend Alan Seeger at first sought anonymity in that celebrity-filled class of 1910, not so Reed. A person of less exuberance might well have been overwhelmed by the rebuffs that he initially encountered—failure to make any of the "better" social clubs, the freshman football team, or even the freshman crew—but Reed, having long since lost most of his youthful timidity, was not so easily discouraged. Finding himself socially ostracized because of his Western origins, but still desiring the power that often comes with recognition, he became what is known in campus parlance as an "activities man." By the end of his senior year he had, at one time or another, been a member of *Monthly*, *Lampoon*, Dramatic Club, Cosmopolitan Club, Western Club, Glee, Mandolin and Banjo clubs, Memorial Society, Round Table, and Oracle.[6] He was also one of Harvard's most enthusiastic varsity cheerleaders. As Reed unabashedly recalled, "I had the supreme blissful sensation of swaying two thousand voices in great clashing choruses during the big football games."[7] His social conscience, however, was far less developed than that of several of his contemporaries, and though he sometimes visited the Socialist Club headed by classmate Walter Lippmann, Reed never became interested enough to join it.

It was during college that Reed began to develop certain intellectual traits which were to become intrinsic parts of his personality. Increasingly he came to believe that ideas which could be experienced or verified personally were more important than ideas which had to be approached theoretically. It is thus not suprising that Reed complained about the artificiality of his educational experiences. He believed that the majority of classes at the university dulled rather than encouraged truly creative minds. "We take young soaring imaginations," he complained, "consumed with curiosity about the life they see all around, and feed them with dead technique." It seemed to Reed that uninspiring courses were too often taught by even more uninspiring teachers whose only qualification was their ability to "plough steadily through a dull round of dates, acts, halftruths and rules for style, without questioning, without interpreting and without seeing how ridiculously unlike the world their teachings are."[8] One of the few classes which did impress him was Charles Townsend Copeland's English 12—a composition course. Reed discovered in Copeland not only a teacher who had something important to say, but also, in time, a close friend who encouraged him to believe in himself and his creative abilities.[9]

By the time of his graduation, in June 1910, Reed had changed physically as well as intellectually. No longer the awkward, sprawling youth of Morristown days, he was now a handsome young man—tall, with broad shoulders, wavy brown hair parted neatly in the middle, greenish-brown eyes, a blunt nose resting impishly over a full mouth, and a noticeably protruding chin. He was alternatingly brash, inquisitive, witty, bumptious, ambitious, intelligent, opinionated, and, perhaps most important of all, extremely likable in a boyish kind of way. Reed's academic record at Harvard was not outstanding but he always considered himself a writer, not a scholar. Yet even as a writer, he had not shown much promise. Although he had composed numerous poems and short stories, essays, several one-act plays, and had even mapped out a novel by the time of his graduation he was not, according to his earliest biographer, a very distinguished undergraduate author.[10] As might be expected, he left Harvard still in search of the proper outlet for his energies and considerable abilities.

Reed spent the next six months gallivanting around Europe without thinking much of the future, but he was back in New York by the end of January 1911, hoping to launch a writing career. Along with three Harvard classmates he rented an apartment at 42 Washington Square, and with the help of Lincoln Steffens, who had moved in directly below, he obtained a part-time position working on the *American*, a periodical run by several muckraking journalists.[11] As an old friend of the Reed family, Steffens continued to take an interest in the activities of the young writer, and at various times served as his personal confidant, intellectual guru, and financial backer. Some years later Reed recalled that his teacher Copeland and his friend Steffens were the most important influences in his life at a time when writing for a living occurred to him as a serious possibility.[12]

The two years that Reed lived in the Village were in many ways far more important in his development as a writer than the four spent in Cambridge. Not only was he enjoying the excitement of living in what was becoming the country's literary Mecca, but also he was finding the city itself to be a virtual treasure-trove of new experiences. He threw himself into the new life with the same youthful energy that had characterized his earlier pursuit of clubbing. Time not spent writing was devoted to sampling the city's divergent life. This was the kind of education particularly meaningful to Reed, for it could be closely observed, fully experienced, and thus more completely savored. Encouraged by Steffens to write about what he saw, Reed found no person too insignificant and no matter too trivial for his attention. The city's diversity of people interested him the most, especially as he later recalled, "the livingness of theories which could dominate men and women captivated my imagination. On the whole, ideas alone didn't mean much to me. I had to see." To discover life as it was being lived, he studiously avoided the well-trodden, publicized attractions of the city, spending countless evenings and early mornings strolling about the Lower East Side. In doing so, like Redburn in his travels through Liverpool, Reed was also observing a side of life he had never bothered to notice before: "In my rambles about the city I couldn't help but observe the ugliness of poverty and all its train of evil, the cruel inequality between rich people who had too many motor cars and poor people who didn't have enough to eat. It didn't come to me from books that the workers produced all the wealth of the world, which went to those who did not earn it."[13] Reed may not have been as radicalized at the time as he later claimed, but clearly he was experiencing the first pangs of an awakened social conscience. It was a social conscience that was being roused, just as it later would be in Paterson, Ludlow, Mexico, and Russia, by what he was seeing with his increasingly acute reporter's eye rather than by anything he had read or heard. Yet it was also a social awareness in its formative stage, and most of Reed's energies were still directed toward the difficult task of trying to earn a living as a writer.

Reed's first year in New York, like his first at Harvard, lacked dramatic success—the failures this time took the form of rejection slips from numerous publishers and periodicals. By the end of the year, however, his work was beginning to be noticed; stories and an occasional descriptive article appeared in *Collier's*, *Saturday Evening Post*, *Forum*, *Century*, and *Metropolitan Magazine*. If not yet fully established as a writer, he was at least less of a financial burden to his family and Steffens, and, at the same time, was enjoying the confidence that only publication can offer. Besides selling articles to the slick magazines, he was also voluntarily contributing material—again mostly short stories—to the new radical monthly *The Masses*. The magazine was in its second year of existence when Reed read one of its issues. He immediately went to its editorial office where he exuberantly offered advice on running the magazine and submitted several of his stories for publication. Max Eastman, the magazine's new editor, later recalled that in his initial meeting with Reed he was both annoyed and overwhelmed by the loud enthusiasm of the Westerner who "stood up or moved about the room all through his visit, and kept looking in every direction except that in which he was addressing his words. It is difficult for me to get the sense of togetherness with a stranger, even if he looks at me. And when he looks at the walls, or the house fronts on the other side of the street, and talks into the air, and walks around in this excessively steamed-up manner, I am hopelessly embarrassed and want to lie down and rest after it is over."[14] Eastman's initial disgust changed to excitement once he sampled the forcefully crisp style and sensitivity to social needs in Reed's stories about city life. He soon named the young writer as one of the contributing editors, and began taking Reed's advice seriously. If *The Masses* benefited from the boundless energy of its newest editor, Reed probably gained more from the magazine through his contacts with its staff. His association with such outspoken socialists as Max Eastman, the illustrator Art Young, and the painter John Sloan, led him to attend public meetings sponsored by the Socialist party and to read all the socialist literature that he could find.[15]

During Reed's second year in the Village two events occurred which were to have important effects upon his life. The first was his participation in the silk workers' strike at Paterson, New Jersey; the second was his meeting Mabel Dodge, hostess of a unique New York salon. In the spring of 1912 Reed visited Lawrence, Massachusetts, where the Industrial Workers of the World had conducted a successful strike against the management of the textile industry. Several months later the IWW brought its organizing methods to Paterson, where 73,000 workers held jobs in the silk industry. Reed's attention was soon riveted on the events taking place in that industrial city located only fifteen miles from New York. Not only did he follow in the press the plight of the Paterson workers, but he also heard a first hand account of their long working hours, frequent lockouts, and squalid living and working conditions. His informant was Big Bill Haywood who lived in the Village while he directed the IWW's fight against the mill owners. Haywood was also a frequent visitor at the Dodge salon and this is probably where Reed met him. Reed was both thrilled and appalled by Haywood's tales of the workers' determined heroism. At the same time he sensed a story in the making and decided to go to Paterson to see for himself. His introduction into the realities of industrial warfare was quick; shortly after arriving in the city he was arrested and jailed for not moving off the the street when ordered. After four days' confinement with imprisoned Wobblies with whom he sang radical songs and shared the *esprit de corps* of a common cause, he discovered that his arrest had made him something of a celebrity. Reed emerged from jail more radicalized than ever. Back in New York, his writing about the experience took on a new militancy: "There's a war in Paterson, New Jersey. But it's a curious kind of war. All the violence is the work of one side—the mill owners. Their servants, the police, club unresisting men and women and ride down law abiding crowds on horseback. Their paid mercenaries, the armed detectives, shoot and kill innocent people." Undoubtedly his job with *The Masses* influenced his interpretation of the situation at Paterson, but, even more important, he had only fully understood what was occurring there after he had seen it for himself. It was only then that he began to understand how all encompassing the power of the owner could be, a power, which he was to discover, included control of the local press. "Their newspapers," he pointed out in the same article, "the Paterson *Press* and the Paterson *Call*, publish incendiary and crime-inciting appeals to mob violence against the strike leaders. . . . They control absolutely the police, the press, the courts."[16] By the time of his return from Paterson, Reed's concern went far beyond journalistic analysis, for he felt increasingly committed to the workers' cause. Thus, once back in the Village he was soon helping to plan a gigantic pageant at Madison Square Garden which was intended to awaken public sympathy and provide funds for the striking workers.

Although Mabel Dodge claims that the idea for the pageant was hers,[17] Reed more than anyone else helped to make the idea a reality. His enthusiasm and penchant for constant acitivity were quickly channelled into what soon became a mammoth undertaking. The energy he displayed in organizing the pageant was even more remarkable in that it was not the only item demanding his attention. Throughout most of May he and Mabel, a woman eight years his senior, were increasingly drawn together, first by their common interest in the pageant and then by their growing interest in each other. The performance on June 7, while something of an artistic *tour de force*, was a financial disappointment, costing more to produce than was raised by ticket sales. For years Reed carried with him the guilt that he felt about letting the workers down, and he was still lamenting the pageant's failures to his friend and fellow writer, Albert Rhys Williams, while both were participating in the Russian Revolution.[18] Frustrated over the pageant's failure to raise money for the strikers, and physically exhausted by too many sleepless nights, Reed let Mabel whisk him away from New York to her villa outside Florence where, like a latter-day Circe, she hoped to keep him for an indefinite period.

Some years later, Hutchins Hapgood, newspaperman, novelist, and friend of the two lovers, observed that "Reed, emerging from jail at Paterson was put in jail by Mabel—a far more difficult prison to escape from."[19] Actually the relationship was doomed from the start, for although Reed was quite willing to let Mabel be his sensual cicerone for a time, he was not likely to remain under anyone's domination for very long. Pouring forth his heart to Hapgood somewhat later, he cried, "Oh, Hutch . . . Mabel is wonderful, I love her, but she suffocates me, I can't breathe."[20] Thus after two and a half months of sunny Italy, the pair returned to New York—Reed to his writing, Mabel to her friends. To them she incessantly complained about her lover's growing inattention. Although they still shared Mabel's plush Fifth Avenue apartment, by early fall the two were drawing apart; the *coup de grâce* came when Reed was asked to go to Mexico to report on the revolutionary events there.

By the winter of 1913 the American press was finding abundant copy in the turmoil of war-torn Mexico. The government forces of General Victoriano Huerta were in full retreat before the peasant armies of Pancho Villa, and it appeared likely that the *Villistas* would soon control the important state of Chihuahua. Largely because of the publicity gained through the Paterson experience, Reed's services were in demand, and both *Metropolitan Magazine* and the New York *World* commissioned him to go to Mexico. With the devotion of a patient Griselda, Mabel decided to go also and followed him first to Chicago and then to El Paso, but after several weeks spent in that dusty border town, she relinquished him to the Revolution: "It was always activity he adored, almost any exciting activity. He was not essentially radical or revolutionary; he loved it when things happened and always wanted to be in the center of events. Any great events."[21] Mabel was correct in her assessment of Reed's love of activity. What she could not have known was that his experiences in Mexico combined with those gained in Paterson were to further radicalize his already exuberant temperament.

Reed crossed the border into Mexico in December 1913, seeking much more than a story. Like Crane's Henry Fleming, he wanted to find out "How I would get along with these primitive folks at war. And I discovered that bullets are not very terrifying, that the fear of death is not such a great thing. . . ."[22] Never becoming totally detached from the events he was reporting, Reed began to admire and sympathize with the Mexican people, whom he saw, like the workers at Paterson, engaged in a courageous struggle to free their country from the clutches of the corrupt and the privileged. As happened during his walks on the Lower East Side and during his excursion to the strike at Paterson, Reed's social conscience was most sharpened by events that he could observe first hand and participate in. As he later wrote in *The Masses*: "If anyone wants to know the truth at first hand, he must do as I did—go through the country and especially through the . . . army, asking the people what they are fighting for. . . ."[23] Aided by luck and his own naïve brashness, Reed was able to meet and interview Pancho Villa. He described Villa as a kind of Mexican Robin Hood who also possessed the military astuteness of a Bonaparte. Granted permission to ride with the *Villistas*, Reed stayed with the army for several weeks. He was greatly impressed by its single-minded determination to fight on until social equality replaced special privilege throughout the country. The mood of the army was symbolized by the attitude of its leader: Reed later recalled the message that Villa gave to a group of departing foreigners: "This is the latest news for you to take to your people. There shall be no more palaces in Mexico. The tortillas of the poor are better than the bread of the rich."[24] This was the kind of simple yet direct statement of purpose that Reed most admired, and he saw in the Mexican general a kind of rough-hewn vitality necessary to aid the working classes in their struggle for equality. For Reed the Mexican Revolution was one step on the road that ultimately led to participation in the Russian Revolution: It was also an unsurpassed opportunity to make a name for himself as a journalist. The training he had received on the streets of New York and Paterson was now used to brilliant advantage, and after but a few weeks in Mexico his colorful stories of personal adventures, interviews with Villa, and his description of the fall of Torréon to the *Villistas* were being compared to the war reporting of Stephen Crane, Ambrose Bierce, and the master of romantic journalism, Richard Harding Davis. By the time Reed returned to the United States in the spring of 1914, at the age of twenty-six, he was already a well-known correspondent considered by many to be among the very best in the profession.

In New York, Reed published a collection of his articles and stories, *Insurgent Mexico* (1914), by far the best and most sustained piece of writing that he had ever done. A few weeks later he was commissioned by *Metropolitan* to go to Ludlow, Colorado, where a group of deputy sheriffs and private detectives had fired into a tent city of striking miners killing forty-five men, women, and children. Reed's reporting dealt primarily with the unmitigated suffering of the miners. It was like seeing Paterson reincarnated. Reed angrily asked what chance for justice was there when the mayor of the town was also the mine superintendent? Or what would it be like to live in a community where "the school board was composed of company officials. The only store in town was the company store. All the houses were company houses, rented by the company to the miners."[25] When Reed returned to the East several weeks later, he was more convinced than ever of the degraded position of the American worker, but in spite of this growing sense of frustration there is no evidence that he was moving toward any specific ideological commitment. Whereas he now referred to himself as a socialist, he was not officially to join the Socialist party until 1918. His radicalism still lacked a theoretical basis, and was more akin to the IWW with its dislike of special privilege, its boisterous sense of élan and belief that the workers must seize the initiative by creating one big powerful union. In Reed's eyes, injustice would not be abolished by ideologies but by action. The deeds of individuals like Haywood and Villa, which Reed observed first hand, attested to that.

As might be expected, the outbreak of World War I created a demand for Reed's reporting skills. *Metropolitan* commissioned him as its European correspondent while he also agreed to send some of his exclusive material to the *New York World*.[26] Although he viewed the causes of the war as largely commercial, and was outspoken in his opposition to American involvement, he was still eager to get to Europe as soon as possible.[27] Arriving in Paris before the end of the First Battle of the Marne, Reed spent the next few months trying to duplicate his Mexican experience by seeing as many sides of the war as possible. But there was something totally different about this conflict—its immensity and mechanized slaughter—that made it difficult for him to get the same feel for what was happening in Europe as he had been so brilliantly able to do in Paterson, Mexico, and Ludlow. Further handicapped by British and French restrictions on civilian access to the front lines, he spent most of his time far removed from the actual fighting, traveling to London, Berlin, and eventually into German-occupied France. It was while visiting France that he and fellow-journalist Robert Dunn were finally able to reach the front outside the city of Lille. Any hope that they might have had of viewing the frontline activities of the Allies as well was ended because of a foolish prank. While inspecting the trenches, the two journalists, following the casual suggestion of a German officer, fired several shots in the direction of the French lines to get the feel of combat. The publication of Dunn's report on the incident in the New York *Post* sealed their fate, and, for all practical purposes, destroyed their effectiveness as reporters on the Western Front since they were permanently barred from entering any of the French sectors.

Finding the Western sectors closed to him by the spring of 1915, Reed and an artist-illustrator, Boardman Robinson, set off on what would become a spectacular journey through much of Eastern Europe and Russia. They began their journey in the Balkans, continued into Russia, and finally concluded it, much to the relief of all officials with whom they had come into contact, in Greece. Conditions in the East were even more deplorable than in the West, and Reed published his articles and Robinson's sketches in *The War in Eastern Europe* (1916). Though the adventures encountered by the two journalists resembled something out of the *Arabian Nights*, Reed's articles lacked the dramatic impact of so much of his writing from Mexico. His reporter's eye no longer caught the unique characteristics of the people he met or focused on the surrounding topography. Instead it remained riveted on the destruction and suffering that he encountered on every side. The war was vastly different from anything he had ever envisioned or expected: "In Europe I found none of the spontaneity, none of the idealism of the Mexican revolution. It was a war of workshops, and the trenches were factories turning out ruin—ruin of the spirit as well as of the body, the real and only death."[28] Unlike the Mexican peons or even the Paterson strikers, the workers of Europe were blind to the way in which they were being used, and, with eyes tightly shut to social injustices, they rushed off to the slaughter while dutifully mouthing patriotic slogans. Reed returned from the Eastern Front more convinced than ever that the war was a calamitous madness, and a conflict in which the United States should play no part. Over the next few years this belief dominated more and more of his energies.

Having already seen enough of what he viewed as the insanity of a senseless war, Reed was content to remain for the time being in the United States. A new romance in his life also influenced him to stay. While on a trip to Portland in the winter of 1915 he met Louise Bryant Trullinger, the wife of a local dentist, and the two immediately fell in love. As impetuous and ambitious as Reed, Louise followed him back to New York where they began living together, writing, making plans for novels, and enjoying the Indian summer of Village life. Louise divorced her husband and married Reed in the fall of 1916. Their continuing relationship, as tempestuous as their personalities, was punctuated by jealousy, unfaithfulness, and competition in their work. As Max Eastman remembered, there was something vital, even heroic about their "joint determination to smash through the hulls of custom and tradition and all polite and proper forms of behavior, and touch at all times and all over the earth the raw current of life. It was a companionship in what philistines call adventure, a kind of gypsy compact."[29]

Although Reed's relationship with Louise and his literary interests occupied much of his time, the war was never totally out of his thoughts. As the 1916 presidential election approached, he was increasingly perturbed by the mushrooming preparedness movement and its implication that the United States must eventually enter the struggle. After viewing a preparedness parade that summer, he wrote in a bitter article for *The Masses* that such events "show that the country is being rapidly scared into 'an heroic mood.'"[30] By November, Reed finally decided to support Woodrow Wilson in the hope that he would abide by his promise to keep the country out of war. Even when promises and campaign slogans were forgotten and war declared, Reed angrily refused to alter his anti-war position. In another article for *The Masses* he warned his fellow countrymen about the course they were bent on following: "I know what war means. I have been with the armies of all the belligerents except one, and I have seen men die, and go mad, and lie in hospitals suffering hell; but there is a worse thing than that. War means an ugly mob-madness, crucifying the truth tellers, choking the artists, sidetracking reforms, revolutions and the working of social forces."[31] Twelve days after the United States entered the conflict, Reed was again protesting the Administration's decision, this time while testifying before a House committee investigating matters concerning conscription. "I have no personal objection to fighting," he told committee members; "I just think that it is unjust on both sides, that Europe is mad, and that we should keep out of it."[32]

Wartime America has never been kind to dissenters, and because of his continuing opposition to the conflict, Reed, like Randolph Bourne, soon discovered that his journalistic talents were less and less in demand. The editors of *Metropolitan* solicited his services only occasionally, while the other slick magazines began to reject his articles. Shortly before the 1916 election, Reed had written an article praising Bertrand Russell for his courage in opposing the war in the face of public outrage.[33] A few months later he found himself in the same position, and for the first time in his life Reed understood how personally damaging an unpopular stand could be. It was a lesson that he should have learned in Paterson and Ludlow, but it had never seemed so real until the spring of 1917.

In many ways the summer and fall of 1917 were the nadir of Reed's life. He was worried because journals would not buy his writing and he was not certain that he could continue to support himself as a journalist. Then, there were physical problems, for he had not fully recovered from the removal of a kidney the previous November. On top of all these troubles, he and Louise were separated and the future of their marriage in doubt. Intertwined with these personal issues was a deep-seated concern about the war; it seemed to him that the American worker was now, like his European counterpart, allowing himself to be herded off to destruction. Nowhere did Reed find the enthusiastic dedication of the Wobblies or the cocky determination of the *Villistas* fighting against the exploitation of the working classes. Like a heavily drugged patient, the entire country seemed mindlessly preparing for war. In September 1917 he wrote: "In America the month just past has been the blackest month for free men our generation has known. With a sort of hideous apathy the country has acquiesced in a regime of judicial tyranny, bureaucratic suppression and industrial barbarism, which followed inevitably the first fine careless rapture of militarism."[34] It was in the midst of the bleak season of political depression and personal self-doubt that Reed wrote an introspective autobiographical essay, "Almost Thirty," in which he somberly concluded: "There seems to be little to choose between the sides; both are horrible to me. The whole Great War is to me just a stoppage of the life and ferment of human evolution. I am waiting for it all to end, for life to resume so I can find my work."[35] Fortunately for his psychological well-being, Reed did not have to wait until the war's end to find this work, for he was soon swept up by a series of events which had been taking place in Russia since early March 1917.

Most Americans, after an initial interest in the abdication of the tsar, soon forgot about events in Russia as their own country became involved in the war. By the end of the summer of 1917, however, the cataclysmic failure of the Provisional government's July offensive and the mounting activities of the Bolsheviks in Petrograd had the American press buzzing with excitement, and John Reed frantically scurrying about trying to find a way of getting to Russia. Max Eastman was also anxious for Reed to go to Russia, to report on the revolution for *The Masses*, but, at the same time, saw no way the magazine could underwrite such a costly trip. An influential supporter of the magazine came to the rescue and helped raise two thousand dollars to send to Russia the one man Eastman believed was capable of capturing the essence of events there.[36] Reed and Louise were reunited by this time, and when she was hired by the Bell Syndicate to examine the Revolution from a woman's perspective, they arranged to make the trip together.[37]

Sailing August 17 aboard the Danish steamer *United States*, they traveled across Sweden and Finland, hearing rumors that General Kornilov was about to enter Petrograd, hang the Bolsheviks, and end the Revolution. They arrived in Petrograd in early September 1917 to discover that the rumors were unfounded. The city's rail workers and other Bolshevik supporters had side-tracked the train carrying Kornilov's Cossacks and thus ended his counter-revolutionary activities. After renting a small apartment, the Reeds joined with Albert Rhys Williams of the New York *Post* and Bessie Beatty of the San Francisco *Bulletin* to explore the city. The four spent the next few weeks almost constantly walking the streets, interviewing anyone who could speak even a few words of English, visiting the Northern Front, and seeing as much as they could. In Russia as in Mexico, Reed was observing workers who were not only willing to unite behind a cause, but were determined to take the governing powers of the state into their own hands. Like Alice in Wonderland, it was as though he had tumbled into another world, for Petrograd and the Russian worker were a welcome relief from European and American workers engaged in a war that was not theirs. In spite of the excitement that he felt in Russia, Reed was handicapped by his inability to speak the language and his ignorance of Russian history. Having picked up a few phrases during his escapades with Boardman Robinson in Eastern Europe a few months earlier, Reed often started conversations with strangers in Petrograd by bounding up to them and enthusiastically announcing: "Ya Americanski Sotsialist."[38] Efforts to go much beyond this initial greeting were usually unsuccessful for, according to his friend Albert Rhys Williams, Reed's pronunciation was terrible. Yet Reed, Louise, and others in their little group were able to surmount many lingual difficulties with the help of some Russian-Americans, a number of whom were already Bolsheviks. These individuals no doubt influenced the American journalists by answering questions, translating and interpreting, and generally helping to explain to them the events that were occurring with dazzling speed.[39] Almost without realizing it, Reed was becoming caught up in the events he was only supposed to be observing, and soon his personal commitment to the Revolution began to encroach upon his duties as a professional journalist.

His first direct participation in Bolshevik activities was totally spontaneous and occurred on November 7, the second day of the "October" Revolution. Upon leaving Bolshevik headquarters late that evening after having attended the first session of the Second Congress of Soviets of Workers and Soldiers, Reed, Louise, Williams, and several other Americans caught a ride on a truck going in the general direction of the Winter Palace. As the truck quickly left the blazing lights of Smolney Institute behind and rumbled at top speed down Suvorovsky Prospekt, a man as Reed recalled, "tore the wrapping from a bundle and began to hurl handfuls of paper into the air. We imitated him, plunging down through the dark street with a tail of white papers floating and eddying out behind. The late passerby stooped to pick them up; the patrols around bonfires on the corners ran out with uplifted arms to catch them. Sometimes armed men loomed up ahead, crying "Stoi!" and raising their guns, but our chauffeur only yelled something unintelligible and we hurtled on. . . ." [40] Reed's actions that night were most certainly impulsive and not very significant; he probably could not even read the leaflets he threw from the truck. But as he tossed the leaflets out, he also abandoned any pretense of neutrality and became actively involved in the cause that was to dominate the rest of his life. His eagerness to be directly involved in the Revolution was not surprising, for he had been heading in such a direction for some time. During the short time he had been in Russia, Reed had already observed amazing differences between the socially myopic workers in the rest of the world and the Russian proletariat who, he believed, were demonstrating a new social awareness in their demands for peace, bread, and land. In Russia he found working people acting in their own defense and Reed was ready to act with them. No amount of reading could have taught him what he learned in Russia. There he decided to participate in a movement he sympathized with but which, like most foreigners, he still did not understand.

A short time later Reed became more directly involved in the Revolution as he and Williams teamed together to contribute their services to the newly organized Bureau of International Revolutionary Propaganda, controlled by the Department of Foreign Affairs. Directed by Boris Reinstein, one of the leaders of the Socialist Labor party in the United States, the Bureau's main function was the publication of newspapers and magazines in German, Hungarian, and Rumanian.[41] It was hoped that this propagandistic material would encourage German and Austrian soldiers to turn their guns against their leaders as many Russian soldiers had done. Under the general supervision of Karl Radek, the Austrian-born Bolshevik who later helped organize the German Communist party, Reed and Williams worked in a section of the Bureau which published a German-language newspaper, *Die Fackel* (which later became *Der Völkerfriede*) and an illustrated weekly, *Die Russiche Revolution in Bildern*. They were paid fifty roubles a month—the same amount given to members of the

Red Army. According to Louise, Reed and Williams used the most modern techniques by introducing "American advertising psychology —briefness and concrete impressions—into the propaganda." The language was kept simple and direct. For example, a picture of the old German Embassy in Petrograd which they placed in *Die Fackel*, had the following caption: "German soldiers and workers—why don't you put a German workman in this place?"[42] In his memoirs, Williams described the kind of work they were doing during their stay with the Bureau. In one picture in which soldiers were removing the tsarist emblem from a building, the caption read: "On the roof of a palace, a soldier is tearing down the hateful emblem of autocracy. Below the crowd is burning the eagles. The soldier in the Crowd is explaining that the overthrow of autocracy is only the first step in the march of social revolution." The caption's conclusion contained the usual obligatory moral in this early form of socialist realism: "It is easy to overthrow autocracy. Autocracy rests on nothing but the blind submission of soldiers. The Russian soldiers merely opened their eyes and autocracy disappeared."[43] The most ironic bit of propagandizing that the two Americans became involved in was their helping to prepare for distribution Woodrow Wilson's Fourteen Points. Leaflets containing the President's peace proposals were to be handed out behind enemy lines as yet another way of demoralizing the armies of the Central Powers.

While continuing his work in the Bureau, Reed also participated in an activity which led to his censure by the official American delegation in Petrograd. On the evening of January 18, 1918, the day the Constituent Assembly was dismissed by the Bolsheviks, Reed stood armed guard in front of the Soviet Foreign Office Building. He did so in response to a rumor that the building would be attacked by the Social Revolutionaries, the old leftist peasant party who now opposed the Bolsheviks. But Reed may have been motivated more by an annoying action of the American Embassy than by a belief that the building was about to be besieged. According to Williams, both Reed and Louise had been followed for some time about the city by "sleuths" under orders from the embassy, which was interested in their activities.

Louise had become frightened by the surveillance. Williams believed that Reed may have stood guard in front of the Russian building and shown his support of the Bolsheviks as a way of retaliating against the American Embassy.[44] Reed's armed vigil was immediately brought to the attention of Edgar Sisson, a member of George Creel's Committee on Public Information who had been sent to Russia to try to keep the Soviets in the war. When he met the journalist a few days after the incident, Sisson warned him that "he had far overstepped the bounds of privileged action by doing Bolshevik patrol duty. . . ." He also chided him for using his journalistic skills for blatantly propagandistic purposes, but Reed shrugged off the admonition and said he hoped that he could continue to be of assistance to the Bolsheviks in the future.[45]

Just how little Reed heeded Sisson's warning became evident when the New York *Times* reported on January 31 that Reed had been named Soviet Consul to New York, an appointment issued through Trotsky's Office of Foreign Affairs. Precisely what the Soviet Government was hoping to accomplish by such an appointment is unknown, but as former Ambassador George Kennan has suggested: "To accredit such a man as consul to a city in his own country, and that without so much as the courtesy of a prior consultation with United States officials, was an act of such flagrant discourtesy as to indicate that the motives were not serious, as indeed they were not."[46] On the other hand, the appointment may have been a clever way to provide Reed, who had decided that he should return to the United States to stand trial for sedition with his fellow staff members of *The Masses*, with diplomatic immunity. Traveling as a Soviet consul, Reed would be assured that his personal belongings—especially notes and other materials on his observations about the Revolution—would not be examined or confiscated.[47] Regardless of the motives behind his appointment, however, it was soon cancelled under the most confusing circumstances.

After learning of the appointment, both Ambassador David R. Francis and Sisson were obviously disturbed by its implications and convinced Colonel Raymond Robins of the American Red Cross Mis-

sion that it was detrimental to American interests. They also persuaded him to help revoke it. Robins contacted a Russian from New
York then living in Petrograd, Alexander Gumberg, who knew important Soviet government officials and American diplomats. It is not
known what specific instructions were given to Gumberg, but shortly
after meeting with Robins he presented to Lenin documents supposedly written by Reed. The documents contained outlines of a plan to
interest American businessmen in investing in Russia. The most de-
tailed document was a prospectus for the creation of an American-
Russian language newspaper to advertise abroad the financial opportunities to be found in the new soviet republic. Ironically, it was
Robins who had first approached Reed on the matter. Like most
American officialdom in the city, Robins was interested in keeping
Russia in the war, but unlike most of his fellow countrymen, he was
willing to accept the new soviet government as a *fait accompli*. He also
believed that if trade could be established between the two countries,
relations would become normalized and it would then be easier to
keep Russia in the war. He thus approached Reed, then in desperate
need of money since he had already spent most of the two thousand
dollars brought with him. From the outset Reed had thoroughly disap-
proved of the capitalistic underpinnings of the project. He had only
reluctantly agreed to provide the technical advice necessary for establishing such a newspaper after it was understood that his only connection with the scheme would be as professional adviser. Yet even this
indirect connection with capitalism proved to be disastrous to the
journalist during this idealistic period of "war communism." Three
years later under the more relaxed conditions of the New Economic
Policy, Reed's connection with the endeavor would probably have
been accepted. But during the early months of 1918 Soviet officials
were disturbed by the documents which seemed to show that Reed was
too closely tied to the American economic system to be a diplomatic
envoy. His commission was revoked. Disappointed by what had taken
place, Reed had no alternative but to return to the United States as a
private citizen.[48]

In spite of his loss of the consulship, Reed remained as enthusiastic as ever about his newfound faith in the Soviet experiment. His commitment to Russia, in fact, made him seem far more serious and determined to old friends. Max Eastman, for example, when he met Reed shortly after his return to America, had the distinct feeling that his friend had undergone a kind of personal metamorphosis: "He was subdued. He was never again so brilliant. Color and metaphor gave place to naked information—and even, let me add statistics—in his writing. From having been a flashing and imaginatively adventuring reporter-poet, he became an earnest propagandist and prose teacher— almost the embodiment of Lenin's austere term, 'professional revolutionist.' "[49] Eastman's appraisal was no exaggeration, for Reed had returned from Russia more seriously committed to an ideal than at any other time in his life. Too late to participate in the first *Masses* trial which ended in a hung jury, he was present during a second and final trial which ended the same way. During the eighteen months that Reed was in the United States he spent part of the time traveling and speaking in major cities on the worldwide significance of the revolution in Russia. He also wrote for the *Liberator*, the magazine which superseded *The Masses* in 1918. In an incredible two-week period of intense work he wrote his classic description of the October Revolution, *Ten Days That Shook the World*. Having completed the book by early January, 1919, he then began to devote most of his energies to the cause of the Revolution in America. By this time he had resigned from the staff of the *Liberator* because it was not revolutionary enough for his liking, and was donating most of his writing and editing skills to such communist-oriented magazines as the *New York Communist*, the *Voice of Labor*, and the *Revolutionary Age*. His writing in these periodicals was even more ideologically oriented than before with frequent references to Marx punctuating his thoughts. He also believed that the workers' struggle for power in the United States was just beginning, and he reiterated a lesson he had learned while observing the strike in Paterson: "As the class-conscious workers develop strength," he wrote in the *New York Communist*, "the capitalist parties sink their differences and combine against them; they falsify the ballot; thus use the police and the engines of the State to prevent the workers' voting; they gerrymander political districts, so that the majority of the voters get the minority of representatives."[50] Reed also returned from Russia more sensitive than ever to criticism of the Soviet government, and spent much of his time in polemical jousting with both real and imagined enemies. For example, he published a pamphlet denouncing the claim made by the spurious Sisson documents that Lenin, Trotsky, and other important Bolshevik leaders had been employed for a number of years by the German General Staff in order to disrupt the Russian war effort.[51]

Aside from his role as propagandist and self-appointed defender of the faith, Reed together with fellow New Yorker Benjamin Gitlow, helped organize the Communist Labor party. Most of its members were native-born Americans who had drifted into the new party from the free-wheeling background of the I.W.W. No sooner was the organizational work completed when Reed's faction became involved in the kind of internecine warfare that characterized the early years of the American Communist movement. The opposition came from the Communist party of the Foreign-language Federations, whose members believed that their close ethnic ties with Russia made them the only true American Bolsheviks. Unfamiliar with American traditions and institutions, they could not understand that the blueprint for sweeping change in the United States might differ from that of Russia. It was their belief that they alone held the key to the revolution in America. Never bothered by their minority position within the Left itself, they argued that the Bolsheviks had seized power in the face of similar odds, and they would not compromise even if their position threatened to destroy the nascent American Communist party. During the spring and summer of 1918, the two competing factions drifted even farther apart. In the process Reed discovered that the Soviet dream was not necessarily in keeping with the American reality. When all efforts at compromise failed in early August 1918, Reed again began making plans to go to Russia with the hope that the differences between the two parties might be arbitrated there.[52]

Reed's departure for the Soviet Union this time was noticeably different from what it had been a little over a year earlier. No longer was he a journalist hurrying off to observe events in another part of the world, but he was now a revolutionary forced to leave his country secretly. Normal departure was impossible since he had been denied a passport by the State Department because of his radical ties. Disguised as a stoker, he boarded a Swedish freighter in New York late one September night and left the United States for the last time. Almost two months later he finally managed to slip across the Finnish frontier into a post-Revolutionary Russia beset by a second "Time of Troubles" —civil war, foreign intervention, and widespread famine. Once back in the only country in the world where he believed any real social progress was being made, he was determined to share the sacrifices made by the Russian people during this heroic period of war communism. When he reached Moscow he refused the offer of comfortable living quarters and the use of a meal ticket, and moved instead into a working-class neighborhood where he prepared his own food in an effort to live as simply as possible.[53] He soon learned that a number of American Communists, including himself, had been indicted by a federal grand jury in Chicago for attempting to overthrow the American government. At the same time he also heard that he and other members of the Communist Labor party had been told by the Executive Committee of the Communist International that the two quarreling American factions would have to settle their differences and unite. Feeling that nothing else could be done in Moscow, Reed decided that he could best aid the revolutionary movement by returning to the United States. There he would stand trial and use it as a forum for publicly expressing his views of the Revolution. Although he faced possible imprisonment in America, Reed was prepared to make what he felt was a necessary sacrifice, and by February 1919 he was ready to leave Russia.

On his return trip to the United States Reed planned to carry with him more than the gospel of the Revolution. To be packed in his luggage were more practical weapons for implementing the class struggle: important propaganda materials, instructions for party leaders, and a large amount of jewels and Finnish marks which were to be converted into dollars for the young American Communist party.[54]

Initially, Reed tried to return along the same route that he had used several months earlier to enter Russia, but he encountered vastly intensified security measures at every point. He finally did manage to slip across the border, but while attempting to board a ship in Helsinki was arrested by the Finnish police. For the next twelve weeks he was imprisoned—most of the time in solitary confinement—without any idea of what charges had been brought against him. Even more frightening and ultimately dangerous was the fact that his imprisonment was not known to the outside world. His fate might have remained unknown had it not been for the assistance of a Finnish liberal, Anio Malmberg, who announced his death to the press.[55] The announcement, in turn, forced the American State Department to acknowledge publicly that he was being held in Finland and thus set the stage for his release. After another period of excruciating delay, it was the Soviet Union which finally arranged his release by exchanging three Finnish college professors held in Russia for the imprisoned poet.[56]

It was thus to Russia and not the United States that Reed returned in mid-June 1919. He was also a markedly different person from the youthful, energetic reporter who had bounded into the country some two years earlier. So physically weakened was he by his long imprisonment that weeks later he still suffered from swollen limbs and his body was covered with rash and scurvy. He was in such poor condition that Emma Goldman, the exiled anarchist, found him living alone in the Hotel International, and helped nurse him back to at least partial health. Indebted as he was to Emma, Reed steadfastly rejected her growing disillusionment with the Soviet Experiment, and much of their time together was spent in friendly argument.[57]

Once he had recovered enough to work, Reed continued to devote much of his energy to writing for the American radical press. He felt it was important for Americans to be aware of the continuing revolution. His work, if less colorful in tone, was thus more pragmatically oriented to swaying public opinion. In the last article that he sent to the *Liberator*—a magazine from which he had never totally broken—he attempted to shame the American public into demanding an end to all foreign intervention in Russia. From Reed's perspective, much of the

suffering of the Russian people and the chaos which spread throughout
the country was a direct result of Allied activity: "The cities would
have been provisioned and provided with wood for the winter, the transport situation would have been better than ever before, the harvest
would have filled the granaries of Russia to bursting—if only the Poles
and Wrangel, backed by the Allies," he bitterly emphasized, "had not
suddenly hurled their armies once more against Russia, necessitating
the cessation of all rebuilding of economic life, the abandoning of the
work on transport, the leaving of the cities half provisioned, half un-
provided with wood, the concentration once again of all the forces of
the exhausted country upon the front."[58] Like Edith Wharton's view of
the invasion of France, Reed saw the Allied activity not so much as an
attack on the Revolution as a devastating assault upon the Russian
people themselves.

Although writing was Reed's greatest talent and perhaps his most
lasting contribution to the Soviet cause, more and more of his time
was taken up by public appearances, speeches, and committee work—
activities which seldom made demands upon his literary abilities. Even
though these new tasks were not ones in which he particularly ex-
celled, he nonetheless displayed his customary enthusiasm in carrying
them out. In July 1920, for example, he helped prepare for the opening of the Second Congress of the Communist International which was
to begin later that month. A First Congress had been held in March
1919, but was sparsely attended because of the combined upheavals of
civil war and foreign intervention. Held under more peaceful conditions, the Second Congress was attended by revolutionists from all
over the world who were as eager as Reed to see the spread of Bolshevism outside Russia. At the Congress Reed divided his time between taking delegates on sightseeing tours of Moscow and trying to
indoctrinate them into the "realities" of Bolshevism.[59] When not with
delegates he was writing reports to present as a member of two commissions—one on national minorities and the colonial question, and
the other on trade union activities. The ideological position that he
took while serving on the second of these commissions led to a personal crisis in his life and a direct confrontation with two of the most

powerful figures at the Congress, Karl Radek and Grigori E. Zinoviev.

Shortly after the Congress opened, two motions made by Reed—that the discussion of the trade-unions issue be placed near the head of the agenda and that English be adopted as one of the official languages used in discussion—were defeated with Zinoviev leading the opposition.[60] Several days later while participating in a meeting of the Trades-Union Commission Reed had a bitter dispute with Radek on whether or not American Communists should work through the trades-unions of the A.F. of L. or should adopt instead the industrial unionism of the I.W.W. Judging that world revolution was not imminent and that a single socialist country was the reality for the moment, the Bolshevik leadership was becoming more expedient and less idealistic in many of its expectations. Radek and Zinoviev therefore argued that from a practical, revolutionary viewpoint, the American Communists should try to dominate the much larger and more important A.F. of L. in attempting to bring revolution to the United States. Reed vehemently opposed such a policy because for years he detested the exclusiveness of the A.F. of L.'s trade unionism. He had grown socially aware while watching the I.W.W. at work in Paterson and had personally known Big Bill Haywood. Now, although the I.W.W. was in a state of almost total eclipse, he insisted that the A.F. of L. should be destroyed and that all support be given to the more militant unionism of the Wobblies.[61] Reed's support of the I.W.W. was not uncritical. Only a little over a year earlier he had denounced an article in a Wobblie publication which attacked the Bolsheviks for failing to dismantle the power of the state once they had seized it. Scoffing at the writer's fears ("Anarcho-Menshevik twaddle"), Reed claimed that it was unreasonable to expect the disappearance of the dictatorship of the proletariat before the destruction of world capitalism.[62] Yet ready as he was to criticize the I.W.W., he was in no way prepared to abandon it completely—especially when the alternative was working through the detested A.F. of L. Believing that the most effective way of radicalizing American workers was through industrial unionism, he continued to fight for this viewpoint in spite of mounting opposition. When outvoted on the Trades-Union Commission, he carried the fight to the general assembly of the Congress where Zinoviev attempted to end all opposition by dictating the majority position to those who remained adament in their dissent.[63] Far from being mollified by Zinoviev's directive, Reed continued to air publicly the dispute in an article which related the accomplishments of the Congress to party members back in the United States.[64]

Although disgusted by the oppositional methods used against him in the trades union dispute, Reed continued to participate in the business of the Congress, and the August 8 edition of *Pravda* carried his report on the "Negro Question" in America. His interest in the treatment of American Negroes can first be traced to a letter written in 1916 enroute from New York to Florida in which he described the way in which white passengers in Southern railway stations threw money from the coaches to see the Negroes fight one another for it.[65] Actually, he knew very little about the overall economic and social position of the American Negro, but dutifully wrote a report that suggested the direction the party should follow in the future: "An oppressed and downtrodden people, the Negro offers to us a two fold opportunity: first a strong race and social movement; second a strong labor movement. . . . In both the northern and southern parts of the country the one aim must be to unite the Negro and white laborer in common labor unions; this is the best and the quickest way to destroy race prejudice and develop class solidarity."[66] Reed was clearly interested in the problems faced by Black Americans, but he was still obsessed with the trades union issue. By suggesting that black and white workers should be united in one big union, he was once again presenting his viewpoint by obliquely attacking the exclusiveness and racism of the A.F. of L. As the Congress continued, Reed's anger mounted. He was particularly distressed by the way in which Zinoviev and Radek dismantled any opposition including his own. Toward the end of the conference he was so infuriated by the tactics of the two party members and what he considered to be a blindness to the labor situation in America that he tried to resign from the Comintern's executive committee. Persuaded to withdraw his resignation, he nonetheless emerged from the conference embittered by the way his views had been overridden. Still suffering the effects of imprisonment, he was also thoroughly exhausted and planned to forget the turmoils of the past few weeks by resting and enjoying a reunion with Louise, who had finally found a way of getting to Russia.

Though Reed had shown himself at the Congress to be a persistent and perhaps even unwelcome voice of dissent, he was still regarded as a valuable asset by the party, and his presence at state functions was still much in demand. Thus near the end of August he was ordered to attend a Congress of Oriental Nations which was to be held at Baku. At the Congress the Soviet government hoped it could strike the first blow against British imperialism in the Near East by spreading the communist ideology among its native peoples. Reed was not enthusiastic about making the long journey to the conference site. He had been looking forward to a long period of rest and was anxiously awaiting Louise's arrival from the United States, where she had been since their return from Russia in 1918. Furthermore, he learned that the conference would be directed by Zinoviev and Radek. His request to remain in Moscow was abruptly denied.[67] Soon Reed was aboard an armored train speeding across the immense Volga plains toward the oil-rich city sprawled on the shores of the Caspian Sea. According to the obviously partisan accounts of several of his friends, Reed returned from the Congress even more disgusted and disillusioned with the antics of his two enemies than ever before.[68] From his perspective, Radek and Zinoviev had cast all restraint aside in their demagogic wooing of the various nationalities. Their lavish entertaining of important delegates seemed even more cynical and exploitative at a time when the vast majority of the Russian people lacked even the basic necessities of life.[69]

Reed returned to Moscow in mid-September 1920, where Louise awaited him. As Max Eastman had noticed earlier in New York, Louise also found that her husband had changed and become more serious. He seemed "older and sadder and grown strangely gentle and aesthetic. His clothes were just rags. He was so impressed with the suffering around him that he would take nothing for himself. I felt shocked and almost unable to reach the pinnacle of fervor he had attained."[70] The trip to Baku had exhausted Reed, and during the first weeks of their reunion he and Louise did little other than make an occasional sightseeing excursion or visit with friends in the city. Near the end of the month he became ill with what was at first thought to be influenza. But as his condition worsened over the next week, it was discovered that he had contracted typhus. A short time later he suffered a fatal stroke. Reed died on October 17, 1920, less than three weeks before the third anniversary of the October Revolution.

Any discussion of the Russian activities of John Reed during the last few months of his life must deal with two critical questions left unanswered at the time of his death: was he disillusioned with the Soviet experiment and was he also in the process of making a definite and perhaps final break with the entire Communist ideology? Since his death, a number of Reed analysts have offered an array of conflicting opinions concerning these questions. Friends like Emma Goldman and Angelica Balbanova and acquaintances like Marguerite Harrison and Jacob H. Rubin, all of whom were in Russia in 1920, insist that during the last part of his life Reed had become increasingly discontented with the Soviet Union.[71] Interpretations made from first-hand observations have a ring of authenticity about them, but these people who knew Reed were themselves disillusioned with the Soviets and may have been projecting their own feelings onto Reed. Most certainly Goldman and Balbanova had heard Reed voice dissatisfaction with various aspects of the Soviet system or the way in which he had been treated at the Congress of the Second International, but this does not necessarily mean that he shared their own more pervasive sense of disgust. Louise Bryant, on the other hand, never referred to Reed's disillusionment in any of her later writings, but did claim that he had grown so unhappy with the Revolution that he personally came to feel as though he were "caught in a trap."[72] Louise was in the best position to gauge Reed's frame of mind during his last days. Unfortunately, due to her own emotional troubles throughout the latter portion of her life, she never stuck to the same story for long and therefore shed little light on Reed's true feelings. One person who felt that Reed never became disenchanted with the Soviet Union was his good friend and fellow worker in the Propaganda Ministry, Albert Rhys Williams. Almost half a century after Reed's death, Williams was still convinced of Reed's commitment to the Revolution, and he suggested that stories about the writer's disillusionment usually tell us far more about the story-tellers than about Jack Reed. "Even now," Williams wrote, "I cannot look at the photographs of Reed taken in that Finnish prison where he lived on frozen fish for more than two months without wanting to fight his traducers. I look at that face, gaunt and defiant, and feel anger at all those who have tried to show Reed as disillusioned when he died. I was not there, nor were they, but Louise Bryant was—and it was only after her death that the legend of the disillusioned Reed was blown up by those who were themselves disillusioned."[73] Reed had experienced a great deal during his last stay in Russia, but Williams was certain that any metamorphosis that took place could not have been so complete as to suggest abandonment of the Revolution and all that it represented.

Reed's major biographers have also differed on the same question. Granville Hicks, whether writing as a member of the Communist party in the 1930s or as a Communist drop-out in the 1960s, nevertheless maintains that Reed continued to believe in the Revolution as he observed it in the Soviet Union.[74] On the other hand, Richard O'Connor and Dale L. Walker, using essentially the same sources as Hicks, but writing from a cold war perspective, have refused to take either Reed or his revolutionary interests seriously and have argued that toward the end of his life he was very much disillusioned with the entire communist system.[75] Though not a Reed biographer, Theodore Draper in *The Roots of American Communism* has also examined the question of his disllusionment and has taken something of a middle position by arguing that he was probably disillusioned at the time of his death, but not to the extent of being willing to abandon the movement. Had his discontent continued, however, Draper believes it would probably have led to a break on the part of both Reed and the Soviets.[76] Finally, Reed's most recent and probably definitive biographer, Robert Rosenstone, has more or less gone full circle and is closest to Hicks's position. Rosenstone argues that Reed's commitment was too strong to be easily abandoned. Reed would not have broken with the Revolution merely because of personal disagreements with individuals like Radek and Zinoviev, and according to Rosenstone he was still the dedicated revolutionist at his death.[77]

It seems likely that an understanding of Reed's last months in Russia will always remain open to further interpretation. In the 1920s, unlike the 1930s, dissent, if not openly courted, was still quite possible within both Russia and the Communist party, and John Reed was never one to hesitate to voice his opposition. That he made his presence felt at the Second International by virtue of his dissent on the trades union question, that he offered to resign in a fit of anger from the executive committee, and that he became increasingly disillusioned with some of the party leaders cannot be denied. Yet to disagree was not necessarily to reject, and Reed had become too personally committed to his newfound faith to turn on it in a matter of weeks. Nowhere else in the world had he found workers so well organized in their efforts to confront working-class exploitation as in Soviet Russia. Nowhere else had he seen such sweeping efforts to create a new and more equitable society. Never before had he played such a direct and sustained role in a cause in which he believed. And finally, never had he paid so dearly in a personal and professional way for his beliefs.

Beginning with his unpopular stand in World War I, Reed's life was fraught with disappointments and personal suffering. Old friends snubbed him. Magazines which once begged for his articles came to reject them. A speech he gave at Harvard, his alma mater, was interrupted by hoots from the audience. Weeks spent in the damp loneliness of a Finnish jail damaged his health and perhaps his spirit. His writing too was adversely affected by his commitment to the Revolution. With the exception of *Ten Days That Shook the World*, most of what he wrote after returning from Russia the first time was either ideological exegeses or propaganda pieces to explain the Bolsheviks' attempts at reforming society. Willing to donate his pen to the cause in which he believed, Reed fully realized what the cost might be in creative terms. He once commented to Max Eastman, "You know, this class struggle plays hell with your poetry."[78] Yet in spite of the

creative sacrifices made for his beliefs, for many he remains the playboy poet—the impetuous, excitement-seeking, fun-loving adventurer
who had been in and out of jails around the globe, sung strike songs
with Wobblies, enjoyed the affections of Mabel Dodge and numerous
other women, ridden with Pancho Villa, been banned from the Eastern and Western Fronts because of "rash deeds," led anti-war protests,
and roamed throughout Petrograd during those ten days that shook
the world.[79] Without question the excitement of the unknown and love
of the adventurous were fundamental aspects of Reed's personality
and his activities abroad. Albert Rhys Williams, in describing both his
and Reed's involvement in Russia, willingly admits this side of their
personalities when he writes, "there was in both Reed and me a good
deal of the romantic, of the love of adventure. To picture either of us
in September 1917 as having profound understanding of Marxism, or
a devotion to the proletariat as Bolsheviks, would be wrong. That
Reed was if anything more a romantic than I did not prevent his
becoming a Communist, which I did not; it may have accelerated the
process."[80] Unlike Williams, however, many of Reed's contemporaries saw only the playful side of his personality which was not
only a misreading of the man, but one that did him a grave injustice.

In spite of a *joie de vivre* that was so much a part of Reed's
personality, he was sensitive to human suffering and, at least during
the latter portion of his life, unyielding in his dislike for its social
causes. Although he enjoyed the advantages of an upper-middle-class
background, Reed increasingly came to detest the special privilege and
social inequality that such a background conferred. He, therefore,
gradually assumed his role of revolutionary because of an eclectic and
impetuous personality, and although the path he traveled was paved
with a bizarre mixture of excitement and adventure it is difficult to see
how he could have reached his final position as a dedicated member of
the Communist party in any other way. Reed was seldom moved by
the theoretical. It was the vibrancy of the October Days rather than the
compelling logic of *Das Kapital*, the exuberant determination on the
faces of Russian workers rather than any belief in the historical
inevitability of dialectical materialism that motivated him. Just as his

best writing reflected what he had either observed in person or participated in, his activism in Russia had a similar inception. Growing primarily out of professional experiences, his radicalization was more the result of a personal sense of anger and frustration than anything else. Eventually the reporting of events became an inadequate response to the events themselves and Reed felt compelled to become involved himself. The unwavering courage he saw at Paterson, the simple revolutionary dedication in Mexico, and the unmitigated suffering at Ludlow were all important experiences leading to his radicalization; but had it not been for the disillusionment that he experienced visiting the front lines in Europe, or, even more important, while fighting against American involvement in the war, it is likely that he would have continued to be a good journalist—indeed, one of the best—but probably nothing more. Campaigning against American entry into the war was truly Reed's first great cause as well as his most personally damaging defeat, a kind of alpha and omega brought to an end only after he had gone to Russia. Thoroughly convinced that the American worker was being duped, he interpreted the country's entry into World War I as a combination of pure ignorance and blatant cynicism. News of the Revolution in Russia, coming as it did at the height of Reed's disillusionment with America, was a life-preserver at which he eagerly grasped. When he reached Petrograd it was as though he had wandered into another world, for there he discovered workers who were still capable of fighting for themselves rather than for some ill-defined nationalism. There he also began to experience again much of the idealistic excitement that had characterized his initial encounters with the *Villistas*. Seeing and then participating in the October events which led to the Bolshevik seizure of power served as the final catalyst in his personal metamorphosis from radical journalist to revolutionary. The things that he saw in the streets of Petrograd, in the Russian trenches, in the countryside outside of Moscow were deeply engraved in his memory and became the idealistic storehouse upon which his enthusiasm continued to feed. He could never forget the time that he had spoken on the day after Christmas, 1917, at a factory in Serpukov where the workers, many of whom had walked long distances, stood "Cold, hungry, ragged, tired"—first listening to him and then in turn promising: "We will not give up."[81] Two years later Graham Taylor, an American Embassy attaché, was also impressed with the intense commitment he found in Russia, but it was Reed and not the workers who he remembered. He specifically recalled the excited way in which Reed had discussed the Revolution at a Christmas dinner sponsored by the American Red Cross. Reed sat next to a New York business executive described by Taylor as a "man whose ideas of democracy had been determined by long identification with Tammany Hall." In his enthusiasm for the Revolution, Reed was completely oblivious to the total lack of communication between him and his dinner partner and through the meal he bombarded the incredulous businessman with information about the new regime.[82] But a minor obstacle such as a lack of communication was of no consequence to a man who had joined the Revolution without being able to speak Russian, and who became a Communist with only a most rudimentary knowledge of Marx. What truly mattered to Reed was that he thought he had seen the first tentative steps toward social justice and had committed his energies to following them. His commitment, then, was not escapist, for he anticipated giving form to a revoluionary movement in the United States.

For the rest of his life, in his writing and organizational efforts, Reed remained dedicated to planting the seeds of Bolshevism in American soil. Most of his disagreements with party members both in the United States and later in Moscow stemmed from their insistence that the revolution in America must follow the same pattern already established in Soviet Russia. Reed thought he knew better and spent the last portion of his life attempting to convince others. It is, of course, impossible to predict how he would have reacted had he lived to witness the struggle for power between Trotsky and Stalin, the five-year plans, or the Purge Trials. His belief in the uniqueness of the American experience might well have doomed him to the same kind of ostracism suffered by the Lovestoneites during the interwar period.

But this is only speculation. What truly matters is that by the time of his death his dedication to the Revolution's ideas had become so intrinsic a part of his personality that the two had become inseparable. Reed died a Communist and no one knows whether or not he would have remained one had he lived longer.

5

Individualism, Professionalism, and Louis Fischer's Search for One World

> *I am most certaintly "for" an "intelligent communism"; no other form or theory of government seems to me conceivable; but even this is only a part of much more, and a means to an end: and in every concession to a means, the end is put in danger of all but certain death. I feel violent enmity and contempt toward all factions and all joiners. I "conceive of" my work as an effort to be faithful to my perceptions.*
>
> James Agee
> *Let Us Now Praise Famous Men*

By FOUR O'CLOCK IN THE AFTERNOON of October 29, 1938, all of Barcelona appeared to be lining the Gran Via Diagonal, the broad street which slants across the face of Catalonia's capital city. Overhead, squadrons of planes were weaving a gigantic protective net for the hundreds of thousands of Spaniards below, assembled to pay their final tribute to the departing soldiers of the International Brigade. Thirty minutes later the parade began. Among the two thousand Internationals who passed before the reviewing stand were some two or three hundred Americans, wildly cheered by the crowd even though their departure from Spain portended defeat for the Republic. The

Americans marching on the Diagonal that day were among the survivors of the nearly three thousand who had fought in the Spanish Civil War.[1]

The decision to send the Internationals home (under the supervision of the League of Nations) had been announced a month earlier, September 21, in a speech given at Geneva by Lopez Juan Negrin, Premier of the Spanish Republic. Negrin had hoped that his announcement might prompt the League to demand a similar withdrawal of German and Italian troops from Loyalist-controlled areas of Spain; but the League powers were then preoccupied with appeasing Hitler in Czechoslovakia. Among those present at Negrin's valiant, but futile, eleventh-hour diplomatic effort to save the Spanish Republic was the first American to join the International Brigade—Louis Fischer. Although his term of service with the Brigade was brief, and his associations with its commander strained, Fischer continued to believe, even during the last oppressive months before the outbreak of World War II, that "those who came back can be proud that they were able to see when the rest were blind and they acted under no compulsion except that of inner conviction and devotion to a good cause. The Brigade's life stands as an untarnished epic."[2] Thus, for Fischer and hundreds like him, active commitment to Loyalist Spain was more than a defiant gesture in the face of world fascism: it was an idealistic act of faith which would weather both defeat and the passage of time.

Like many of those whom he served with in Spain, Fischer had known poverty firsthand. He was born in 1896 in a small apartment above a delicatessen in the Philadelphia slums. His parents, David and Shifrah (Kantzapolsky) Fischer, had left their native town of Shpola, near Kiev, in search of a new life only to find that America was no promised land. After several years of factory work, David Fischer turned to selling fish and fresh fruit from a pushcart. A family of four needed more than the meager profits of sidewalk vending, so Louis's mother supplemented the family's income by taking in washing from neighbors. Until he was sixteen neither Louis nor his sister had ever lived with electricity, running water, an inside lavatory, or warmth except that provided by coal stoves. The family moved so often—

usually to escape unpaid bills—that the security of permanent relationships or familiarity with any one neighborhood was also lacking
from his youthful experiences. Except for a weekly meal shared with a
more prosperous aunt, Fischer later recalled that neither he nor his
sister had enough to eat. It was, in fact, only on election days that the
family was able to escape temporarily from the dreadful monotony of
poverty. In most elections Louis's father was assured of the customary
two dollars for his ballot, but should the vote be anticipated as an
extremely close one, the family could expect as much as a five-dollar
income supplement.[3]

From an early age Fischer dreamed of escaping the poverty that so
dominated his existence. He worked hard in grammar school, graduated from Southern High School in 1914, and spent the next two
years at the Philadelphia School of Pedagogy (a part of the University
of Pennsylvania) to obtain a trial certificate which allowed him to
teach in the city's public school system. His first job was an eighth
grade teacher in one of the Philadelphia public schools. Fischer enjoyed teaching, but like his father, he abhorred the set schedules of a
regular job, and soon began hunting for a more flexible employment.
Any final decisions about his future, however, were abruptly postponed when the United States entered World War I. Like so many
other young men of his generation, Fischer was caught up in the maelstrom of the conflict. His wartime service, however, followed a decidedly different course, largely as a result of his youthful environment.

Having grown up in a poor predominantly Jewish neighborhood,
Fischer was familiar with the socialist and Zionist thought that usually
dominated any political conversation.[4] His own economic plight as
well as that of those around him led him to read Henry George's
Progress and Poverty and the memoirs of the Russian anarchist, Peter
Kropotkin. Both books so impressed him that for the rest of his life
he believed that cooperation among people rather than competition
would best restructure the social order. Yet Fischer disagreed with
Kropotkin on one important point. While the Russian saw revolution
as the only way of dealing with an oppressive social order, Fischer

sought less violent means of change. In a moment of reminiscence
about his youth, he claimed to have supported "the trust-busting spirit
of the Theodore Roosevelt era and the liberalism and populism that
were part of every poor American's heritage."[5] Such may have been
the case, but when Fischer expressed this view of his youth he was
about to break with the Soviet Union. It does not do justice, therefore,
to his more radical viewpoints that so dominated his activities and
commitments during the 1920s and 1930s. Yet it was neither socialism nor Progressivism which first attracted his youthful support. Instead, it was a movement which struck an intensely personal chord
—the call for the establishment of a Jewish homeland in Palestine.

The seeds of Fischer's interest in a Jewish homeland had been
planted in early childhood when he and his sister had listened with
fascinated horror to their parents' stories of Jewish life in Czarist
Russia. These tales were reinforced by the harsh realities of ghetto life
in Philadelphia and made the vision of a Jewish state in Palestine not a
dream but a goal. When he was seventeen, Fischer joined the local
Zionist organization. Eager to work and displaying an effective ability
to organize, he rose quickly in the movement. Eventually he supervised the holiday sales of small Zionist flags and flowers on street
corners around the city. Later Fischer was given even more responsibility and promoted to secretary of the central Zionist organization
for all of Philadelphia. Quite unexpectedly, his Zionism took a more
militant turn with the outbreak of World War I. Like other young
Jewish men in the United States, he was excited to learn in 1917 that a
Jewish Legion was being formed by the British. It was to be used to
liberate Palestine, and, more important, Jews living in the United
States were encouraged to get involved.

From the beginning the Jewish Legion was essentially a British
creation.[6] By 1917 with the war dragging on, the British, desperately
needing more men, were willing to consider any plan that might hinder
the Central Powers. As a result they decided to form a voluntary
Jewish military force which, it was hoped, would help push the Turks
out of Palestine. The recruits were to come largely from Russian Jews
living in Britain. But with American approval the British decided to

seek recruits in the United States from among the alien Jewish population not subject to the draft.[7] The British and American volunteers were to be known as the 38th and 39th Battalions of the Royal British Fusiliers. Not only did they share the military objectives of the Legion, but many American recruits apparently signed on with the intention of settling in Palestine when the war was over.

Fischer was twenty-one years old when he joined the Jewish Legion. His initial military training in Nova Scotia in the spring of 1918 and his transfer to England several months later gave him his first glimpse of the world outside Philadelphia. He never actually fought in the war. By the time he arrived in Palestine in 1919, the conflict was over.[8] But Fischer remained in the Legion, and spent much of the next fifteen months touring ancient Hebrew ruins and observing a kind of Jewish life that he had never seen in Philadelphia.

Considering Fischer's natural abhorrence for prescribed routine and bureaucratic control, it is not surprising that he found a soldier's life difficult. He particularly objected to forced attendance at synagogue every Saturday, to having to march to worship, and to the contemptuous way in which many of the officers acted toward the enlisted men. On one particular occasion when Fischer informed an officer that two "gentlemen" (privates) wished to speak with him, the officer curtly replied " 'In the British army . . . the only gentlemen are the officers.' "[9] As Fischer's discontent grew, his conduct began to reflect his distaste for the British military tradition. He quickly acquired the reputation of a troublemaker and as a result was singled out for punishment when the discipline of the battalion became too lax.[10] Like most of the other enlisted men, Fischer had occasionally taken advantage of the Legion's casual discipline by going on leave without permission. As long as the absence was brief the officers usually took no notice, but the next time Fischer departed camp without permission he was arrested and sentenced to twenty days in a prison camp located in the middle of the desert. Each morning, with a full pack strapped to his back, he did exhausting exercises under the glaring heat of the Egyptian sun. Each afternoon, under the supervision of a "brutal-faced sergeant," he dug and then refilled large holes in the desert floor.[11] Such futile, monotonous routine was anathema to Fischer, who had gone to Palestine to build a new Jewish state in the desert; this dream now seemed a hopeless nightmare.

Fischer may have survived his short time in prison by remembering the pleasant experiences of his soldier's life. Having enlisted with the intention of ultimately settling in the Holy Land, he had spent much of his free time exploring rural Palestine. He was most interested in the communal activities of the Jewish settlers living in a number of Kibbutzim scattered over the area. Twenty years later, he recalled that it had been the example of diverse nationalities living and working together that first attracted him to the Kibbutzim. What impressed him most was the fact that the Kibbutzim were collective endeavors where "work and income were shared alike and the emphasis was on egalitarian community living rather than personal needs. They renounced for the common good; it was a religious way of life shaped by persons who were not religious."[12] The communalistic and international composition of these early Zionist communities had great appeal for the young Philadelphian. He was attracted to the idealism of the communes as well as to their collective leadership. Social cooperation stood in stark contrast to the Legion where decisions were made according to rank, and prison sentences were given out on official whims. The communes, of course, also seemed to be laying the foundation for a future Zionist state whereas the Legion, at least from Fischer's perspective, seemed to exist primarily for the harassment of its enlisted members. At the same time the more Fischer observed the exciting life of the Kibbutzim, the more he became bored with the Legion, and finally in mid-1920 he decided to do something about it.

Several months after his return from the prison camp, Fischer took a prolonged unexcused leave of absence from the Legion. This time, however, he departed with a definite goal in mind. Having heard that several isolated Jewish settlements in Upper Galilee were under frequent attack by wandering groups of Bedouins, he decided to go there to help. Dressed in British uniform with a three-day pass in his pocket, Fischer made his way to the besieged colonies of Bel Hai and Cfar

Gileadi near the mouth of the Jordan River and the ancient town of Dan in northern Palestine. Once there he stood armed guard at the colonies' blockhouse for almost two weeks. It was a monotonous job relieved only occasionally by the need to fire into the air to frighten away lurking marauders. Once, however, snipers gave him a taste of the terrible realities of war when a young settler, standing by his side, was shot.[13] Seventeen days after having left, Fischer returned to his battalion. Dusty and tired, he blamed his absence on a missed train connection. The new commanding officer, perhaps a supporter of the Zionist movement himself, listened to the story and then curtly dismissed the wandering private without further comment. Later he sent for Fischer and then swamped him with questions about how the settlers in that most remote area of Palestine were faring.[14]

As the end of his term of enlistment drew near, Fischer was faced with the decision of whether or not to settle permanently in the area. Like many other recruits he had joined the Legion with a vague intention of doing so, but fifteen months later he was no longer certain that he wanted to remain in Palestine. During the course of traveling —literally from Dan to Bathsheba—his earlier ideas about Zionism underwent a transformation. Life on the Kibbutzim was by far the most magnetic lure of the Zionist ideal, and many years later he could still recall the appeal that these struggling communes had had for him. On the other hand, he also recalled the concern he had felt at the time about the ever increasing hostility between Arabs and Jews.[15] In conversations with his best friend and fellow legionnaire, Gershon Agronsky, the future editor of the English-language Palestine *Post*, Fischer had voiced his fears that an expanding conflict would inevitably grow from increased Jewish nationalism in Palestine.[16] Zionism from his perspective in Philadelphia had existed in a kind of void and, as might be expected, had never been tied to the troublesome social and political realities that existed in Palestine. Once Fischer joined the Legion and traveled through the area, these realities became apparent to him. Certainly the two weeks spent on the Kibbutzim in Galilee had been a sobering experience for the young Zionist who had never associated the movement with death, Arab opposition, and the possibility of perpetual conflict. Fischer's enthusiasm for Zionism was clouded by what seemed to be its impossible future. When his enlistment ended, he was ready to leave the Near East, and for that matter the Zionist movement itself.

Although there were theoretical reasons for Fischer's disillusionment with Zionism, these explanations must be placed in their proper context since they were articulated long after his service in Palestine and represent a deeply felt mistrust of nationalism that had been over three decades in the making. Personal reservations may have dampened Fischer's Zionist fervor—reservations that had little or nothing to do with the conflicting interests of Arab and Jewish nationalists. For example, his extreme dislike for the discipline of military life suggests he might find membership in other organized movements uncomfortable as well. How attractive then would life on a Kibbutz be for someone who had found teaching school too restrictive and monotonous? Would not discipline, order, and routine have been essential to the survival of these isolated agricultural communes? Did Fischer's disillusionment with Zionism and his decision to leave Palestine, perhaps, stem from a realization that by abandoning the Legion for a Kibbutz he would be merely discarding one set of restrictions for another? Whatever his reasons for leaving, Fischer resigned from the Legion in 1920 and returned to the United States.

Back in Philadelphia by late 1920 Fischer spent several months working at odd jobs and reading everything available about the recent war of which he had never really been a part. Reading about the war whetted his appetite for foreign travel, and a Europe which had simultaneously given birth to war and revolution seemed tremendously fascinating to him. Yet there was the problem of how to get there, and, once having arrived, how to support himself. Fischer reasoned that if he could first understand the world, he could then, perhaps, write about it. With all the naïve bravado of youth, he went to see the managing editor of the New York *Evening Post* to ask for a job.[17] The editor refused, of course, but he agreed to read anything that Fischer sent and to pay for whatever the paper published. With this encouragement, Fischer scraped together enough money to book passage; shortly before the end of the year he left for London. Thus in a rather haphazard way began what was to become a lifelong career as writer and freelance journalist. Unlike Reed, Fischer turned to journalism and then to the writing of books primarily as a way to view European politics firsthand. It would be a career well-suited to his individualism. Although, like Reed, he would eventually become emotionally committed to a foreign cause, Fischer differed from him in that he was incapable of ever abandoning his profession completely. Once he became used to viewing and analyzing events from the relatively detached position of a freelance journalist, he was never able for long to devote himself totally and uncritically to a foreign cause. In short, his individualism and professionalism kept getting in the way of his foreign activism.

During his first nine months in Europe, Fischer spent most of the time in Berlin where, because of postwar inflation, he could live on the twenty-odd American dollars a month that he was earning from the sale of articles to the *Evening Post*. By the end of the summer of 1922 he had traveled throughout much of Germany and had also managed excursions to Vienna and Warsaw. Everywhere he went he found a new militant nationalism. It was the same kind of nationalism which had pushed Europe into the most destructive war in history and which was re-emerging from the ruins with a new shrillness. To some degree it was a similar concern about the nationalistic ramifications of Zionism which had made him question the efficacy of that movement and now, the more he saw of Europe, the more he became convinced that the same malady was attacking its foundations.[18] At the same time he read with mounting interest about the new, internationally oriented state that the Bolsheviks claimed to be building from the ruins of Czarist Russia. To a young journalist who had grown up in a Philadelphia slum, their promises were electrifying. A program calling for world peace, economic equality, and an immediate end to all forms of imperialism was infinitely more appealing than the "dull 'normalcy' of the Harding-Coolidge era in the U.S.A., and the aimlessness of

Europe. . . ."[19] Like John Reed before him, Fischer felt that the future lay not in Europe but in Russia, and he began searching for a way to get there.

In 1922 Fischer knew Russia only through the stories of his parents and his reading of Russian literature. As a youth he read Tolstoy, Dostoevsky, Turgenev, Gogol and was tremendously impressed by Kropotkin's autobiography.[20] Like most who knew Russia mainly through her literature, he meshed fact with fancy. To Fischer, Russia was an exotic mixture of mystery, idealism, and misery. But the new Russia that Fischer was reading about in 1922 seemed quite different from the mythical place that he had imagined since childhood. In fact, the new Russia seemed unlike any other country he knew. Years later, when he looked back on this time in his life, Fischer recalled: "The unique appeal of the Bolshevik Revolution was its universality. It did not propose merely to introduce drastic change in Russia. It envisaged the world-wide abolition of war, poverty, and suffering. In all countries, therefore, the little man, the laborer, and the intellectual felt that something important had taken place in their lives when revolution took root in Russia."[21] Perhaps Fischer was merely replacing an old myth with a new one, but he left for Russia in late 1922 with tremendous excitement. He also left Western Europe hoping to find new copy that might well help a young journalist in an already crowded field.

Much as John Reed had done earlier, Fischer entered the Soviet Union in the late fall of 1922 with no real knowledge of the people or the language, no contacts, and very little money. What he had plenty of was luck. On the long journey by train from Riga to Moscow, he met Sidney Hillman of the Amalgamated Clothing Workers of America who was also traveling to the new capital city to help the Soviets build clothing factories. When they arrived in Moscow, Hillman got Fischer a cab and told the driver to take him to the Hotel Savoy, which turned out to be the watering hole for foreign correspondents. Within a short time Fischer was initiated into the one group in which he always felt comfortable—a fraternity which had "no name, no officers, no meetings, no dues, and no fixed membership." Among its members competition was extreme to the point of being excessive, but, paradoxically, a remarkable degree of comradeship also existed. No one in the fraternity, wherever his reporting took him, had to be alone. As Fischer recounted, "whenever an American newspaperman arrives in a foreign capital he has friends whom he has never seen. He need only telephone one of the resident American journalists and say, 'This is Charles X of Chicago so-and-so,' and the reply will be, 'Where are you? Come on over. Will you know how to get here?' "[22] Unlike the Kibbutzim, this was the kind of community in which Fischer thrived, for it placed virtually no checks upon his individualism.

During his first months in Russia, Fischer lived in Moscow but took occasional trips to the provinces. When in the capital he walked wherever possible to familiarize himself with the city's inhabitants and their language. Before learning to speak or read Russian, he spent part of each morning with a translator who read the newspapers to him. If there was no story to cover or interview to be held, he usually spent the afternoon reading, writing, playing tennis, studying Russian, and, more often than not, chatting with other journalists. Paul Scheffer of the *Berliner Tageblatt*, Walter Duranty of the New York *Times*, and William Henry Chamberlain of the *Christian Science Monitor* were the friends with whom Fischer talked and played a seemingly endless game of poker.

In 1923 Fischer's personal life took a dramatic turn when he married Bertha (Markoosha) Mark, whom he had met several years earlier in New York and with whom he had lived for some time in Germany. They had decided to marry only after Markoosha became pregnant with their first son, Yura, born in 1923. A second son, Vitya, was born a year later. Fischer's marriage was far from conventional. As a freelance correspondent, he was often separated from his family for long periods of time. From 1923 to 1927 Markoosha and the boys lived in Berlin and Louis visited whenever he could. Reunited in 1927, the family remained together until the children were again sent to Berlin to live with friends from 1931 to 1933 because of the hardships generated by the first Five Year Plan. Hitler's seizure of power ended this arrangement, and the family returned to Moscow in 1933.

Fischer's unconventional marriage seemed to meet his professional and personal needs. So too did his job as a freelance journalist because it enabled him during his fourteen years in the Soviet Union to work without a set schedule. The job apparently suited him well. Very quickly he developed excellent journalistic skills, and in 1923 a youthful dream became reality when the *Nation* bought three of his articles. At first he was paid a penny a word, then two cents, then four, and finally considerably more when he became a contributing editor, although neither the *Nation* nor any other publication for which he wrote ever paid him a regular salary. To supplement what was still a small and unpredictable income in the mid-1920s, he usually returned to the United States every year to lecture on the Soviet Union. Beginning in 1934 and continuing until he left for Spain in 1936, he also spent a part of each summer leading Open Road Tourist Groups through the Soviet Union, lecturing and interpreting for them the workings of the new communist state. Throughout the 1920s Markoosha worked and supported the family, and not until 1929 did Fischer earn enough to help.[23]

By the mid-1920s, in addition to journalistic activities, Fischer was devoting more time to researching and writing books. His decision to move in this direction was but another example of his aversion for any restrictions on his intellectual activities. After several years of working as a freelance journalist he began to feel that only writers of books were completely free to express themselves without censorship. Journalists, on the other hand, like Bunyan's Pilgrim, had to travel continually the tortuous road between the slough of the capricious whims of an editor and the "despond" represented by the policy position of specific magazines.[24] In 1926, after eight months of research, he published a first book, *Oil Imperialism*, which was a history of how the international oil cartels had tried to gain control of the oil fields of Russia, Persia, and Turkey. A short time later he began the far more ambitious project of writing a history of Soviet foreign affairs, an undertaking which he naïvely estimated would take another eight months. More than three years later, after extensive research throughout much of the Soviet Union, including interviews with such a galaxy of diplomats as Georgi Chicherin, Maxim Litvinov, Leo Karakhan, Nikolai Krestinsky, Gregory Sokolnikov, and Christian Rakovsky, he published in two volumes, *The Soviets in World Affairs* (1930). The book received rather mixed reviews. Some critics praised his dedicated research and frankness while others attacked what they considered to be a pro-Soviet slant.[25] This was not the first time, nor would it be the last, that Fischer was accused of being little more than a Soviet propagandist. Earlier, in 1925, for example, the anarchist Alexander Berkman had criticized him for being less than candid in his reports concerning the fate of political prisoners in Russia. Fischer, in turn, charged that by leaving Russia, Berkman and fellow anarchist Emma Goldman had completely lost touch with Soviet reality and were thus creating a distorted picture in their lectures and books.[26] The criticism which angered Fischer most was that he found it profitable to write with a pro-Soviet viewpoint. "You can tell the narrow-minded provincials who suspect me that I am not an agent of the Soviet Government, paid or unpaid," he indignantly announced to one such critic in 1927, "and you can suggest that they kick themselves and know that some people do things not for money considerations but out of deep conviction. I realize it will be difficult for Babbitts to get this."[27] Although he never joined the Communist Party, Fischer, as historian Frank A. Warren has shown, continued throughout the 1920s and 1930s to write articles and books in which Soviet means usually justified Soviet ends. Such works as *Why Recognize Russia?* (1931), *Machines and Men in Russia* (1932), and *Soviet Journey* (1935) as well as numerous articles were all highly favorable in their treatment of life in the Soviet Union.[28] Not since viewing the Kibbutzim had Fischer been so excited by planned social activity, and what made the Soviet plan especially impressive was the vast scale upon which it was being carried out. Even when he doubted the Revolution he still believed that it had brought forth a "new freedom to workingmen, peasants, women, youth, and national minorities, and that, in time, the dictatorship would yield to democracy which would be real and better."[29] Fischer was writing at a time when scores of other American liberals, and radicals were fleeing the excesses of unregulated capitalism and then the catastrophe of widespread depression. Thus many others besides Fischer believed that they had sensed some hint of the future in the work of the Soviet planners.[30] Indeed, it became intellectually fashionable to make a pilgrimage to Moscow during this period, and while Fischer was living in Russia he met and helped a great many American visitors including John Gunther, Vincent Sheean, Anna Louise Strong, Maurice Hindus, Negley Farson, Eugene Lyons, Theodore Dreiser, Paul Robeson, Agnes Smedley, and Waldo Frank. Many of them saw only what they wanted to and left the country with their faith in Russia intact. And like many of the visitors he shepherded about Moscow, Fischer also was "blind" to much that was going on in Russia during the interwar period. As he later tried to explain in /The God That Failed, his myopia was caused not so much by a lack of information as by an enthusiastic belief in the soundness of Soviet goals and a willingness to trust the means that were being used to accomplish them: "One's general alignment with a cause is more compelling than all but the most shocking facts about it. Just as religious conviction is impervious to logical argument and, indeed, does not result from logical processes, just as nationalist devotion or personal affection defies a mountain of evidence, so my pro-Soviet attitude attained complete independence from day-to-day events."[31]

Throughout his stay in the Soviet Union, Fischer remained a sympathetic interpreter rather than an active participant in the events occurring there. Why he showed little desire to participate directly in Russian affairs may relate to an unpleasant experience he had in 1925 when he actually tried to play a direct role. At this time he took a salaried job with the Soviet Telegraphic Agency (TASS) office in London as a journalistic expert on international politics. After only four months he quit. While from the start he disliked the monotonous routine of regular supervised employment, he was also professionally disgusted by the official "slant" he was expected to give all news items that passed across his desk. Although his reporting had been decidedly pro-Soviet for some time, he resented being told to follow the party line.[32] When Fischer decided to quit, his streak of independence clearly took precedence over his activism. But was this the only issue involved? To be sure John Reed was angered by the rejection of his arguments on the trades-union issue. But Reed did not quit his job in protest. Fischer's lack of sustained active involvement may have stemmed from a realization not immediately apparent to other Americans in Russia—that because they were foreigners the Soviet Union would always view them as outsiders. Or, how significant was it that Fischer first came to Russia only after the early glow of revolutionary enthusiasm had already burned off, and was in the Soviet Union when the government was faced with the more prosaic yet equally troublesome problems of how to maintain and use power rather than simply seize it? It was one kind of experience to be in the country during the heady days of "war communism," and something quite different to be there during the more pragmatic days of the New Economic Policy. While visiting villages outside of Moscow, for example, Fischer found that the partial return to capitalism had failed to appease the most important group toward which it had been directed: the peasants he interviewed claimed to be getting less for what they produced and paying more for what they purchased. Even more disillusioning was the fact that everywhere the enthusiasm for the Revolution appeared to be waning: "In one village I asked the wife of a former justice of the peace what difference the Revolution had made. She replied, 'People talk more.' "[33] These viewpoints and the Revolution's declining idealism may well have influenced Fischer in his decision to remain on the sidelines, but in the end he probably restricted his support of the Soviet Union to writing because any fuller commitment would have required a kind of discipline that he was unwilling to accept.

By the time of World War II, Fischer had become an outspoken critic of Soviet Russia. Apparently he had harbored doubts about the Soviet experiment for many years, but had not publicized them because of his support for Russia's foreign policy. His growing disillusionment with the Soviet system during the 1930s may help to explain his lack of a direct commitment, but Fischer's objections never developed in as clear-cut or as constant a process as he would have us believe. The TASS experience in 1925 probably planted the first seeds of doubt. Further disillusionment grew out of his attendance three years later at the Shakhty Trial—where fifty engineers were accused of sabotaging coal production, and by implication the entire Soviet economy.[34] As he sat through the proceedings and listened to the fantastic charges brought against the defendants, Fischer was uncertain of how much to accept. "I believed part. I wondered about the remainder."[35] By the early 1930s he was also becoming disgusted by the glorification of Joseph Stalin throughout the country, and as the decade wore on his private notes were filled with misgivings about this new cult of personality. Not only was the dictator's portrait becoming a new iconic symbol, but also his name was beginning to appear in the most unexpected places. While scanning, for example, the Soviet Encyclopedia, Fischer noted with disgust the way in which glorification of the Georgian was even creeping into such improbable areas as the section dealing with metaphysics or the one on myths and mythology.[36] Fischer was also bothered by the Kremlin's policy, even in the face of disorders produced by industrialization and the Nazi threat abroad, of quietly encouraging, as a socially cohesive force, the growth of Russian nationalism. Old Czarist heroes were rescued from historical dustbins, the beauty of the Russian language was suddenly rediscovered, and Pan-Slavism was regarded as a national obligation. "The fact that Bolshevism would want to drink at the mouldy wells of Czarism . . ." was all the more distressing to a professed internationalist who had broken with Zionism in part because of its militant nationalism.[37]

If the cult of personality and the renaissance of Russian nationalism dampened Fischer's enthusiasm for the Soviet system, the nightmarish atmosphere of the Great Purge Trials nearly destroyed it. Even while that witches' brew was in the making, first by the party's "cleansing" efforts in 1933, and later by the series of executions following the assassination of Sergei Kirov in 1934, Fischer was happily leading groups of tourists around the countryside describing the effectiveness of the new revolutionary system.[38] But doubts began to grow. By the spring of 1936, with Hitler in the Rhineland, Mussolini in Addis Ababa, and the Purges in Russia escalating, he was more confused and morally tormented than ever. Fischer genuinely believed that Russia alone of the major world powers was willing to act against the emerging fascist threat. In spite of any doubts that he might have had about internal events in Russia, he praised Soviet foreign policy, claiming that "the new United Front policy of the Comintern has really brought fruit in that Fascism has been checked."[39] But as the purges continued Fischer could scarcely ignore the gloom and fear settling like a volcanic ash over the country. His interest in the trials went far beyond that of a journalist, and he became so obsessed with their apparent madness that he kept lists of all those reported in the newspapers to have been arrested.[40] At times these names were of friends or acquaintances. While Fischer shared his doubts and anxieties with intimates he still believed that if he reported his concerns he might jeopardize the Soviet Government's continuing efforts at collective security. Throughout the spring and early summer of 1936 he floundered like a shipwrecked sailor as he desperately grasped at anything that might keep afloat what remained of his sinking faith in Russia. Perhaps the trials would soon end and the government would reform itself. Certainly the outbreak of civil war in Spain in July 1936 made continuing support for the Soviet Government seem valid, especially in view of the aid that Russia offered to the besieged Republic.

A little over a month after news of the Spanish Civil War reached Moscow, party papers through the country announced that two of the originators of the Revolution, Leo Kamenev and Gregory Zinoviev, had been arrested and would be brought to trial. Conducting an Open Road tour in Kiev when the announcement was made, Fischer was in no way psychologically prepared for such a frightening escalation of terror. Thoroughly confused about what was happening, he still believed it necessary to give public support to the Soviet Union. In a letter to Max Lerner he tried to place the purges in historical perspective by explaining them as "part of the past which is not dead."[41] If Fischer was finding it hard to justify to others what was happening to the Revolution, he was finding it even more difficult to explain it to himself. By late summer, he finally decided that the gloomier period of Soviet history which apparently lay ahead was not one of which he wanted to be a part. Instead of going back to Moscow to report on the trials, he decided to leave for Spain where it appeared, at least from a distance, that the issues were more clearly defined.[42] Departing Russia with his tourists in the late summer of 1936, he left them in Warsaw and then joined his wife and youngest son at a health resort in Czechoslovakia. Eleven days later he was in the Paris apartment of André Malraux inquiring about events in Spain while making final preparations to go there. After obtaining letters of recommendation from Malraux and the Spanish Embassy in Paris, he left for Madrid. Fischer arrived in mid-September, and took a room in the Hotel Florida where a number of other foreign journalists were staying.

For the next two weeks Fischer spent most of his time shuttling the forty miles back and forth between Madrid and Toledo where, since July 18, some thirteen hundred Nationalists had been repelling all Republican attempts to dislodge them from the Alcazar, the medieval fortress where they had taken refuge. As Franco's Nationalists daily drew closer to Toledo, the siege of the Alcazar became a kind of obsession for Fischer that went far beyond journalistic interest. Each morning he felt as though he were being drawn magnetically toward Toledo to watch and hope for victory; each evening he would return dejectedly to Madrid swearing that he would not go again, only to repeat the journey the very next morning.[43] On one occasion, after several days of watching the siege from the sidelines, he impulsively followed the Republican troops in an attack on the fortress, ostensibly to satisfy his curiosity to see how it felt to be under fire again. When the attack was routed by murderously accurate mortar fire and hand-grenades thrown down on the Republican soldiers, he cast any remaining professional detachment aside and helped carry the wounded to the field hospital. Further attacks on the fortress were equally futile, and Toledo fell to Franco on September 27. Most observers felt that Madrid would be next. Fischer's initial involvement in the affairs of Spain had been little more than a gesture and no more significant that Reed's throwing leaflets along the way to the Winter Palace. Yet it was a beginning, and his involvement would soon take a dramatic turn.

On the morning of November 5, Fischer awoke to find Madrid in a state of panic. The streets were clogged with refugees, and the air was saturated with rumors that Franco's Moorish troops were fighting on the city's outskirts. Hoping to find out what was actually happening, Fischer made his way to the Russian Embassy only to learn that its staff had already been evacuated. He met André Malraux a few minutes later and learned that the situation was indeed serious and that he should make plans to leave Madrid immediately.[44] The next day Fischer caught a ride with several other journalists who were driving south toward the village of Albacete, where the newly organized International Brigade had its headquarters.

Two days after the battle for Madrid began, Fischer became the first American to join the International Brigade. For all practical purposes, eighteen years had passed since his first involvement in Israel. But now in Spain he was much clearer in his own mind about what he was doing. The decision seemed just as correct years later as it had that November day: "I am as proud of that as I am of anything I have done in my life. A nation was bleeding. Machine guns were being mounted on the ivory tower. It was not enough to write. For fifteen years I had written and spoken about what other people did. This limitation always irked me. But I never felt tempted to work in the Soviet Union or in any Communist movement. Now men were dying; I wanted to do something."[45] In the Brigade, Fischer met volunteers from all over the world. Like Fischer they were fighting for something far larger than the Spanish Republic since they saw Spain as the front line against Hitler and Mussolini and as the place where a stand was being made against fascist aggression.[46] Many writers, whatever side they supported, apparently believed like Fischer that the time to do something other than write had come, and they flocked to Spain.

The International Brigade was created at the suggestion of several people.[47] Once the idea was approved by Moscow, the Comintern was charged with carrying it out. This was in keeping with its call in 1935 for the creation of a Popular Front against fascism. Although non-communists were encouraged to join the Brigade in an effort to uphold the Popular Front concept, about 60 percent of Brigade members were Communists before volunteering, and another 20 percent became Communists before leaving Spain. At least 80 percent of all volunteers who served the Brigade were of working-class origin with almost half the total number coming from France, Germany-Austria, and Italy. When completed, the Brigade had its own *troika* in command of its base at Albacete. French communist André Marty was the supreme commander, and two Italian communists, Luigi Longo and Guiseppe di Vittorio were Inspector-General and Chief Political Commissar.[48]

The first group of volunteers arrived in Albacete on October 14, 1936. This small, provincial town, drowsing in the encrusted dust from the surrounding wastes of La Mancha, was ill-suited to meet the needs of large numbers of soldiers. Almost overnight the Bank of Spain was turned into a combination barracks and storage depot, the bull-ring became a temporary mess hall, and the church was converted to a prison."[49] By the time of Fischer's arrival in early November, the town's main thoroughfare was overflowing with men dressed in a variety of military undress and speaking such a number of different languages that he might well have thought himself in a modern Babel.

Because of his organizational experiences, Fischer agreed to be quartermaster general for the International Brigade. Although given the rank of major, he never took an oath of allegiance, refused to observe the military salute, and studiously ignored all other signs of military courtesy. Like most of the other volunteers he wore a uniform of corduroy pants with large flaps on the sides, a corduroy jacket, and heavy army boots. The duties of a quartermaster general in a volunteer brigade were numerous, at times inordinately difficult, and for the most part as unspectacular as they were essential. "I had to feed the brigade in Albacete. We sometimes had as many as three thousand at the base. I had to clothe the new arrivals from head to foot, keep the barracks clean, and distribute arms. Each one of these tasks was a nightmare because of the disorganization, the shortage of supplies, and the crowding."[50] Once he was told to prepare for the arrival of a detachment of six hundred men, only to find when they marched into town that eleven hundred had come. When organizational breakdown led to discomfort it was always Fischer who was blamed. On one occasion, for example, an irate battalion commander threatened to arrest him because requested supplies had not been received. Fischer's most persistent problem was supplying the newly arriving volunteers with adequate weapons. For emergencies he kept several hundred old rifles—many with an 1896 marking—under armed guard in a local church; but even these were useless since he had no bullets to fit them. In a desperate but imaginative effort to arm the Brigade, its commander André Marty sent Fischer all the way to Valencia to plead the International's cause when it learned that a shipment of arms from the free port of Danzig had arrived. How successful Fischer was is unknown.[51]

Of all the difficulties Fischer faced as quartermaster, however, none were as troublesome as those encountered while working with André Marty. After growing up in a French working-class family, Marty had first gained international fame in 1919 when he led a mutiny in the French fleet as it was preparing to lend aid to the White Russian armies. Joining the Communist Party in 1923, he rapidly rose within its ranks and eventually was elected a Communist deputy to the French Parliament. When the Civil War began in Spain he was one of the most prominent communists in Europe and was thus selected to head the International Brigade. Fanatically loyal to the Party, during the course of the war he seemed obsessed with the activities of a fifth-column within the Brigade; according to the Civil War's most thorough historian, he was also "arrogant, incompetent and cruel."[52] Also frustrated by Marty's antics was German novelist Gustav Regler, then a foreign activist in Spain and eventually a disillusioned ex-communist. In later years Regler recalled that the Brigade's commander "covered his forgivable inadequacy with an unforgivable, passionate spy-hunt; he was genuinely convinced that many of the volunteers who came to his headquarters were Fascists spies." Most certainly there were ample grounds for Marty's fears, but, as Regler claims, he carried his paranoia to such an extent that "he put all his energies at the service of his mistrust, and did not shrink from conducting daylong, soul-destroying interrogations, or even from sacrificing the tranquility of his nights and his peace of mind by promptly liquidating doubtful

cases, rather than harm the Republic by what he called 'petty-bour-
geois indecision.' "[53] Regler's assessment may have been colored by
his personal dislike for Marty as well as by disillusionment with the
Party, but Marty was known to be suspicious of those whom he considered to be outsiders. In the eyes of the commander of the International Brigade, Louis Fischer was just such a person.

From Fischer's perspective the trouble between him and Marty
stemmed from the fact that he was not a communist and, therefore,
not totally subject to Marty's discipline.[54] Another likely cause of
friction was Fischer's ability to talk with the Soviet officers who occasionally visited the base. Marty, who could not speak Russian, was
suspicious of these conversations. Relations between the two steadily
deteriorated until the day one of Fischer's closest assistants, a Pole by
the name of Wolf, disappeared and was never seen again. Although
Marty claimed he knew nothing about it, Fischer learned that, under
orders from the Brigade's commander, Wolf and four others had been
secretly arrested and charged with Trotskyism.[55] For Fischer the incident reeked of the malodorous purges in Russia. The rupture shortly
became public when Marty reprimanded Fischer in an order of the day
for not being on duty to receive complaints about the quality of the
food which he had procured. A final break between Fischer and Marty
was now all but inevitable. It came during the first week of December
1936; and as Fischer later recalled it was remarkably anticlimactic:
"Marty returned from a trip to Valencia. He was cordial and warm
when he met me, and called me into his office, and said, 'I talked to
some of your friends in Valencia. They feel it is such a pity for you to
waste your time with kitchen problems and clothing distribution when
you could be doing far more important things.' "[56] Knowing that
Marty was at last asking him to resign, Fischer turned over his duties
to a new quartermaster. Thus ended his brief career in the International Brigade.

Although he never again served in a military capacity, Fischer
continued to devote much of his time and energy to the Loyalist cause.
He returned to Spain some eight times between his departure from the
International Brigade and the fall of Barcelona in January 1939. In

1937 and 1938 he gave lectures in the United States to help raise money for Spanish relief. Although his experiences in the International Brigade had been disillusioning, his interest in the Civil War was unaffected. In a letter to Freda Kirchwey, the editor and publisher of the *Nation*, he tried to explain his enthusiasm for the Loyalist cause: "Spain is so thrilling because it is one of the few places where courage still lives, perhaps the only antifascist country where it still lives, there and in Russia."[57] Much to his anger and frustration, few Americans felt this way. Fischer's disdain for their lack of interest sometimes got him into trouble. At a Hollywood extravaganza to raise money for the Loyalist cause, an event Fischer viewed as an utter waste of time, he confused his host's wife with his mother and insulted Dorothy Parker, one of the invited celebrities.[58] Fischer was, perhaps, a more effective exponent of the Republic's cause when he directed his efforts toward getting Congress to lift its arms embargo against Spain. In 1938 he met with Secretary of State Cordell Hull and corresponded with Eleanor Roosevelt.[59] Articles appearing in the *Nation*, and a pamphlet, *The War in Spain*, combined hymns of praise to the courage of the Spanish people and graphic condemnations of the fascist practice of bombing civilian population centers.[60] From the middle of 1937 until the fall of 1938, Fischer's activities became more officially oriented. At the request of Premier Juan Negrín, he acted as liaison between the Loyalist Government and the American volunteers who were returning to the United States at the Republic's expense. To facilitate the repatriation process, funds were deposited by the Republican Government in a bank in Paris and Fischer was given the authority to use them. International Brigade volunteers returning to the United States received $125 for passage home. Fischer also tried to give the men a little money to spend on board ship and an extra bonus of twenty-five dollars.[61] Although he left Spain for the last time in December 1938, Fischer certainly did not sever his ties with the country; as late as 1941 he was still trying to help Spanish refugees resettle elsewhere.[62]

While Fischer's commitment to the Spanish Republican cause never wavered, even in the face of defeat, the same is not true of his support for Russia. With the signing of the Nazi-Soviet Pact in August

1939, Fischer announced his personal "Kronstadt." The break would have come sooner, he later claimed, had it not been for his hope that the Spanish Civil War would be a kind of "spiritual blood transfusion for the prostrate élan of Bolshevism."[63] Even when it failed to have this effect, Fischer still supported the Soviets. Since only Mexico and Russia were significantly aiding the Spanish Republic, he rationalized that a denunciation of the Soviet Union could only harm the Loyalist cause. When the war in Spain was over, he no longer felt so constrained. The Nazi-Soviet Pact, which he viewed as "the gravestone of Bolshevik internationalism and the cornerstone of Bolshevik imperialism" only reinforced his resolve to break with Russia.[64] To be sure, it would not have been easy to relinquish support for an experiment in which he had so long believed. In fact, it was only possible once he had left Russia for good.

Disillusionment did not mean inertia in the years ahead. Fischer continued to be active as journalist, author, and defender of humanitarian causes, although he was never again to be actively involved in a foreign cause. An ardent critic of neo-colonialism, he championed the Indian and Indonesian independence movements after World War II. During the 1930s he had become an admirer of Mahatma Gandhi. Later he became a friend as well and eventually wrote what is considered to be perhaps the best biography of the Indian leader. He also wrote masterful studies of Lenin and Stalin as well as works dealing with Soviet foreign affairs. In 1961 he joined the staff of the Woodrow Wilson School of Public and International Affairs at Princeton University as a research associate and visiting lecturer. He remained there until his death in 1970.

To understand the foreign activism of Louis Fischer is, to some degree, to understand his ever increasing commitment to an idea—the need for an international approach to human affairs. His youthful involvement in the Zionist movement and the Jewish Legion grew in part from the same romantic longings for a grand adventure or a new experience which propelled Seeger into the Foreign Legion, Cowley into the Ambulance Crops, and Reed into the Soviet Union. But Fischer, unlike these writers, came from an impoverished background, and to someone who had known the realities of ghetto life, the idea of a Jewish homeland in Palestine offered something more than merely excitement. "Life as I had seen it could certainly stand improvement," Fischer later wrote in *Men and Politics*. "Especially did I feel that society has an obligation to help us overcome the accident of birth."[65] Zionism thus offered Fischer what seemed the best means of altering the world as he knew it, and he went to Palestine not only to fight but also, perhaps, to settle.

Only after reaching Palestine did Fischer have the chance to test his theory. At first he was thrilled by the spectacle of a heterogeneous group of idealists collectively building a home in the midst of a desert. Eventually, however, the idealism, the willingness to sacrifice, the intermixing of nationalities, and the social and material equality which he so much admired were overshadowed by his concern about the widening gulf between Arabs and Jews. In 1920 he left Palestine realizing that Jewish nationalism was a troublesome but necessary part of Zionism. "My interest in Zionism and, indeed, my special interest in Jewish affairs left me completely during the years between 1921 and 1939 which I spent in Europe," he recalled in the 1940s. "I understood the concentration of Jews on the painful Jewish problem. It cannot be ignored or neglected. But I am not attracted by nationalist movements unless they are part, as the Indian or Indonesian nationalist movements are, of an attempt to end imperialism and its evils. Zionism however is a nationalist movement which is tied to British imperialism."[66] The ideas that he articulated twenty years later were not so well focused in 1920, but he left Palestine then simply because he was not committed enough to Zionism to fight for it. Thus, while his involvement in the Zionist movement was actually the beginning of Fischer's interest in internationalism, his interest in internationalism, by necessity, marked the beginning of his rejection of Zionism.

In the 1920s both the United States and Europe offered rather meager fare to a young internationalist who was also interested in social planning. Having rejected the League of Nations, the United States was steadily withdrawing into its traditional shell of isolationism. Throughout the 1920s and on into the 1930s there seemed to be too little being done in the United States to overcome the "accident of birth," a task which Fischer felt was the obligation of all governments. The entire economic system appeared to be at fault; in a letter to a friend, Fischer wrote in 1932: "I think capitalism cannot plan. . . . I maintain that as long as production exceeds consumption—and it must given the profit system—we will always have cycles of prosperity and depression."[67] Moreover if life in America appeared empty, life in Europe seemed even more absurd. Incessant quarrels over reparations, indemnities, and national boundaries suggested that European diplomats had learned nothing and forgotten nothing since the Great War. Only the international brotherhood promised by the Bolsheviks seemed to offer an acceptable alternative to the decadence of Europe and the indifference of America. Fischer thus rushed off to the Soviet Union hoping there to find a new civilization in the making.

In Russia, Fischer sought the collective spirit and enthusiastic zeal of the Kibbutzim, stripped of all nationalistic trappings. For fourteen years he observed, usually praised, and seldom criticized what he saw, but, except for his brief fling with TASS, never felt compelled to commit himself completely to the Soviet experience. Even as he grew disillusioned with the Revolution, he still believed that Russia, with all her problems, offered more hope for the future than any other country in the world. The Purge Trials changed his mind: "I changed because Russia changed. There were no personal, private, or professional reasons for my dissent. I was reacting against new policies and new conditions in Stalin's Russia. I was reacting against nationalism, the inhuman growing cynicism . . . and the personal dictatorship with all its concomitant evils."[68] It was thus with relief that he learned of the outbreak of civil war in Spain.

Fischer always looked upon his service in Spain as a high point in his life.[69] Like many Italians and Germans in the International Brigade, he too went to Spain as a refugee—a refugee who no longer felt comfortable in a country he had once admired. Spain seemed to him everything that Russia was not. The issues were clear. There was a well-defined cause to defend and a clearly outlined enemy to fight. Perhaps he might even find the old revolutionary idealism of the Soviet

Union being rekindled through its aid to the Spanish Republic. For Fischer the war in Spain was a kind of escapism; by serving a new cause he could forget his loss of faith in an old one. At the same time his presence in Spain meant more. Like the other forty thousand Internationals, Fischer was taking his stand against the destructive spread of fascism. By going to Spain he was also participating in a conflict that his own country officially ignored. He hoped that his involvement in Spain would encourage other Americans to participate. "You mustn't allow America to get away with passivity in this great fight," he pleaded with Freda Kirchwey and the other editors of the *Nation* in 1936. "Spain will suffer, but America too."[70] Unlike most Americans of his day, Fischer saw the war in Spain as much more than a local affair. The nations of the world, in his opinion, were interdependent, and therefore, the need for collective security was clear. He expressed these views in *The God That Failed*: "no nation can enjoy successes that are not shared. There is no real peace or happiness while your neighbor down the street or ten thousand miles away is suffering."[71]

A world united through international cooperation emerged over the years as the essence of Louis Fischer's political philosophy; by the time he arrived in Spain, it was the foundation of his commitment. Yet, even in Spain he worked for the Republic on his own terms and at his own pace. In this respect his foreign activism conformed to an individualism which came to be the most pronounced part of his personality. As a freelance journalist he had covered the part of the world that most interested him and interpreted it freely. During most of the 1920s and 1930s he saw himself as a citizen of the world, owing no special allegiance to any country, political party or ideology. Nor did he tie himself to material possessions; at the age of forty-five he boasted "I never owned any property—beyond a typewriter and now a steel filing cabinet—or any stocks or bonds. I have never held any insurance of any kind."[72] Marriage and children likewise did not impede his personal freedom. Until 1929 it was largely his wife Markoosha who reared and supported the family. In later years he was away for long periods traveling throughout the Soviet Union and then shuttling back and forth between the United States and Spain. Even Fischer's wholehearted support for the Soviet Union was offered, as he always maintained, of his own free will. He was always, in fact, something like the Transcendentalists in his eagerness to be guided by his own vision, even, if at times, it became a bit blurred: "I have all my life been devoted to one cause or another. I cannot imagine life without something higher than myself in which I can have faith. Naturally that colors my writing. But who is objective? Only a jellyfish has no prejudices. I endeavor to reduce mine to a minimum. Truth with me is a passion, and I do not hold that a cause is worth much if it must live on lies. I write as I please and what I believe to be true."[73]

Unlike other American writers who became active in foreign causes, Fischer always allowed his personal feelings and attitudes to take precedence over the cause in which he was involved. He was never prepared, like John Reed, to "go the limit." By the time he reached Spain, Fischer could not remain long committed to a cause that infringed on his personal life-style. This explains why he left the International Brigade, but continued to work for the Spanish Republic. Even after his involvement in Spain, Fischer still hoped it was possible to transform the human experience into something better, and his commitment to the idea of one world grew. By the end of the 1930s Fischer had discovered that it was easier for him to believe in an ideal rather than something as specific as a Jewish state, the Soviet Union, or even the Spanish Republic, since commitment to an ideal carried with it no specific rules, duties, or limitations. This belief in one world, while not actually a commitment, was perhaps all that Fischer's concern with individual liberty would allow. "I am essentially a libertarian and resent shackles," he wrote in *Men and Politics*, "even personal ones. I can impose discipline upon myself but I would fight its imposition on me by others."[74] Thus Fischer's desires to act and to be free were in continuous conflict.

6

Swords and Ploughshares:
Hemingway and Dos Passos in Spain

> *One friend in a lifetime is much; two are many; three are hardly possible. Friendship needs a certain parallelism of life, a community of thought, a rivalry of aim.*
>
> Henry Adams
> *Education*

In may 1918 the paths of two young Americans crossed, briefly, in the little Italian town of Schio, some fifty kilometers west of the Piave River, where Italian and Austrian armies faced one another across rugged terrain. Both were natives of Chicago, both aspiring writers, and both volunteer ambulance drivers in the American Red Cross. The older, who was twenty-two, had been driving ambulances in France and Italy for more than a year and was preparing to return to Rome for assignment. The younger, not yet nineteen, had only recently arrived from the United States and hoped to get closer to the fighting. After a short conversation, each went his separate way—John Dos Passos to Rome and Ernest Hemingway back to his Fiat ambulance.[1] But the two eventually came to know each other well, and nineteen years later when they both actively supported the Loyalist cause in the Spanish Civil War, Hemingway and Dos Passos were close friends. Both went to Spain in early 1937 with the intention of making a film that would help the Republican cause. Two months after their arrival, however, they departed separately once again, having disagreed not only over the nature of the film but, more importantly, over the nature of the war itself. Thus, their active involvement in Spain, rather than bringing them closer together, had the unhappy effect of breaking their friendship apart.

Foreign travel may have attracted many young volunteers to World War I, but not John Roderigo Dos Passos, for he had spent much of his youth traveling abroad. His wanderings through Europe were in a sense an escape from his family history. Born in January 1896, Dos Passos was the son of John Randolph Dos Passos, one of the country's foremost corporation lawyers, and Lucy Addison Sprigg, daughter of an old Maryland and Virginia family. His parents were not married to each other. John Randolph Dos Passos, in fact, refused to divorce his wife and did not publicly acknowledge his son's existence until after her death in 1912. But Dos Passos and his parents could openly travel together in Europe and there John spent much of his early life. Shy, self-conscious, and introverted, Dos Passos attended the best schools and always did well, but he made few close friends. In 1912 he entered Harvard.

Like so many other young writers of his generation who attended prestigious universities during the prewar years, Dos Passos became dissatisfied with most of the curriculum and the overt snobbishness of many of his classmates. Still something of a loner, he devoted most of his efforts to an independent reading program. He also helped edit the *Harvard Monthly* during his senior year. Hoping to become a writer, Dos Passos was captivated by the impressionistic journalism and romantic adventures of fellow Harvard graduate, John Reed. In reviewing Reed's books for the *Monthly*, he grew increasingly envious of Reed's exciting life and was determined to volunteer for the war in Europe. But his mother's death and consideration for his father's wishes led him to take no action until he graduated in the spring of 1916.

After failing to obtain a position in Herbert Hoover's Belgian Relief Organization, Dos Passos signed on to drive in France for the Norton-Harjes Ambulance Service. But his father vetoed the idea and persuaded him to go instead to Spain to attend classes in preparation for architectural school the following autumn.[2] Three months later, however, his father died suddenly and Dos Passos hurriedly returned to the United States. In New York he settled the estate and tried again to enlist in the ambulance service. At this time anti-war sentiment was on the rise throughout the city, and although Dos Passos attended several pacifist meetings he was still determined to go to Europe. As he wrote to a friend in April 1917, "Don't think that I've gone militarist or believe in conscription—far from it. I merely want to see a little of the war personally—and, then too, I rather believe that the deeper we Americans go into it, the harder we put our shoulders to the muskets and our breasts to the bayonets, the sooner the butchery will stop."[3] Two months later he sailed for France aboard the *S.S. Chicago*.

Ernest Hemingway led a far less exciting and more conventional childhood. He was born on July 21, 1899, the second of six children. His father was a successful doctor and a devoted outdoors enthusiast, while his mother was a domineering woman who sought to impose on the children her own ambitions for a musical career. The Hemingways lived comfortably. They spent winters in a large Victorian house in the prosperous Chicago suburb of Oak Park and summers at a family cottage in northern Michigan. Ernest was an outgoing, active child. While a student at Oak Park High School, he was a member of the football, swimming, and water polo teams, managed the track team, and wrote for and edited the school newspaper. His journalistic model was Ring Lardner whose column was one of the most popular then appearing in the Chicago *Tribune*.

By the time he graduated in the spring of 1917, Hemingway experienced the same war fever that was affecting thousands of young Americans. But as with Dos Passos, parental objections prevented him from going to war; instead, he obtained a job as a reporter on the Kansas City *Star*. For the next few months Hemingway covered news of the courthouse, police stations, and city hospitals, all the while improving his writing style under the critical supervision of the assistant city editor. These stories, however, seemed dull when compared with exciting reports on the war and Hemingway became even more determined to enlist in the conflict. When nearsightedness made him ineligible for the army, he wrote his sister Marcelline, "I'll make it to Europe some way in spite of this optic. I can't let a show like this go on without getting into it."[4] Persistence finally yielded results and he was permitted with family approval to enlist in the American Red Cross as an ambulance driver.

By the time Hemingway reached Europe in the spring of 1918, Dos Passos was a veteran with a year's experience driving for the Norton-Harjes and the American Red Cross Ambulance Services. Dos Passos had arrived at Bordeaux a year earlier, gone immediately to Paris and had then begun his training in a hunting reserve outside the city. He had his first taste of combat in August when he and his partner transported the wounded for twenty-four hours at a time in the Châlons-sur-Marne sector during the second Battle of Verdun. It was an experience he never forgot.[5] At one point he and another driver had to wear gas masks during a prolonged attack. Dos Passos recalled a "hellish experience," and, as he wrote to a friend, it increased his sympathy for all of the common soldiers who had been through three years of similar attacks.[6]

Despite dangers and hardships, Dos Passos was discovering, as Alan Seeger and others already had, that there was something irresistible about life at the front. More important to him personally, however, was the variety of experiences that he was encountering—experiences which he felt were essential to all potential writers. "I want to be able to express, later—all the tragedy and hideous excitement of it," he wrote in a late August entry in his diary. "I have seen so very little. I must experience more of it, more—."[7] Thus when the Norton-Harjes was taken over by the medical corps of the American Expeditionary Force in 1917, Dos Passos was not yet ready to go home; he and another Harvard friend signed on to drive for the Red Cross in Italy.

After a brief waiting period in Paris, the two young men drove their Ford ambulances in convoy to Lyon, Marseilles, and then up the coast to Genoa. Upon reaching Italy, Dos Passos and yet another of his seemingly endless string of Harvard acquaintances were assigned to the small town of Bassano, several kilometers to the north-east of the Piave River. There the Italian army was frantically attempting to regroup after its disastrous retreat from Caporetto the previous fall. In this quiet sector of the front, ambulance drivers had an abundance of free time. Dysentery and frostbite were the most common casualties they faced and boredom was their worst enemy.

By the time of his arrival in Bassano, Dos Passos's initial excitement about being a part of the conflict was wearing thin, and nothing he saw or did there modified his outlook. To some degree he was becoming politicized, for what he had seen of the war convinced him that it was being conducted in the most stupid, blundering, and inhumane way possible. His anger at the utter disregard for life that daily confronted him spilled over into his letters home.[8] Dos Passos allowed his emotions to overcome his discretion, for he knew that the correspondence of the volunteers was censored. In fact, shortly after arriving in Italy in 1918, Dos Passos learned that his friend and classmate E. E. Cummings and another young American, Slater Brown, both members of the Field Service in France, had been arrested for allegedly holding pro-German views expressed in Brown's correspondence. Dos Passos probably hastened his own troubles by writing in defense of Cummings to the Field Service offices in Paris.[9] He had also written a sympathetic letter to Cummings's mother in which he light-heartedly shrugged off his own indiscretions. "I sympathized with him so thoroughly, and my letters being anything but prudent that I expected I'd be in the same boat; but the censor evidently didn't notice me—so I'm still 'at large' as the blood & thunder militarists would say of us."[10]

Rumors of the investigation of disloyal attitudes in his section of the Field Service continued into 1918, but Dos Passos was not affected. His life went on uneventfully as he tried without success to escape from the rain, cold, and an overwhelming sense of restlessness. While disillusioned with both the war and life in Bassano, he was still determined to see it through to the end. When his term of enlistment ended that spring, he immediately set out for Rome and what he assumed would be reassignment. When he arrived at Red Cross Headquarters there in late May 1918, he learned that the censors had read his letters carefully. An irate Red Cross official confronted him without actually placing any charges.

> I tried to explain that while I was cheerfully giving what service I could, I felt that as an American citizen I had a right to my own ideas. He muttered something about letters. He seemed embarrassed to have to tell me that he wasn't at liberty to explain anything further. I confided in him that I might have written injudiciously to Arthur McComb in Madrid, or to Pepe Giner, who was of the pro-Allied faction in Spain. I'd written Pepe that if he wanted to serve the course of civilization he would work to keep his country neutral. Then there were the letters in behalf of Cummings and Brown.[11]

Failing in Rome to clear his name, Dos Passos went to Paris to plead his case at the supreme Red Cross headquarters. There he was advised to return immediately to the United States to avoid further trouble.

Despite his Kafkaesque experiences in Rome and Paris, Dos Passos returned to New York in late summer 1918, still believing that he had to see the war through to its end. Perhaps he merely wanted to clear his name, or simply complete what he had started. Six weeks later, through the persistent intervention of family and friends, his nearsightedness and Italian misadventures were "overlooked," and he was accepted as a private in a medical corps "casuals company." But Dos Passos never saw combat. Instead he spent the remainder of the war washing windows and raking leaves in a dreary camp near Allentown, Pennsylvania. Ironically, his company was sent to France on the day of the Armistice, and Dos Passos was discharged early the next summer.

While Dos Passos had been struggling to clear his name, Hemingway was driving ambulances in Europe, and in the opinion of his sometime partner, Frederick Spiegel, he was "extremely conscious of the war as the 'crusade for democracy,' and was burning with desire to have a share in it."[12] Regardless of how he viewed the war, the eighteen-year-old Oak Park native had gone to Europe determined to see as much of it as possible. No sooner had he arrived in Paris in May 1918, than, like a small boy loose on a carnival's midway, he charged about the city in a hired cab hoping to anticipate the site where Big Bertha, the long-range gun with which the Germans daily bombarded the city, would drop the next shell. Several weeks later Hemingway was sent to section IV of the Red Cross Ambulance Service in Italy. Assigned to drive in a relatively quiet sector near the village of Schio, he spent most of June fretting because the fighting was far away.[13] Concerned that he would never see the war driving an ambulance, he managed to transfer his activities to the Red Cross canteens. Something like makeshift USO clubs, these canteens were located at various points along the front, providing the soldiers temporary relief from the discomforts of the trenches. Each canteen usually consisted of two huts. The Red Cross volunteer lived in one while the other was for the soldiers' use, containing writing materials, candy, jam, cigarettes, soup, coffee, and often a phonograph. In late June, Hemingway was assigned to operate one of these canteens in the small, burned-out town of Fossalta, which lay close to the front lines.[14] He finally satisfied his thirst for combat when the local commander allowed him to enter the trenches and distribute the provisions to the men. With the joyful abandon of Icarus, he thrilled to the new experience of being under fire at last. Close to midnight on July 8, he entered the trenches ladened as usual with supplies. Then, as he stood and talked with a group of soldiers, an Austrian shell exploded nearby, wounding him severely in both legs. Hit again in the right knee by a machine gun bullet as he carried another wounded soldier to the command post, Hemingway's wartime service came to an abrupt and painful end.[15] When he returned to the United States months later he bore his own red badge—a noticeable limp and was firmly convinced that war was one of the most brutal and fascinating of all human experiences.

Dos Passos and Hemingway had thus both rushed off to Europe propelled by the same curiosity, desire for adventure, and determination to be part of the conflict that had motivated Cowley, Seeger, and other young writers of their generation. Both drove for the ambulance services, both experienced the horrors of war, and both returned home restless and disillusioned. Yet Hemingway's homecoming, unlike that of Dos Passos, was that of a hero, for he had been the first American to be wounded in Italy and had been decorated by the Italian government. In his biography of Hemingway, *Ernest Hemingway: A Reconsideration*, Philip Young has perhaps overemphasized the impact of the writer's war wounds on his life. But they no doubt had an important effect and help explain Hemingway's postwar disorientation, his preoccupation with courage as well as his fascination with violent death.[16] While Hemingway wrote one of the best anti-war novels of his generation, superbly describing the horrors of combat and the absurdities of war, he never lost his fascination for it. After he sampled it in Italy, war had the same effect on him that a good wine has on a connoisseur: it made people, places, and sensations all seem larger than life.

Like Hemingway, Dos Passos also returned home with a wound but a wound of a different kind. Years later he could still recall the sense of anger and frustration which he and so many other soldiers had felt when they re-entered civilian life:

> We experienced to the full the intoxication of the great conflagration, though those of us who served as enlisted men could hardly be expected to take kindly to soldiering, to the caste system which made officers a superior breed or the stagnation and opportunism of military bureaucracy. Waste of time, waste of money, waste of lives, waste of youth. We came home with the horrors. We had to blame somebody.[17]

While Hemingway shared many of these feelings, Dos Passos's anger always seemed much deeper, his bitterness more profound, and his determination to find somebody to blame more compelling. The variation in their reactions may have resulted from the differences in their ages as well as the fact that Dos Passos had served longer. The scandal revolving around the *lettres compromettantes* no doubt influenced Dos Passos's view of the war, and perhaps explains why he was convinced, as his contemporary and fellow writer Randolph Bourne had warned, that war was, indeed, the health of the state. During wartime Dos Passos, like Bourne, saw the state beginning to dominate all aspects of human activity until there was little room for individuality or spontaneity. He developed this view while still driving ambulances in Italy,[18] and his concern carried over into the postwar period in his first creative endeavor: "The vividness and resiliency of the life of man is being fast crushed under organization, tabulation," a French soldier warns a group of young Americans in *One Man's Initiation: 1917*. "Overorganization is death. It is disorganization, not organization, that is the aim of life."[19] Dos Passos's wound was not, therefore, like Hemingway's, the kind that either courage or stoic resignation could heal. Their different responses to the war led Dos Passos and Hemingway to engage in different postwar activities. Years later, when the two worked together as friends for a common foreign cause, these differences would surface again.

Wartime experiences did not harm the creative talents of the two writers, and the literary careers of both Dos Passos and Hemingway prospered during the 1920s and 1930s. Beginning with the appearance in 1923 of a thin volume entitled *Three Stories and Ten Poems*, and *To Have and Have Not*, published while he was involved in the Spanish Civil War, Hemingway wrote three other novels including *The Sun Also Rises* and *A Farewell to Arms*, compiled three collections of short stories, wrote a book describing bullfighting and another on big-game hunting in Africa. Equally productive and even more diversified, Dos Passos completed six novels, three of which composed the *U.S.A.* trilogy, a book of poetry, three plays, and a travel account of Spain during the same period. When not writing the two were engaged in a variety of activities as different as the styles and themes of their books.

Until the mid 1920s Hemingway supported himself and a wife and son primarily through newspaper work, writing mostly for the *Toronto Daily Star*. As his literary reputation grew, so too did the range of his activities. When not writing, he lived a strenuous life, testing or exhibiting his own skills and courage or avidly pursuing a fascination with violent death in Paris, Pamplona, Madrid, the Swiss and Austrian Alps, Italy, Wyoming, Key West, Cuba, Bimini, and Africa. A full life to Hemingway meant boxing, fishing, hunting, drinking, loving, observing horse races and bullfights, and, of course, writing.

To be sure, Hemingway's life did not readily lend itself to political involvement or even social concern, but as a Hemingway scholar, Robert O. Stephens, has suggested, Hemingway was by no means as politically naïve as many of his critics imply.[20] Before his twenty-fourth birthday he had already interviewed such important world leaders as Clemenceau and Mussolini, and attended the Genoa and Lausanne Conferences. As early as 1922 he was already describing the opportunistic nature of fascist ideology while suggesting that "The fascisti make no distinction between socialists, communists, republicans or members of co-operative societies."[21] Contemptuous of Italy's new dictator, he portrayed the Duce as "the biggest bluff in Europe," and then added, "you will see the weakness in his mouth which forces him to scowl the famous Mussolini scowl that is imitated by every 19-year-old Fascisti in Italy."[22] For the most part, however, his writing in the late 1920s and early 1930s did not deal with social issues and he was aware that many critics viewed him as essentially an apolitical writer. The appearance of his book on bullfighting, *Death in the Afternoon*, in the midst of the Depression was seen by several critics (Malcolm Cowley among them) as proof of the writer's fundamental lack of social concern. Disliking criticism of any kind, Hemingway was particularly incensed after this attack: "It's damned funny when I used to get the horrors about the way things were going those guys never took the slightest interest nor even followed—" he wrote to Dos Passos shortly after the book was published. "They were all in Europe and got worked up over Tristan Tzara when the goddamnest things were happening—when you've gotten as hot about something and as burned up and finally completely disillusioned on the *working* of anything but intelligent political assassinations when they start out and say 'Don't you see the injustice, the Big Things that are happening, why don't you write about them etc.'" Although not usually given to personal political analysis, Hemingway was so angered by the criticism of his book that in the same letter he tried to categorize his own beliefs: "I suppose I am an anarchist—but it takes a while to figure out . . . I don't believe and can't believe in too much government—no matter what good is the end. To hell with the Church when it becomes a state and the hell with the state when it becomes a church. Also it is very possible that tearing down is more important than building up."[23]

Yet even if Hemingway was more politically astute than many of his critics have been willing to admit, his role during the 1920s and 1930s was almost exclusively that of observer, and a not very interested one. Insisting that he mistrusted all forms of government, he failed to become involved in the social activities that dominated the lives of fellow writers like Dos Passos.[24] In the midst of the Depression he had no qualms about going to Africa on a safari, and he seemed almost oblivious to the economic turmoil that pervaded the nation. Motivated by a driving passion to write well while living his version of a full life, Hemingway simply found little time for anything else, including an interest in the social and political issues of the day. His personal philosophy was relatively simple: "I've got only this one life to live and by Christ I want to go where it interests me. I don't feel any romance for the American scene. It doesn't move me. It's that I just want to make enough dough now so I can go back to Africa."[25]

Although Hemingway's and Dos Passos's paths crossed frequently during the 1920s and 1930s, their interests could not have been more diverse. Dos Passos was a socialist and by the time the Great War was over he was anxious for sweeping social change: "We came home with the feeling that bottom dog must be boss. We must restore self-government at home. If the people had had their way none of these disasters would have happened."[26] His observations of postwar America left him thoroughly disillusioned. In *Manhattan Transfer* (1925) he gloomily suggested that the artist could not survive in such a mechanized and materially dominated society. A trip to the Soviet Union in 1928 convinced him that the Russians were making greater strides in adapting their social institutions to the demands of industrialism than were his own countrymen.[27]

During these years Dos Passos, unlike Hemingway, became increasingly socially committed and politically active. While his friend was becoming expert in the techniques of bullfighting, wing shooting, and game fishing, Dos Passos was becoming a radical. In 1926 he helped found *The New Masses* and was a leading contributor for several years. That same year he became passionately involved in the defense of Sacco and Vanzetti, and wrote a Zolaesque pamphlet, "Facing the Chair," which proclaimed the innocence of the two anarchists. Utterly convinced that two innocent men would be executed for their political views, he picketed the State House in Boston and spent a night in jail for his efforts.[28] The execution of Sacco and Vanzetti left Dos Passos deeply embittered. He soon channeled his anger into helping organize and then writing biting satires for the socially conscious New Playwrights' Theater. When he learned of the low pay and wretched working conditions of Appalachian coal miners, he became chairman of the National Committee to Aid Striking Miners Fighting Starvation. To publicize the miners' hopeless plight he accompanied several writers, Theodore Dreiser among them, on a trip to Kentucky in 1931 to report on a strike in Harlan County. His radicalism peaked the following year when his name appeared on a list of writers who supported Communist Party candidates in the presidential election.

Although Dos Passos never joined the American Communist Party, he supported it as a kind of gadfly which jarred Americans into an awareness of basic social inequities. His enthusiasm for the Party was checked by his reservations about its methods, and by late 1932, these reservations were mounting. What had always made Dos Passos uneasy about the Party was its insistence on ideological orthodoxy and its bureaucratic control over members. His trip to Harlan County added to his doubts for he suspected that in its activities there the Party was more concerned with publicizing the coming revolution than in helping the striking miners.[29] Like John Reed, Dos Passos believed that lasting social change in the United States could best be achieved by cultivating a native-grown radicalism rather than by trying to weave more exotic foreign strands. "I've been reading the *Industrial Worker* weekly with considerable pleasure," he wrote to playwright John Howard Lawson in 1934, "I still feel more in common with the wobbly line of talk than any other—and their clever absorption of technocracy data and their cheerful kidding of the comrats is a great relief after the humorless monotone of the *Daily Worker*—I think what's needed is a caustic testing of all the marxian premises in view of a psychology of defense . . . and an entirely refurbished view of people and events. . . ."[30] His disillusionment with the American Communist Party was also affected by his discontent with the efforts of the Soviet Government to organize every facet of human activity. Writing to his good friend Edmund Wilson, Dos Passos complained that elements of the Revolution which he had most admired had long since been replaced by ones more draconian: "The thing has gone into its Napoleonic stage and the progressive tendencies in the Soviet Government have definitely gone under before the self-protective tendencies. The horrid law of human affairs by which any government must eventually become involved in power for itself—killing for the pleasure of it, self perpetuation for its own sake, has gone into effect."[31] During the early 1930s Dos Passos shared his doubts with only a few friends, but in 1934 he publicly expressed them. Along with twenty-four other intellectuals he protested, in an open letter to *The New Masses*, the breaking up of a socialist meeting at Madison Square Garden by members of the Communist Party. In his eyes the American Communist Party had now become identical to its counterpart in Russia—arrogant, bureaucratic, and sectarian.[32]

Although political interests dominated most of Dos Passos's activities, they apparently played little or no role in his friendship with Hemingway. There is, for example, nothing to suggest that Dos Passos objected to his friend's apolitical lifestyle, nor is there any indication that Hemingway was bothered by the radicalism of Dos Passos. "None of it makes a god damned bit of difference—" Hemingway wrote to his friend in 1932—"I can't be a communist because I hate tyranny. . . . But if you're one it's swell with me—I can't stand *any* bloody government I suppose—."[33] What did seem to matter, however, was that both writers enjoyed enough of the same things to overcome any political differences. Thus, while playing the youthful Gulliver during the early 1920s, Dos Passos was a frequent visitor in the Hemingways' Paris apartment and even joined them in the summer of 1924 to see the running of the bulls in Pamplona. It was Dos Passos who first experienced Key West and then sold its unique attractions to his sports-minded friend who later made it his home. Neither Hemingway's second marriage in 1927 nor Dos Passos's first in 1929 affected the friendship, and together with their wives they met in Montana, Cuba, Bimini, Key West, or any other of Hemingway's athletic watering spas.

Despite their close friendship, their personalities could not have been more different. Quiet, unassuming, intellectual, reflective, and often bothered by poor eyesight and fragile health, Dos Passos was a most unlikely companion for the exuberant, athletic, opinionated, bossy, often quarrelsome, and robustly healthy Hemingway. Although occasionally subjected to the temperamental outbursts and irrational jealousies for which Hemingway was famous, the friendship prospered largely because the two seemed so thoroughly to enjoy one another's company. There were times, of course, when the sportsman's pace set by Hemingway overwhelmed his less athletic friend, as Dos Passos wrote to his wife from Painter, Wyoming, in 1930: "I feel pretty silly carrying Hem's damn blunderbuss over all these damn hills, perpetually nervous for fear of injuring the damn popgun. Have already managed to put the telescopic sight on the blink but Hem was extremely decent about it."[34] Hunting and fishing trips were, perhaps, more relaxing, for Hemingway was inevitably so intent on the prey that Dos Passos was left alone to enjoy the climate and scenery.

The closeness of the friendship carried over into the private lives and literary activities of the two writers. In 1925 Dos Passos joined with Hadley Hemingway in an unsuccessful attempt to dissuade her husband from publishing his novel, *The Torrents of Spring*, which contained a spitefully petty satire of Sherwood Anderson.[35] In 1928, when Dos Passos was about to get married, Hemingway warned him to keep money away from the new bride and firearms away from her father, who had suicidal tendencies.[36] In 1930 it was Dos Passos who was giving help by pulling an injured Hemingway out of a wrecked automobile while the two were on a hunting trip near Billings, Montana. Three years later it was Hemingway's turn to help. He sent Dos Passos a thousand-dollar check to ease financial worries caused by a lengthy recuperation from a recurring attack of rheumatic fever.[37] Always earning far more as a writer than Dos Passos, Hemingway continued to lend money to his friend during the 1930s so that his writing would not be interrupted. Dos Passos and Hemingway may have been critical of each other's writings, but their friendship was held together by the consuming interest they shared in a common craft.

As their friendship grew, Hemingway and Dos Passos came to admire each other's work. You are the "king of the fiction racket," Dos Passos wrote Hemingway in the fall of 1929. In the same message he described how rival publishers were even approaching him in the hope that he might persuade Hemingway to leave Scribners.[38] The compliments did not flow one way, however, and shortly after reading *1919*, Hemingway was lavish in his praise: "It comes off all the time and you can write so damned well it spooks me that something may . . . happen to you—wash and peel all the fruit you eat—."[39] On other occasions, however, Hemingway did not hesitate to give advice or criticism. Displeased that Dos Passos was moving into a different genre, Hemingway in 1927, warned his friend that he was spreading himself thin by writing too much: "What the hell do you write a play for . . . ? Lay off. What is the use of trying to screw if you are dry. Lay off and it always comes back. Lay off and don't try and do a damn thing and let the juice come back. You've done too bloody much writing and you are stale as hell on it. . . . You ought to go to grass and not when you ought not to be writing a damn thing be working on a bloody play."[40] By 1932 Hemingway was still worried about the direction in which his friend's career was heading, but this time it was a question of Dos Passos's politics becoming entangled in his writing. As usual Hemingway found it easy to advise: "You can write the best of any of the bastards writing now and you've been around the most—you write better all the time—For Christ sake don't try to do good—If you try to do good you'll not do any good nor will you show it—."[41] Dos Passos also offered advice. Shortly after reading *Death in the Afternoon* in 1932, he enthusiastically wrote: "The Bullfighting book —is absolutely the best thing that can be done on the subject—I mean all the description and the dope—It seems to me an absolute model for how that sort of thing ought to be done. . . ." But Dos Passos tempered his praise by also offering a word of caution. "I'm only doubtful, like I said, about the parts where old Hem straps on the long white whiskers and gives the boys the lowdown."[42] Having been given the "lowdown" enough times on numerous hunting and fishing trips, Dos Passos was obviously trying to sidetrack it when he saw it creeping into his friend's writing.

While criticism from one another was welcome, from others it was often rejected. Frequently, in fact, Hemingway and Dos Passos were involved in one another's literary battles. When the second volume of the *U.S.A.* trilogy appeared, Hemingway praised the work and advised Dos Passos to ignore "a turnip" like Malcolm Cowley who had criticized several of the novel's more innovative techniques.[43] In 1934 it was Dos Passos's turn to defend Hemingway when Cowley and other critics attacked *Death in the Afternoon* for its lack of a social message. "Say about Hemingway—" Dos Passos wrote to Cowley from Key West, "he has his hunting license in the fact that nobody living can handle the damn language like he can. I suppose they are all sore at H. because they think he's in on the big money. If they had any professional feelings about the trade they'd be glad to see one of the boys making good. And for Christ's sake people aren't all black and white—or communist & fascist—When there's shooting going on you have to take sides I suppose though I'm not as sure of it as I was a few years ago—."[44] Uncertain as he might have been at the time about committing himself to a cause, when the shooting actually began in Spain two years later, Dos Passos joined Hemingway in taking sides.

The involvement of Hemingway and Dos Passos in the Civil War was more than a desire to check the spread of fascism, for, over the years, both had developed a deep admiration for Spanish life and culture. Dos Passos enjoyed long visits to Spain in 1916, 1920, and 1933, traveling through much of the country and never ceasing to be excited by its diversity.[45] Each time he returned he became more deeply immersed in the culture and more fascinated with its traditions. "As I learned the language I began to feel enormous sympathy for the people of this nation so various and so much themselves," he later recalled, "so unaffected by the standardization of the life of our day."[46] In the United States all activities seemed to be directed toward the needs of an urbanized and mechanized life. In Spain people still seemed to live in harmony with their surroundings and, more importantly, in harmony with themselves. This kind of harmony had tremendous appeal for Dos Passos since he believed it was almost totally lacking in most industrial states. "In America they don't do anything except work and rest so's to get ready to work again," a character states in his Spanish travel book, *Rosinante to the Road Again.* "That's no life for a man. People don't enjoy themselves there. An old sailor from Malaga who used to fish for sponges told me, and he knew. It's not gold people need, but bread and wine and . . . life."[47] Such life-sustaining needs were to be found, in Dos Passos's opinion, most completely in Spanish villages, for there the rhythms of human existence seemed to flow simply and vitally. Traveling in Spain was thus always a revitalizing experience, and this is why, like a votary's repeated pilgrimages to a sacred shrine, he was always eager to return.

Unlike Dos Passos, Hemingway had not discovered Spain until after World War I when, at the suggestion of Gertrude Stein, he had gone to Pamplona to view the bullfights held there every July. He too had become infatuated with the country, its rugged landscapes, the joy of trout fishing in its mountain streams, the gaiety of Madrid cafés, and the pleasure of viewing the treasures of the Prado. But most of all, Hemingway found in Spain what he had previously discovered only in war—the opportunity to study the courage and dignity of individuals as they stood close to death. In the Spanish bullfighter, Hemingway could observe all the human qualities he most admired: professional skill, honesty, courage, and grace in the face of pressure or death. Whereas Dos Passos found the uniqueness of Spain in the harmonies of its village life, Hemingway, the inveterate sportsman, predictably discovered it in this most dangerous of national amusements. Yet Hemingway always viewed bullfighting as something more than a sporting event, for, as he wrote in *Death in the Afternoon*, it was the only "art in which the artist is in danger of death and in which the degree of brilliance in the performance is left to the fighter's honor.

In Spain honor is a very real thing, called *pundonor*, it means honor, probity, courage, self-respect and pride in one word. Pride's the strongest characteristic of the race and it is a matter of *pundonor* not to show cowardice."[48]

While Hemingway and Dos Passos were attracted to Spain for different reasons, they shared enough interests to have contemplated in the 1930s working together on a film that would portray various aspects of Spanish life. In 1933 Hemingway suggested that Dos Passos and his wife come to Spain both to vacation and write a script. Buoyed by a royalty check from Scribners, he promised to help finance the trip to Spain and guaranteed a summer of traveling and writing together. "We can have a damned good time doing the movie thing i.e. getting it all set in our heads and much enjoyment withal. Then with it all clear I will sell some bastard on the idea of making it even if [I] have to be polite."[49] Although this project never got beyond the planning state, three years later the two writers were in Spain jointly working on a film. At this time Spain was in the midst of war, and the friendship of Hemingway and Dos Passos was stretched to the breaking point by their activities there.

In late 1934, some nineteen months before General Franco made his clandestine flight from the Canary Islands to Spanish Morocco, the two writers had already become involved in the political turmoil that was pushing Spain toward civil war. They had both tried to help a Spanish friend, the socialist painter Luis Quintanilla, when he was arrested for participating in the Madrid riots of October 1934. The riots had occurred to protest the inclusion of the Spanish Catholic Party in the Republican government. Hoping to obtain his release by publicizing his imprisonment, Hemingway and Dos Passos sponsored a showing of his etchings in December at the Pierre Matisse Galleries in New York.[50]

Dos Passos was more aware of the political situation in Spain than Hemingway; as soon as the war began, in July 1936, he began a letter-writing campaign to the Roosevelt Administration to persuade the government to sell arms to the defenders of the Spanish Republic.[51] While Dos Passos was thus involved, Hemingway was bear hunting in

Wyoming, fishing in Key West, and completing his novel *To Have and Have Not*. Although he was interested in the conflict, Hemingway had no plans to go to Spain until mid-November, when he received an offer from John Wheeler, general manager of the North American Newspaper Alliance, to cover the war for his syndicate. Not wanting to miss a war, Hemingway accepted at once. By this time his concern about the fate of the Spanish Republic had also been awakened; in late November he financed the passage to Spain of two Americans who had volunteered to fight against Franco. He then made a second financial contribution to help the medical bureau of the American Friends of Spanish Democracy to buy ambulances.[52] Early in January 1937, while in New York signing a contract with Wheeler, Hemingway became even more actively involved in the Loyalist cause. He agreed to head a committee which was attempting to send an entire ambulance corps to Spain.[53] Soon, however, another activity closer to his literary interests began to occupy his time in New York, for he had begun to collaborate with the young novelist Prudencio de Pereda in revising the scenario of a propaganda film dealing with the civil war. Filmed earlier by the Loyalist government, *Spain in Flames* showed in newsreel sequence incidents of the war including the siege of Alcazar, the fighting in the Guadarama sector, and the fascist bombing of Madrid.[54] Hemingway had been displeased by the original narration and replaced it with his own which he believed was a more realistic description of the fighting.[55] When the film was released at the end of January, he had already returned to Key West to make final preparations for his trip to the war zone.

While Hemingway was working on *Spain in Flames*, Dos Passos was about to become involved in a similar venture. For years he had been interested in the cinematographic theories of Sergei Eisenstein; he had met Russia's greatest director while visiting the Soviet Union and he had incorporated several of his theories into his own writing. Dos Passos had been impressed by the ability of Soviet directors like Eisenstein to create with so little technical assistance. He described their innovativeness in a letter to E. E. Cummings: "The great thing is that they have little money for elaborate studio work and have to use

actual scenes and people and inventive photography."[56] An awareness of such techniques was soon to prove beneficial, for, having failed
to get the Roosevelt Administration to sell arms to the Spanish Republic, Dos Passos, joined with Lillian Hellman, Archibald MacLeish,
Dorothy Parker, and several others in a project to awaken public
support for the Spanish Republic through a documentary film.[57] They
organized themselves into a corporation, Contemporary Historians,
and engaged a talented, thirty-nine-year-old Dutch communist, Joris
Ivens, as director. Through the corporation they planned to finance
and distribute a film dealing with the anti-fascist struggle in Spain.
Work on the film was just beginning when Hemingway agreed to join
them.[58]

From practically the first moment that Hemingway joined Contemporary Historians, he and Dos Passos began to disagree over what
the film should be. Dos Passos wanted to focus on the common people
in the villages by showing how the war was affecting their lives. That
day-to-day village life continued much as before, even under the most
deplorable wartime conditions, symbolized for him the courage and
determination of an entire nation. Hemingway, on the other hand,
believing that the American public needed a sharper vision of the war,
wanted to place more of an emphasis on the fighting.[59] Their disagreement was briefly put aside when Ivens and his cameraman, John
Ferno, left for Spain in February 1937. With them they carried a
hastily composed scenario which, according to Dos Passos, had been
written by himself, Ivens, and Hemingway in a single evening. It was a
scenario apparently more to the liking of Dos Passos for it centered on
the experiences of a village first captured by the Nationalists and
then freed by the Loyalists.[60] Ivens soon discovered that the script
which had seemed so effective in New York was now unworkable. The
basic difficulty was that few villagers were willing or able to portray a
life under fascist domination. All were willing to chase the Nationalists
out of their village, but few were willing to admit that the enemy could
have taken it in the first place. While searching for a more workable
theme, Ivens stumbled on the tiny village of Fuentedueña perched high
above the Tajo River and lying close to Madrid on the important

Madrid-Valencia Road. The villagers, as Ivens discovered, were engaged in a cooperative irrigation project through which they hoped to increase their agricultural contributions to the war effort while, at the same time, building for the future.[61] Used to improvising, Ivens immediately recognized his theme. He hurried to Paris to confer with Hemingway who had arrived there in March 1937. Hemingway readily agreed to scrap the old scenario, and the two made plans to return to Fuentedueña to begin filming *The Spanish Earth*.

Meanwhile, Dos Passos had also arrived in Spain in mid-March and had traveled from Barcelona to Valencia, where he planned to consult his long-time friend José Robles about the film.[62] He had met Robles during his first visit to Spain in 1916, and they had rapidly become good friends. In the early 1920s Robles had moved to the United States, taught language for a number of years at Johns Hopkins, and translated several of Dos Passos's novels into Spanish. When the civil war began he was vacationing with his family in Spain and had immediately volunteered his services to the Loyalists. Because of language ability, Robles was given a job in the Minstry of War. When Louis Fischer met him in October 1936 he was acting as the Spanish language interpreter for the Russian General Goriev, who, according to Fischer, was in charge of the entire Madrid sector.[63]

Arriving in Valencia in late March 1937, Dos Passos could not find Robles or even learn if he had been in the city. After several days of frustrating inquiry he finally found Robles's wife, who told him that her husband had been arrested and was secretly being held without trial. Perhaps recalling his own troubles during World War I, Dos Passos immediately began trying to find out where Robles was being held. Although he failed to locate him, Dos Passos was told by government officials that Robles was in no danger and that the charges against him were not serious.[64] Dos Passos therefore decided to go to Madrid, where he hoped to clear up the Robles affair and also begin work on the film of *The Spanish Earth*.

In Madrid, Dos Passos made no headway in finding Robles. To make matters worse, he and Hemingway had almost immediately renewed their argument concerning the content of the film. After visiting

Fuentedueña, where he acted as interpreter for Ivens, Dos Passos was delighted with what he saw and argued even more vehemently for the irrigation project as the film's major theme. To Dos Passos the irrigation project symbolized the courage of the Spanish people, for it transcended the tragedy of the moment and built for the future. "In hopeful moments one could feel that perhaps here were the seeds of a new order that would remain in the soil and spread from once the dreadful exigences of civil war had passed."[65] Hemingway, on the other hand, was caught up in the excitement of being at war once again, and as Dos Passos recalled, his friend's mind was consumed by "military scenes, soldiers, and machine guns." Thus the argument that had begun in New York continued in Madrid, and there was even more bitter disagreement over whether the irrigation project should be the film's central theme or whether the human drama of suffering and courage that Hemingway was rediscovering through his numerous visits to the front should be its primary focal point.[66]

It might have been far easier to compromise on the film had there not been an even greater source of disagreement between the two friends. By early April, Hemingway was convinced that Dos Passos, through his persistent inquiries about Robles, was endangering the success of the entire project. He had even warned his friend that his questioning about Robles might throw suspicion on the entire group and jeopardize the film project even before it was begun. Dos Passos was not persuaded, however, and continued to ask what Hemingway viewed as embarrassing questions. Finally, when the American novelist Josephine Herbst arrived in Madrid later that month, Hemingway asked her, as an old friend of Dos Passos, to convince him to forget about the Robles affair. This request was particularly disturbing to Herbst, for shortly before she left Valencia for Madrid she had been told in the "strictest confidence" that Robles had been shot as a spy.[67] When she told Hemingway this startling news he was surprised, but, according to Herbst, seemed to accept the verdict. Later that same day while lunching with Herbst and Dos Passos at the Russian Brigade headquarters, Hemingway took his friend aside and broke the news to him. For the rest of the meal Dos Passos said nothing about Robles, but merely sat in silence. When lunch ended, he approached Herbst and in "an agitated voice asked why was it that he couldn't meet the man who had conveyed the news, why couldn't he speak to him too?" Herbst later recalled that at the same time she could think of nothing very comforting to say and muttered that it would probably be best if Dos Passos ask no more questions while in Madrid. If he really wanted to know the details, she suggested that he would have to return to Valencia.[68]

The news of Robles's death left Dos Passos deeply troubled. He paid almost no attention to the work being done on *The Spanish Earth*, but instead doggedly continued the inquiries about his friend. Besides trying to find out what had happened to Robles, he openly proclaimed Robles's innocence. When at the end of April Hemingway, Sidney Franklin, an American bullfighter from Brooklyn, and John Ferno were shooting the last scenes of the film, Dos Passos was besieging Republican officials in Valencia, where he had already lodged a protest about Robles's death with the American ambassador. Before leaving Spain for Paris in early May, he finally obtained, with the aid of the Republic's Minister of Foreign Affairs, a death certificate which would enable Robles's wife and son to collect his insurance money.

Arriving in Paris during the first week in May, Dos Passos joined Hemingway and Ivens who had brought with them the film's rushes and were beginning to piece together a finished product. For almost a week the three worked together in a temporary studio borrowed by the Dutch director. Dos Passos later recalled that when he left Paris the rough version of *The Spanish Earth* contained about half war scenes and half material pertaining to the irrigation project, but there was a later editing of the film in which he had no part. As a result of this second revision, he claims that additional footage portraying the irrigation project was cut.

Disagreements about the film and the Robles affair began to drive a wedge between Hemingway and Dos Passos; the final split was saved for the day that Dos Passos left Paris on the boat train for London. As Hemingway accompanied him to the Gare St. Lazare, he warned his disillusioned friend not to write anything about Spain which would hurt the Republican cause. Heated words followed. Dos Passos finally shouted that he would write what he considered to be the truth. Although nothing more was said at the station, the tensions of their activities in Spain had taken their toll, and the friendship was at an end. Each went his separate way just as each had done nineteen years earlier after first meeting at Schio. By the middle of May, Hemingway was bound for New York to complete work on *The Spanish Earth*, while Dos Passos was heading toward Provincetown, where he would soon begin writing a virulent anti-communist novel dealing with the Spanish Civil War, *The Adventures of a Young Man.*[70]

In New York, Hemingway, Ivens and his editor, Helen van Dongen, worked together for several days on a final version of the film at the Preview Theater. The sound track was not finished until late June with Hemingway doing both the written, and after considerable persuasion, the spoken narration. Later Virgil Thomson and Marc Blitzstein provided a musical score by arranging a medley of Spanish folk songs. When completed the total cost for making *The Spanish Earth* came to only a little over $13,000—almost a fourth of which was personally donated by Hemingway.[71]

Hemingway's precise and unaffected narration added immensely to the film's starkly perceptive scenes of the Spanish people struggling to make the earth more productive while fighting to defend the democratic government which had given them the land in the first place. The film begins with the camera focused on the earth and gradually shifts to show the villagers at work on their irrigation project. Yet the viewer never loses sight of the war. Even though the village occasionally reappears as a unifying motif, most of the remaining scenes center on Madrid and the fighting. There are scenes of soldiers going into battle, of the German novelist Gustav Regler and the famous La Pasionara addressing the troops, of the tragic residue of an air raid on the civilian population and of Loyalist soldiers successfully defending the Madrid-Valencia Road which leads to Fuentedueña. *The Spanish Earth* ends on an optimistic note. The road and the village have been saved through the defense of the highway, and water is seen trickling through the recently completed irrigation ditches into the arid fields of Fuentedueña de Tajo.

The film was generally well received by the few critics who reviewed it; several agreed with John T. McManus in the New York *Times* that it emphasized the war, while the irrigation project was "little more than a pianissimo counterpoint."[72] Two reels, without the soundtrack, were previewed in June 1937 at the Second Writers' Congress in New York. After the showing, Hemingway made one of the few public addresses of his life. He told his fellow writers that "There is only one form of government that cannot produce good writers, and that system is fascism. For fascism is a lie told by bullies. A writer who will not lie cannot live or work under fascism."[73] On July 8, Hemingway and Ivens showed the film to the Roosevelts at the White House. The President was interested in the Russian tanks being used by the Loyalists, and Mrs. Roosevelt asked questions about the possibility of a Republican victory.[74] Three days later, accompanied by Lillian Hellman, Ivens and Hemingway attended a fund-raising showing of the film in Los Angeles where over $20,000 was collected for the purchase of ambulances. Divided as Americans were over the Civil War, not all reactions to the film were favorable. The Pennsylvania Board of Censors, for example, refused to allow *The Spanish Earth* to be shown in September 1937 because of its obvious pro-Loyalist bias, and only a drastically cut version was seen in New York two months later.[75] By far the most dramatic viewing was the April 25, 1938, premiere in Barcelona, where the projection was interrupted by an air raid and the audience waited in the dark for almost an hour before the film resumed. When the lights were finally turned on and Hemingway's presence was noticed, the audience spontaneously applauded him for over five minutes.[76]

In spite of the opposition they sometimes encountered in showing the film, the producers of *The Spanish Earth* accomplished much of what they originally had set out to do. Thousands of Americans viewed it, and, in the process thousands of dollars were raised to buy ambulances, provide aid for Loyalist refugees, and help returning members of the Abraham Lincoln Brigade.[77] Dos Passos contributed little to the final production of *The Spanish Earth* because he had been so involved in the Robles affair, but he had worked diligently to get the project started and had continued his efforts through its early stages. He had also been largely responsible for the film's unifying theme, although its overall emphasis had been changed during final editing. Hemingway, Ivens, and Ferno, on the other hand, were most responsible for *The Spanish Earth* as it was eventually viewed, and it was Hemingway's work on the film that constituted his most significant contribution to the Republican cause.[78]

Long after *The Spanish Earth* was completed the controversy between Hemingway and Dos Passos that had begun in Spain continued. In a brutal letter written to Dos Passos in 1938, Hemingway accused his old friend of intentionally harming the Republic's faltering war effort through his anticommunist writing. "A war is still being fought in Spain between the people whose side you used to be on and the fascists," Hemingway scolded. "If with your hatred of communists you feel justified in attacking, for money, the people who are still fighting that war I think you should at least try to get your facts straight."[79] Although Dos Passos had for years patiently listened to his friend's advice, by this time he was apparently ignoring it, and he continued to write about his disillusionment in his novels and articles. Despite his criticism of the Republican cause, Dos Passos still followed the Civil War very closely and personally supported the Republic by trying to end the American arms embargo which hindered its military efforts. Long after Franco's victory Dos Passos still maintained a direct link to the past by serving on the board of an organization which assisted a colony of Republican refugees in Ecuador. There were other, more bitter links to the past as well, for he also kept in contact with the Robles family and was still trying to help them in the mid-1940s.[80]

Dos Passos and Hemingway personally aided the Spanish Republic for reasons both similar and unique. Both writers were attracted to Spain and her culture in much the same way that Edith Wharton and Alan Seeger were to France and Henry James to England. Both deeply

hated fascism—particularly the presence of German and Italian troops
on Spanish soil. In this respect, as Allan Guttmann has suggested, they
were committed to the Republic in so far as it may have symbolized to
them the struggle of the individual against the machine and a machine-
oriented civilization. The British-dominated Non-Intervention Committee and the American embargo were, for the most part, so successful in keeping arms out of Republican Spain, and so incapable of
preventing German and Italian aid to Franco that almost from the
beginning of the war the Nationalists possessed an overwhelming
technological advantage. To observers such as Hemingway and Dos
Passos, the war appeared to be a heroic struggle by the Spanish people
against the impersonal armed might of German and Italian tanks and
planes—of People against machines.[81] Had not, in fact, *The Spanish
Earth* suggested as much by portraying the people of Fuentedueña
irrigating their land while their comrades in Madrid fought for its
survival?

That Dos Passos and Hemingway also had quite different reasons
for going to Spain helps to explain their conflicting reactions to the
war once they became actively involved. It can be argued that Hemingway's commitment to the Republic did not fully develop until after
he had reached Spain and seen for himself the celebrations following
the Loyalist victory at Guadalajara, the heroic defense of Madrid, and
the senseless fascist bombings of civilians. Never very interested in the
political affairs of his own country, it is unlikely that he was very
much aware, at least at the outbreak of the war, of the ideological
differences between the Loyalists and the Nationalists. Matthew
Josephson remembers meeting Hemingway at a cocktail party in 1936
and being asked: "Have you any idea of what is going on? Do you
really believe in the Loyalists? Are they on the level?"[82] Perhaps
Hemingway's questions stemmed from the fact that so many of his
Spanish bullfighting friends had gone over to Franco. Supposedly,
when Hemingway asked his friend Sidney Franklin if he was interested
in going to Spain, Franklin enthusiastically responded: " 'Sure Pop,
which side we on?' "[83] Thus, even though Hemingway had shown an
occasional interest in the Spanish political situation, Dos Passos may

have correctly judged that Hemingway had gone to Spain to see the show.[84]

Hemingway's initial involvement in the Civil War probably hinged more on his hatred of the "bullying personalities" of Hitler and Mussolini than on any deeply felt commitment to the ideals of the Spanish Republic. He initially understood few of the complexities of the war. Upon meeting the Russian novelist Ilya Ehrenburg in Madrid he confessed: "I don't understand much about politics and I don't like them. But I know what Fascism is. The people here are fighting for a good cause."[85] Consistent with his beliefs was Hemingway's willingness to accept the communists in Spain because he was convinced that they were doing more than anyone else to defeat the fascists. He might have ignored certain communist activities because of his desire for victory, but he was never as naïve in this respect as some of his critics have thought.[86] His devastating treatment of André Marty in *For Whom the Bell Tolls* shows that he was in no way beguiled by the International Brigade's commander, and, as he told Joseph North, former editor of *The New Masses*, during a drinking bout in Spain, "I like communists when they're soldiers. When they're priests, I hate them."[87]

Even if Hemingway had no interest in the politics of the Spanish Civil War, he inevitably would have found his way to Spain, for war was something that drew him like a magnet. He saw it as one of life's truly unique and exciting experiences, and as a writer's greatest challenge. He wrote in *The Green Hills of Africa* that as a subject war was "one of the hardest to write truly of and those writers who had not seen it were always jealous and tried to make it seem unimportant, or abnormal, or a disease as a subject, while, really, it was just something quite irreplaceable that they had missed."[88] Determined as he was to be the greatest war writer of his age, he approached the task with the same deliberateness that he applied to his sporting activities. Just as he believed there were rules to be followed while marlin fishing in the Gulf Stream or big-game hunting in Africa, there were also rules to be followed in war. Thus, once in Spain he readily adopted the role of soldier as well as the soldier's creed—"When one has become involved in a war, there is only one thing to do: win it."[89] Knowing how to act in a war zone was equally important to him. Since he was happiest when demonstrating a learned skill or displaying professional know-how while involved in a demanding activity, he knew how to conduct himself at war. Once in Madrid he immediately became the seasoned veteran, far more at home at the frequently bombed Hotel Florida than most of the other correspondents. He had also come prepared, bringing with him Sidney Franklin—a man admired throughout Madrid because of his bullfighting skills. Able to buy "essentials" unobtainable to less knowledgeable visitors, Franklin kept a wardrobe in his and Hemingway's room filled with ham, bacon, coffee, marmalade, and eggs which they often shared with others. While most correspondents scurried frantically about the city in search of transportation to the front, Hemingway had the use of two cars and a gasoline allowance because of his work on *The Spanish Earth*.[90] Other correspondents lacking war experience listened to Hemingway's advice and sought his leadership. The dangers shared, the comradeship, even the hardships were all parts of the wartime atmosphere which Hemingway so much enjoyed. In an interview many years later Dos Passos commented on this aspect of his old friend's personality: "He loved to collect a gang of men around him. He had his gang in Spain and this made him happy."[91]

Just as there were physical rules that had to be followed in adjusting to war, there were mental ones as well which Hemingway believed had to be maintained. In his view there were certain modes of conduct that were simply not permissible; during her stay at the Hotel Florida Josie Herbst recalled the indignant way in which he reacted when several jars of jam were stolen from his room. "He could give an ambulance," she recalled, "but would not be able to stomach stealing jars of jam on the sly. It wasn't soldierly. When I laughed at the whole thing, he was indignant."[92] It was also not "soldierly" to flinch in the face of war's more brutal aspects. Since treachery, for example, was a by-product of war, Hemingway, the hardened veteran, could accept the possibility that José Robles had been guilty of spying. But even had Robles been innocent, Hemingway could rationalize his tragic death as an ugly but inevitable part of war. The loss of a friend was indeed a sad business, but it had to be placed in proper perspective so as not to interfere with the soldier's ultimate goal—victory. To survive at war was to follow without exception this code, and Hemingway expected those around him to follow it as well.[93] The stolen jar of jam represented a small but discernible crack in the code—a fact which Herbst had failed to understand. Later the persistent questioning of Republican authorities about the death of Robles threatened to weaken the code even more, and Dos Passos, in Hemingway's opinion, was guilty of much more than an indiscretion. Hemingway's view of what was appropriate during wartime left no room for the public expression of disillusionment. Thus, on that day in 1937 when Dos Passos boarded a train at the Gare St. Lazare, Hemingway boldly demanded that he keep his criticisms of the Republic to himself so as not to hinder the Republican cause.

Hemingway's efforts were in vain, however, for by the time of their final confrontation Dos Passos was following his own code of war. It was the dirty side of the conflict which he was least prepared to accept, and in his opinion the communists were largely responsible for it. Although he too admired the fighting and organizational abilities of the Communist Party during the civil war, he believed then as he would later that they had "brought into Spain along with their enthusiasm and their munitions, the secret Jesuitical methods, the Trotsky witchhunt, and all the intricate and bloody machinery of Kremlin policy."[94] Unlike Hemingway, Dos Passos was never able to lose himself in the excitement and exigencies of the battlefront because he had come to believe that what happened to people behind the lines was as important, if not more so, than the fighting itself. Thus, over the years he, like Louis Fischer, had come to mistrust anything which threatened to limit the freedom of the individual. He had returned from World War I detesting the dehumanizing authority of the army, and from Russia disgusted by the immensity of the Soviet bureaucracy. In the United States the gigantic industrial corporations repelled him. With the outbreak of the Spanish Civil War he saw yet another ingurgitating specter—the specter of international fascism threatening to destroy the individuality and agrarian simplicity he regarded as the essence of Spain.

While Dos Passos had gone to Spain to aid the Spanish people in their fight against tyranny, the death of José Robles engaged him in his own personal battle against oppression. To him Robles's execution symbolized the tragic fate of Spain and Europe as both tried to exist in the midst of fascism and communism. At the same time, his reaction to the death of Robles reflected his inability to harmonize an active social conscience with an obsessive commitment to individual freedom. During the 1920s and early 1930s this conflict punctuated most of his activities, but never to such an extent as in Spain. Unable to accept or understand the death of Robles, he severed himself almost completely from the Republican cause, abandoned other political activities, and withdrew, for the moment, to the "ivory tower" of literature. Explaining his withdrawal into the ivory tower to his notoriously apolitical friend E. E. Cummings, Dos Passos wrote in the summer of 1937: "It takes a little trip out to the firing line now and then to make you appreciate its excellence."[95]

Having followed strikingly different routes to Spain, the reactions of Dos Passos and Hemingway there were remarkably reflective of the vast differences in their personalities and interests. Although Hemingway remained the more loyal to the Republic, many of his activities suggest that he had gone to Spain in search of the same kind of excitement that he had sought years earlier in joining the Red Cross. He may have thoroughly detested fascism and lent his wholehearted support to the Republican cause, but, at the same time, the lure of combat always had a magnetic effect upon him, and the Spanish Civil War was the most romantically compelling spectacle of the 1930s. Once in Spain he fully supported the Loyalists, conducted himself as he felt a soldier should while subordinating all else, including a friendship, to victory. The soldier's code applied to his writing as well, and while the war was still in progress he praised in *The Fifth Column* the heroism of the defenders of Madrid. Disillusionment remained a private matter and it was only when the war ended that he added his voice to those criticizing communists and failures in Spain. Dos Passos, on the other hand, had long believed that he had found in Spain values lacking in his own country, values well worth crossing the ocean to defend. Yet once in Spain his enthusiasm was shattered by Robles's death—a tragedy he refused to rationalize by accepting Hemingway's explanation that war knows its own necessities. Instead he came to view his friend's death as a terrifying symbol of a world torn between dehumanizing extremes. Perhaps, as Hemingway suggested, Dos Passos was too naïve in his understanding of the nature of war. Or perhaps his involvement in the Civil War was doomed from the beginning in that he had arrived in Spain already distrusting the communists. Whatever the case, as his grief deepened, that which he most admired about Spain—the villages, the people and their simple idealism—was lost in an angry blur of confusion and bitterness. He departed the Civil War as though fleeing an area stricken by plague, and, in the process, abandoned many of the political beliefs that had motivated his activities during the 1920s and 1930s. If anything, his short-lived involvement in the Spanish Civil War made Dos Passos an ardent anti-communist and moved him toward the extreme Right in the post-World War II period.

Once the immediate rancor of their wartime disagreement had passed, Dos Passos and Hemingway both seemed willing to bury it along with their friendship. It was not until almost thirty years after they had parted ways at the Gare St. Lazare that Edmund Wilson finally reopened the issue by asking Dos Passos why he had not dealt in his memoirs with the disagreement that ended his friendship with Hemingway. "Why didn't you tell about your experiences during the Spanish War and the reasons—execution of Robles, etc.—for the coolness between you and Hemingway?—all this, so far as I knew about it, seemed so characteristic both of him and of you."[96] Wilson was correct on both counts, for whereas the disagreement in Spain had undoubtedly characterized both writers, Dos Passos had ignored it in *The Best Times* and, instead, recalled only pleasant memories of his former friend: "We had gotten to calling Hem the old Master because nobody could stop him from laying down the law; or sometimes the Mahatma on account of his having appeared in a rowboat with a towel wrapped around his head to keep off the sun. He had more crotchety moments than in the old days, but he was a barrel of monkeys when he wanted to be."[97] Immediately after returning from the Civil War Hemingway had continued to attack Dos Passos for stabbing both him and the Republic in the back through his writing.[98] But time had also tempered much of this bitterness. In writing Dos Passos from Cuba in 1951, Hemingway obviously still relished the pleasure the two had shared when he asked: "Do you remember the fine times we used to have in Pamplona and the Voralberg and Paris and in Key West and on the ocean?"[99] Out of these fine times a friendship had been welded, but it was one not strong enough to withstand the tensions of a foreign commitment so very characteristic of both writers.

7

Waldo Frank:
Egoism, Activism, and
The Dream of American Unity

Now you will not swell the rout
Of lads that wore their honours out,
Runners whom renown outran
And the name died before the man.

A. E. Housman
"To an Athlete Dying Young"

ALL TOO OFTEN American writers have looked to countries other
than their own for initial literary recognition. Edgar Allan Poe, for
example, was virtually ignored until Charles Baudelaire's transla-
tions of several of his works gave him an appreciative European audience. Robert Frost, discouraged by the publication of only fourteen
poems over an eighteen-year period, went to England, and there,
within three years, published his first two books of verse. T. S. Eliot
was also courting poetic oblivion in London working in a bank until
his work was discovered by fellow expatriate, Ezra Pound. And finally, William Faulkner was recognized as a literary genius in Europe
—particularly France—long before most Americans had read or even
heard of *The Sound and the Fury*.

Such "discovery" abroad has frequently given the American writer
a springboard to recognition in his own country even if it comes well

after death. Such, however, was not true in the career of the philosopher, historian, novelist, lecturer, and cultural ambassador, Waldo
Frank, who had a literary reputation in the United States well before
being adopted by Latin America. Yet Frank's literary star followed a
descending orbit. While his reputation grew in the southern hemisphere, it rapidly declined in the north: by the time of Frank's death in
1967, not one of his twenty-nine books and plays was still in print.[1]
As his good friend and fellow writer Lewis Mumford lamented,
Frank's recognition had reached such a low point that he had "become
too obscure even to be attacked."[2] Such profound failure would have
been disturbing to any writer, but Frank's enormous ego turned it into
a dominating motif of his career.[3] His obsessive need for recognition
in the United States was never satisfied. But Frank was read and
admired during the 1920s and 1930s in Spain and Latin America,
where he came to be widely acclaimed. It is not surprising, therefore,
that when World War II began and the spread of fascism throughout
much of Hispanic America seemed imminent, Frank donated his aid
to that part of the world where he had traveled and lectured and
been well received. He went to Latin America in 1941 because he
feared that fascism might destroy the very hemispheric unity he had
been promoting for so many years. He also went because it was
where he enjoyed the literary recognition and public acclaim which he
felt was his due. In Latin America his views would be taken seriously.
Thus, as was true of most American writer activists, social commitment and self-interest were welded together to shape the course of
Waldo Frank's life.

Waldo David Frank (1889–1967) grew up in an atmosphere of
sheltered, material comfort and artistic indulgence provided by a father skilled in the business world and a mother who was a talented
musician. Julius J. Frank, a second generation German Jew, was a
model of the successful European transplant, and his skills as a Wall
Street lawyer were attested to by his family's imposing four-story
brownstone on West 78th Street. Helene Rosenberg, descended from a
family of internationally successful Alabama businessmen, devoted
herself to her musical interests and her family. The Frank household

was dominated by intellectual and ethical ideas rather than traditional Judaic customs or religious beliefs. It was only as an adult that Frank became truly aware of his cultural heritage. The youngest, the most precocious, and by far the most rebellious of the four Frank children, he at times exhibited some of the characteristics of an *enfant terrible*. He spent much of his early youth happily locked away in the family library reading a wide variety of books—over a thousand before entering college—and by age twelve had already cast aside Scott, Dickens, and Thackeray for Balzac, Tolstoy, and Flaubert, to whom he felt more temperamentally drawn. Two years later he was seriously mapping out a literary career—an early evidence of a growing ego which his friends remembered as his most striking trait. While accompanying his father on a number of European business trips, Frank not only broadened the range of his interests but also became more wedded to the world of ideas. As a student at De Witt Clinton High School his interests were always inclined toward intellectual activities. In addition to being captain of the debating team he was also an associate editor of both the yearbook and the school's literary magazine. A most mature fifteen-year-old, Frank's first literary idol was a poet: he found Walt Whitman "as remote—and holy—as a Hebrew prophet."[4] Perhaps motivated by Whitman's praise of the unconventional and certainly driven by his own intellectual precocity, Frank decided that he knew far more about Shakespeare than did his senior English teacher and thus decided not to attend class. He refused to alter his stand— even when threatened with not graduating—but he had already passed the Harvard entrance examinations.

Although Frank was ready to begin college, his parents thought otherwise. Their sixteen-year-old son seemed too young and impetuous. Instead, they sent him to Les Chamettes Pensionnat in Lausanne, Switzerland, where he spent the next year (1906–07) studying French and improving his musical skills on the cello.[5] After almost a year abroad, Frank was so enamored with European life, especially that of the university students he had met, that he decided to attend the University of Heidelberg. Although his parents agreed, an older brother, Joseph, did not and came to Switzerland to retrieve the budding expatriate. Joseph issued a fraternal ultimatum: "You are not going to Heidelberg. . . . You are going to be an American by gum! And what's more, you are not going to Harvard. You're queer enough as it is. You're going to be not only an American," he insisted, "but as human an American as I can make you. I'm going to send you to a place that will smooth out your angles and your crochets. Yale for you. . . ."[6]

Somewhat less malleable than his brother had hoped, Waldo was ill-prepared for American collegiate life, and his taste for European living added to his discontent. He felt, for example, that his classmates at Yale were immature compared with his European friends. Frank especially missed the many evenings that he had spent in Switzerland sharing and debating ideas. He found little stimulation outside the classroom, and recalled some years later: "It surprised me that my classmates . . . almost the whole student body got along without a stir or tremor in search of life's meaning."[7] Much as he had done in high school, Frank directed most of his energies toward intellectual pursuits. Always an avid reader, he became very interested in drama, continued to take cello lessons, and, perhaps most important of all with respect to his future career, began taking classes and reading widely in philosophy. When not involved with academic responsibilities, during his junior and senior years he wrote theatrical reviews for the New Haven *Journal Courier*. He completed all of the requirements for the B.A. in only three years, but stayed on an extra year in order to complete a master's degree and graduated Phi Beta Kappa with his class in 1911.

By the time of his graduation, Frank was still determined to pursue a literary career, and, like many other aspiring writers, he believed that the only place to begin was in New York. From the fall of 1911 to January 1913 he worked as a reporter, first for the New York *Evening Post* and then for the New York *Times*. In the process he quickly discovered that the transition from life on the Yale campus to working in the newspaper world was "a leap from a nursery to a sort of jungle."[8] Journalism as a career, however, came to an abrupt end when he failed to verify information used in a story and was fired after the *Times* was sued for libel. By early 1913, Frank was not only without a job but was also growing tired of life in New York. He decided to join the hegira of writers flocking to cities in Europe in the hope of finding a more stimulating atmosphere in which to write. For almost eight months he lived in the Latin Quarter of Paris, once again enjoying the pleasures of Continental life. In spite of the excitement of the cafés and newfound friends, he tried to devote a part of each day to serious writing and to reading Nietzsche, Spinoza, and Freud. European life was tremendously appealing to Frank, but after some months in Paris, he decided that he could write more easily in his own country. He left Europe, took a brief trip to North Africa, and then returned to the United States in the fall of 1913. Once back in New York, he rented a room in the Village and continued to write short stories and plays, none of which were published, and a novel, which was published in 1917. Even though Frank had chosen to return home to write, like most of the literati of the Village, he continued to regard the United States as a discouraging place for the serious but unknown young artist. At the heart of the problem, as he later tried to explain, was the fact that "there were no magazines hospitable to virgin efforts, there were no little theatres, no liberal weeklies. The land seemed a hostile waste, consumed by the fires of possession."[9]

Never shy when expounding his ideas about the need for new aesthetic outlets in America, Frank met at a Village gathering one evening a man of similar mind—the poet James Oppenheim.[10] Within a few weeks the two were feverishly planning a new magazine which they hoped would revolutionize the arts in America and provide an outlet for fresh talent. Taking the lead, Oppenheim obtained most of the necessary capital from a wealthy patron, and, with Frank as his associate editor, launched the *Seven Arts* in the late fall of 1916. As the editor of a newly established journal, Oppenheim faced a number of unexpected problems. Perhaps the most difficult was the monumental ego of his young, often imperious associate. Oppenheim later recalled how Frank voiced opinions on editorial policy, lobbied for the publication of his own writing, and unabashedly predicted that in a "hundred years from now people would make pilgrimages to his model-tenement apartment just to see the place where he had lived. . . ."[11] Oppenheim's difficulties were multiplied in the spring of 1917 when Randolph Bourne joined the magazine's staff. The articles that Bourne contributed contained a heavily pacifistic stance which proved unpopular in war-excited America. In a few months the financial backers of the *Seven Arts* withdrew their support and the magazine failed. In the meantime, Frank had expressed his disapproval of the war by registering, in June 1917, as a conscientious objector. But a lingering illness resulting from a needless appendectomy spared him from official persecution.

Shortly before the end of 1917, Frank married Margaret Naumburg, a woman he had met two years earlier. Having a career of her own, she had studied with Montessori and then founded The Children's School (later the Walden School) in New York—one of the first educational institutions to make use of psychoanalysis. Soon after his marriage, Frank published his first novel, *The Unwelcome Man* (1917), and a book of literary criticism that same year. Like many first novels, *The Unwelcome Man* received mixed reviews. Van Wyck Brooks, for example, praised the writer's potential, but suggested that the novel was an interesting rather than a successful work of art.[12] Early in 1919, disillusioned by the political climate of post-war America, Frank made a bow towards radicalism by working in Kansas for a month as an organizer for the Non-Partisan League. Although he sought the sweeping political and economic changes that he believed the League was capable of implementing, Frank had also gone to Kansas for other, far more personal reasons: "I knew I was only a poet," he later wrote in his memoirs, "a queer kind of metaphysical poet. I needed a great audience and was looking for it."[13] There is no indication that Frank found a receptive audience in the Midwest. Moreover, the trip to Kansas marked an end to his political activism for a number of years. Although continuing to follow political events with interest, over the next decade he devoted most of his energies to writing and to a growing interest in Hispanic culture.

Frank always took his literary career extremely seriously, and he was a disciplined, prolific writer. During his most productive years he averaged two thousand finished words a day, and the range of his interests was always Leonardesque in scope. Between 1917 and 1929, he lectured on the arts at the Rand School and the New School for Social Research in New York City and spent most of his free time writing. During this period he published six novels, three books of literary criticism, three books dealing with cultural history, including *Our America* (1919) and *The Re-Discovery of America* (1929), a play, *New Year's Eve* (1928), and an English translation of Romain Rolland's *Lucienne*. In addition, he accepted a position on the *New Republic* as a contributing editor in 1925, and a similar post on *The New Masses* a little less than a year later. Although he saw himself primarily as a novelist, Frank used most of his works as vehicles for discussing his deeply mystical cosmological views. In later years friends such as Van Wyck Brooks and Lewis Mumford claimed that Frank's approach was less that of a novelist than of an intellectual or cultural historian.[14]

To a great extent Frank's metaphysics was influenced by a variety of sources, including the Transcendental mysticism of Thoreau, Emerson, and Whitman, the pantheism of Spinoza, and the studies of the subconscious made by Freud and Jung.[15] Gradually, over the years, Frank became convinced that the essence of life—indeed, the very nature of all being—could only be fully understood in terms of the organic unity of the universe. This belief, in turn, meant that the individual must view his existence as but a small part of an overall unity or whole. Frank had first become personally aware of his own relationship to the cosmic whole through a mystical experience that he had undergone while visiting in Richmond, Virginia, in 1920. He later tried to explain the nature of his newly discovered awareness in *The Re-Discovery of America*: any person once "moved by the image of himself as a focus within the whole, will act in unison with his sense of the Whole. When he feels, does, thinks, it will be no longer in sufferance to an 'I' that images itself as separate, impervious, alone: it will be the whole—the Universe—God (Choose your own word) that feels, does, thinks of his person."[16]

Frank's biographer argues that although his subject was a mystic,

Frank differed from Eastern mystics because he believed in activism rather than quietism in analyzing existence.[17] In this respect, wholeness—according to Frank's definition—could never be purely self-centered, but instead had to be *"both personal and social in order to be either. Individual man cannot achieve his health unless he lives, consciously within a whole that holds all life."*[18] At the same time, Frank was also convinced that Marx had given modern civilization the best possible guideposts for social and economic change, but he accepted Marxian theory only with serious qualifications. Quite simply, Frank believed that Marx's materialism had to be tempered with the pantheism of Spinoza. Whereas Marx had provided a workable blueprint for the society of the future, it was Spinoza who had dealt with the overall unity of the universe and in doing so most effectively "established the organic being of God in matter and in human thought; who has made rational the ancient mystic intuition that the cosmic dwells within the man insofar as the man grows self-conscious."[19] Both revolutionary social change and a sense of organic unity were needed to transform the world, and like two horses of the same team, Marx and Spinoza were to work in tandem pulling Frank's theoretical carriage.

When Frank attempted to use his metaphysical views to interpret his own cultural heritage, his writing, at times, became almost Spenglerian in the sweeping scope of its pessimism. Viewing the Middle Ages as the period of the greatest human synthesis, he believed that intellectual and spiritual decomposition had first begun during the Renaissance when thinkers of all varieties for the first time depended almost exclusively upon rationalism, science, and materialism to explain their universe.[20] The process had continued unchecked into the twentieth century, a time which in Frank's view reflected a new plateau of atomistic disintegration and spiritual bankruptcy. Human existence seemed without purpose, for no longer did everything move together toward the perfect whole. Instead, like the slivers of a broken mirror, "spirit goes one way, mind goes another, body goes a third. Spirit is disembodied; body is lightness. . . ."[21] The legacy of the past was continuing into the present, and Frank was particularly pessimistic about the mainstream of Western Civilization which seemed doomed to chaos because of prolonged fragmentation.

As a child of Europe, the United States had inherited most of the parental maladies, compounded many times over. In an attempt to explain this phenomenon historically, Frank concluded that the Puritans and the pioneers were the two arch-villains. He argued that both denied life in its fullest, and richest, sense. The Puritan had "slain life" by subordinating everything—beauty, creativity, and the use of the senses—to a relentless struggle for power which had at first been sought for religious reasons, but ultimately as an end in itself.[22] Equally as repressive and as life-denying was the pioneer, although for different reasons. Pressed by a hostile environment into a constant struggle for survival, the pioneer had at first neglected, but then gradually and even happily forgotten, the aesthetic and nonmaterial side of existence.[23] These were the legacies bequeathed to twentieth-century Americans. No wonder, in Frank's view, it was an age dominated by the desire for power and financial gain, an age in which man worshipped not God but the machine. In short, twentieth-century America was a fragmented, purposeless world.[24] By the end of World War I, it seemed to Frank as though the United States was in the midst of yet another Dark Age in which the person who "dreamed, loved, created rather than possessed was a byword and a pariah. Life retreated—its mystery and infinite passion—to the domain of failure."[25] Yet unlike other writers, Frank never abandoned his attempts to rejuvenate the nation's depleted spiritual values. Redemption, however, could only come through a massive infusion of spiritual idealism and a radically new kind of lifestyle which he gradually came to believe existed relatively close to home. Many of the values, in fact, which he so desperately wanted his own country to adopt were to be found in the Americas, but only in those areas touched by the influence of Spain.

During the 1920s while much of the country cheerfully embraced an expanding economy and an optimistic view of the future, Frank came to believe that much of the organic unity so obviously lacking in both Europe and the United States was flourishing in the culture of the Hispanic world. Like his mystical self-awareness, this cultural realization had come about quite suddenly and in a most unexpected fashion. While on a trip through the Southwest in 1919, he was one day waiting for a train in Pueblo, Colorado. Frank decided to pass the time by visiting a steel mill located on the outskirts of the town. The bus which took him to the mill was filled with a group of Mexican laborers. Observing them during the ride, Frank was suddenly struck by the fact that, unlike the pioneers, here was a people who had "settled down and sought life by cultivation rather than exploitation."[26] The Mexican workers symbolized to him a sense of permanence and a cultural wholeness that he had failed to detect anywhere in America. Although at the time he knew almost nothing about Spanish culture, Frank later explained to a Latin American audience how he had immediately sensed that Hispanic culture had a vital message for him: "something for my people; something which my world . . . lacked; something I had missed and sought blindly, since I was a boy. Something whose absence made the then triumphant successes of the world a danger and delusion. My intuition sent me to Spain, to Mexico, to Argentina, to learn what that intuition was."[27]

Frank's attraction for Hispanic culture took him to the Iberian Peninsula in the summer of 1921. There, for the first time in his life, his thirst for literary recognition was quenched. While waiting between trains in the old city of Badajoz he bought a book entitled *The Yankee Peril,* by Luis Araguistain. Unfamiliar with the author, but intrigued by the title, Frank was delighted to discover that Araguistain not only quoted from *Our America,* but also praised its author's style, independence of mind, and "historical sagacity." Exhilarated by this discovery, Frank soon learned that he was a respected literary figure in Spain: "I was not unknown in Spain! I could find friends in Spain! The thought came like a leap of the heart."[28] A similar thought would also sustain him later in his life and would be a motivating force in his foreign activism as his books continued to be read in Latin America and ignored in the United States.

Soon after returning to the United States in 1921, Frank felt that his research in Spanish culture was incomplete, and he began planning a return visit to Spain. Leaving New York in February 1923, he was determined to be more thorough in his investigations. He divided the next year and a half between traveling throughout the Spanish provinces and writing what he termed a "symphonic history" of Spain. Published in 1926, *Virgin Spain* was neither a travel book nor an uncritical hymn of praise; rather it was Frank's attempt to explain the essence of the Spanish character and the uniqueness of Spanish civilization. In his most descriptive, impressionistic style, he suggested that the enduring tragedy of Spain, like that of Don Quixote, lay in its misdirected idealism, and its inability to distinguish fact from fantasy. Yet, despite these flaws, he argued that Spain, alone among European nations, possessed an organic unity which enabled its people to have meaningful lives on both the "horizontal" and "perpendicular" planes.[29] The Spaniard's "horizontal life consists of his social, economic, class relations; of the relations of his village, town, province, state, with their neighbors. Its roots are in the abyss of passion and instinct; its heights reach for God."[30] Thus, unlike the United States where the machine had taken on Brobdingnagian proportions, and where people mindlessly genuflected at the altar of a shallow, materialistic creed of accumulation, Spain remained a country where the whole person lived in harmony with life's more permeating unity.[31] Consequently, Spanish society was one worthy of imitation. Frank symbolically concludes the book with a dialogue between Columbus and Cervantes in which, at one point, the Genoan invokes Spain to aid the New World: "Your spirit, Spain. They above all will need it, in the north: they whose speech is English and who have led in the building of the Towers which are the Grave of Europe. For it is written that these shall also lead in the birth of the true New World—let them take from you O mother. For their spirit is weak and childish. They are cowards, not masters, before life."[32]

Although *Virgin Spain* received mixed reviews in the United States, it was praised lavishly in Spain and Latin America.[33] And even though several of Frank's works had already been welcomed in the Hispanic world, it was *Virgin Spain* that won for him the critical acclaim and affection of a large number of Spanish-speaking intellectuals.[34] Leading the chorus of praise in Spain was philosopher

Miguel de Unamuno, who was so impressed by the last chapter of the book—the dialogue between Columbus and Cervantes—that he personally translated it into Spanish.[35] In Latin America the reception was even greater, especially after the publication in 1927 of the Spanish poet León Felipe's authorized translation, *España virgen*.

For the next two years Frank's literary reputation continued to grow in Spain and Latin America. The interest in his work was so great that portions of *The Re-Discovery of America* were serialized by several Spanish-language periodicals well before the completed version appeared in the United States.[36] As his fame spread, a number of Latin American intellectuals and writers, led by the Argentinean Emigul Espinoza (Samuel Glusberry), who was helping Frank collect materials for an anthology, *Tales from the Argentine* (1930), suggested that he make a lecture tour. Final preparations for the tour were completed by the late spring of 1929. In June, Frank embarked on a seven-month journey, giving over forty lectures in nine countries, beginning with Mexico and continuing on to Argentina, Bolivia, Peru, Chile, Uruguay, Brazil, Colombia, and Cuba.[37]

At the time of his departure Frank was forty years old. Short and stocky with black thinning hair and a dark mustache, in both appearance and intensity of expression he seemed a cross between a Hebrew prophet and the stereotype of a Latin revolutionary. From the very beginning of the tour he insisted upon speaking in Spanish, which immediately won for him the affection of his audiences. When not lecturing on American literature, Frank emphasized what he considered to be the primary mission of his trip—the awakening of the American peoples of both continents to the fact that Europe was dead and that the world was awaiting the birth of a new leadership, the birth of a new America.[38]

Frank would usually declare that each America had something the other half needed and, as parts of an organic whole, each would thus complement the other by making its own unique contribution. In an article written shortly after his return to the United States in 1930, he summarized what he considered these contributions to be:

Politically, and in all matters of external organization, the Hispano-American countries are for many complex reasons inferior to ourselves. And in these respects we can help them greatly by aiding them to develop and to mobilize their forces, to establish their communications; making thus more possible the body of Hispano-America which the spirit of these peoples calls for.

On the other hand, in respect of vision, of cultural values, of personal sensibility, of aesthetic expression, and of a common American ideal, these peoples, through their intellectuals, are more intact than we are. They have what we need: the clear consciousness of the universal menace, which is the uncontrolled dictatorship of economic forces, and the strong devotion to the American tradition of a true new world.[39]

Frank's trip was a *tour de force*. During his seven months in Hispanic America a day seldom passed in which his ego was not amply nourished. In Mexico the audiences were unusually large and appreciative; years later he still recalled that he had "been welcomed and loved like no other intellectual in Mexico's history."[40] The reception in Argentina was even better. In fact, throughout the entire trip, Frank was often front page news even in countries which he did not visit.[41] Almost daily he received the kind of attention that he felt had been denied him in the United States. For example, an editorial in the Mexican newspaper *El Universal*, claimed that Frank, unlike most Americans who had visited that country, was not limited by Anglo-Saxon prejudices. When he was awarded a *Doctor Honoris* at the University of San Marcos in Lima, Peru, it was stated that all of Latin America recognized him "as ours, and of our race; of that race which he defined so well—the race of discontent and discomformity, but, as well, of hope."[42] So great, in fact, was the acclaim that Frank received during his trip, that it remained a high point of his entire career, an experience that he could always vividly recall. "My reward was to experience popularity," he remembered, "as no writer does in our country: to know what it was to be 'the rage' among both the men and elegant ladies. But I was to learn that I also had the masses with me." Frank even felt that in Argentina he had done something more than merely speak: "It is indicative to note that the accounts of my meetings in Buenos Aires describe my person. I was acting out a monodrama."[43] If he had been acting out a monodrama throughout much of his life, it was only in Latin America that Frank found audiences willing to grant him the attention tha he believed his career and his message deserved.

Back in the United States by late 1929, Frank's vital interest in the development of Pan Americanism continued; he made brief return visits to South America in 1934, 1937, and 1939.[44] Gradually, however, his attention was drawn more toward the United States. During the 1930s he became increasingly involved in the affairs of his own country. Even before the end of his first successful Latin American tour, the rumblings of economic collapse were belying the optimistic incantations of American business. During the economic disaster that followed, Frank, like so many of his angry and disillusioned fellow writers, began to move leftward into the arena of political activism.

As the country continued to experience massive economic upheaval, Frank, perhaps hoping to learn by example, made in 1931 the obligatory pilgrimage to the Soviet Union. After returning from a four-month visit he dutifully discussed the workings of the Soviet system in *Dawn in Russia* (1931). While engaging in the customary panegyrics of the converted, Frank tempered his praise somewhat by warning of various danger signs on the Soviet horizon. In particular, he was disturbed by the seemingly unchecked growth of centralized power, what he considered to be a noticeable degree of ideological inflexibility on the part of officials as well as intellectuals, and the scope of economic privilege among the selected few.[45] Although the book received no special attention in the United States, just the opposite was true in America Hispana. So eager, indeed, were Latin American publishers to release *Dawn in Russia*, that the official Madrid edition was soon pirated by a number of enthusiastic if unscrupulous editors.[46] Unhappy over the loss of royalties, Frank was nonetheless pleased that Latin American readers were so eager to read his opinions. He must have wondered why the same was not true to the north.

A year after *Dawn in Russia* appeared, Frank became involved in a coal miners' strike in Kentucky. When local authorities in Pineville, Kentucky, interfered with relief shipments being sent to striking miners, he led to the area a group of strike sympathizers which included Malcolm Cowley, Edmund Wilson, Quincy Howe, and lawyer Allen Taub. As it turned out, the efforts of the group were both brief and futile. Shortly after arriving at the county seat with several tons of food and supplies, the entire delegation was kidnapped by a gang of night-riders and unceremoniously escorted out of the state. Frank and Taub were severely beaten in the process.[47] Several months later Frank participated in a far less dangerous activity when he headed yet another group of writers seeking a meeting with President Hoover in order to protest the government's treatment of the Bonus Army.

During this period of political activism Frank never actually joined the Communist Party, although he remained during the early 1930s one of its most enthusiastic fellow-travelers. "Most of all Communism, although I could not accept it, tempted me, I believe and—when I saw the Communist youth—moved me—because it seemed to offer a community"; he later recorded in his memoirs, "and to belong to a community was what I needed."[48] In May 1935 he was rewarded for his loyalty to the Party by being chosen president of the first League of American Writers. A month later he accompanied the communist writer Mike Gold to Paris where they officially represented the League at the first International Congress of Writers for the Defense of Culture.[49] A year later while accompanying the Communist presidential candidate Earl Browder on the campaign trail, Frank, as he already had done in Kentucky, sampled the "tolerance" of the democratic process when both he and Browder were jailed in Terre Haute, Indiana, on vagrancy charges.

By late fall 1936, with the beginning of the Spanish Civil War, Frank's activism quickly shifted from the domestic to the international scene. In December of that year he agreed to head a group calling itself The American Society for Technical Aid to Spanish Democracy. He explained in his initial statement to the press that the organization hoped to aid the Republic by helping American workers with technical skills to get to Spain to replace Spanish workers in the factories. With production assured, the Spanish workers would then be freed to fight against the fascists.[50] As concerned about Spain as Frank was, any hopes that he may have had about directly participating in the Civil War ended when, shortly after returning from a writers conference in Mexico City, he publicly criticized the Purge Trials then being conducted in Russia. Perhaps influenced by two interviews that he had had with Leon Trotsky while in Mexico City, Frank also wrote an open letter to the *New Republic* demanding that in the future Soviet authorities prohibit secret trials and publicly exhibit all evidence.[51] Frank was immediately branded a Trotskyite, and unmercifully hounded by the communist press during a three-week trip that he made to Spain two months later. Although the Madrid section of the Spanish Popular Front voted to welcome him officially as a friend of the Republic, Frank soon realized that his criticism of the Soviet Union had rendered him powerless—he decided that there was little that he could personally accomplish in Spain.[52] Unable to aid the Republic directly, he returned to the United States where he continued to write in support of the Republican cause.[53]

The two years following his return from Spain were to be perhaps the most agonizing that Frank had ever known. A second marriage of some twelve years was nearing an end. With his writing at a standstill, his literary future was uncertain. Events in Europe added to Frank's depression. Franco was about to win in Spain, and Hitler had successfully invaded Poland. Further disheartened by the smug complacency that he detected in a number of fellow writers, during the early months of the Phony War period, Frank began writing a book which he hoped would awaken America to the growing threat of totalitarianism. Appearing in April 1940, *Chart for Rough Waters* attempted to explain the worldwide appeal of fascism, and warned that communism was an equally dangerous totalitarian movement. Most important of all, however, the book offered a vehement argument against continuing American isolationism. As if to demonstrate his sincerity, Frank, along with Lewis Mumford, resigned in June as contributing editor to the *New Republic*. A joint statement announced that their resignations were in response to the magazine's editorial apathy and continuing blindness towards the spread of international fascism.[54]

By the time of his break with the *New Republic*, Frank was almost fifty-one. Exhausted by more than a decade of political activism, and still bearing the Trotskyite label, he was convinced that other than writing there was little that he could do personally to counter the fascist threat. With these thoughts in mind, he decided to retire to his home in Truro, Massachusetts, to devote all of his energies to writing. During the winter of 1940–41 he stuck by his decision, even when he received letters from many Latin American intellectuals asking him to make a lecture tour to speak out against the rising tide of fascism. By early January and February 1941 the letters were becoming more urgent, especially those from Argentina where a reactionary government appeared to be moving toward the fascist orbit. Early in April the American State Department added its plea by offering him four thousand dollars if he would make a personal tour of South America.[55] Frank, who was in the midst of a novel and convinced that his writing had been put aside far too often, refused to consider any of the offers. But during the summer and fall of 1941, feelings of guilt began to overshadow his creative urge; late in November he confided in a notebook that the decision not to go to South America was probably the worst one of his life.[56] The following month he at last made up his mind. No doubt aroused by the attack on Pearl Harbor, he once again put his writing aside and began to plan yet another trip south.

The financial arrangements for the trip that Frank and several others eventually worked out were complex, involving the cooperation of the New York publishing house of Duell, Sloan, and Pearce as well as the United States Office of the Coordinator of Inter-American Affairs. As finally set up, Frank accepted an advance from Duell and Company for a book, tentatively to be entitled *The ABC of South America*, which he was to write upon returning from the tour.[57] Viewing the trip as a way of combatting fascism in South America, the Office of the Coordinator of Inter-American Affairs agreed to reimburse Duell and Company for Frank's expenses, although this did not make Frank a representative of that office. Near the end of the tour, in fact, a spokesman for this government agency emphasized that while it had helped to make arrangements for the trip, Frank was not a member of its staff, or that of any other government agency.[58]

Even though the State Department used Frank to speak out against fascism, there is no evidence that his mission resulted from anything other than a personal sense of commitment. By the time that he left for Latin America, Frank had long since adopted a Popular Front kind of mentality, and believed that all shades of political opinion should combine in a united effort against fascism. Also, like Lewis Mumford, Gilbert Seldes, Max Lerner, Archibald MacLeish, and others, Frank had become far more sympathetic to traditional American institutions. At this time he was thoroughly convinced that such institutions could best be protected by confronting the fascist threat everywhere.[59] Acting upon his beliefs, Frank became a member of the Committee To Defend America by Aiding the Allies which had been organized by William Allen White in May 1940. He also joined the Fight for Freedom Committee in 1941—an organization that advocated direct American intervention in the war. He believed that his most significant contributions could be made not only through writing and joining committees, but also by acting on his beliefs. His determination to act, however, reflected his concern not just for the well-being of his country, but also for the health of all of the Americas. From the late 1920s onward he had held that a symbiotic relationship should exist between the two Americas, and by 1941 he believed more than ever that a cancerous growth in one was bound to invade the other. Most certainly the very fact that the Office of the Coordinator of Inter-American Affairs indirectly supported Frank's trip makes Frank's foreign involvement different from that of the other writers discussed thus far. Yet there is no evidence that Frank ever believed he was representing the government on his Latin American tour. To him the trip was simply a personal gesture, freely given, and not an official act. From Frank's perspective, then, his lecture tour through Spanish America was a voluntary commitment motivated by a cultural philosophy which viewed the Americas as a single unit.

Frank spent more than half of his Latin American tour in Argentina. Since his triumphant visit there in 1929, he had kept in contact with a number of Argentine writers and intellectuals. By the early 1940s he was concerned that the country was moving along a collision course with fascism. As he later explained, either:

> she must go forward, must re-integrate in clear creative action; or she will have failed of her destiny. She must perform a part of leadership in the family of American nations; or she will turn against herself, all her weaknesses will become positive, and rend her. The ideal of the new world as an organic hemisphere of Ameri-can nations, each ful-filling its personal genius by devotion to the Whole, is the incentive, the challenge, and the medicine Argentina sorely needs. She must be cured of her false European nostalgias; of her false sense of separation from her neighbors. She must for her own sake, and for the sake of us all, be mobilized into American action.[60]

Even before Frank had left on his tour, he had become increasingly concerned by the activities of Argentine President Ramon S. Castillo, who had risen to power in July 1940. Unlike his predecessor, who was pro-English and pro-Allies, Castillo professed a policy of "neutrality" while he carried on a torrid flirtation with the fascist powers—particularly Germany. Castillo was known to overlook the clumsily veiled activities of Nazi agents in his own country, and to allow the various pro-fascist Argentine newspapers to publish freely. At the same time, he censored all public meetings and lectures and silenced publications that criticized the government or openly support the Allies. A month after Pearl Harbor, Castillo refused to accept a resolution adopted at a meeting of American foreign ministers at Rio de Janeiro, calling for all American governments to sever relations with the fascists.[61] Thus, when Frank boarded his plane in April 1942 he strongly believed that it was the Castillo government and not the Argentine people that was inclined toward fascism. Moreover, he was certain that the people of Argentina wanted to know the truth about the world situation, and, with customary modesty, Frank believed that he alone was capable of telling it to them.[62]

Before embarking on his Latin American tour, Frank spent a few days in British Guiana. He then relaxed for two weeks in Brazil while he prepared for what he called his "Argentine Campaign." Arriving in Buenos Aires early in May 1942, he diplomatically told the reporters who met him at the airport: "I have come here to learn. I have not come here on a new mission. I have come here to continue my *old* mission of many years in America Hispania. That mission," he emphasized, "consists of trying to understand Argentina; and of telling the truth about my own country. . . ."[63] Although the Castillo government gave no indication that it was even aware of Frank's presence, the intellectual community publicly welcomed him. Soon after his arrival, Frank was asked by the *Sociedad Argentina de Escritores* to speak at a dinner given in his honor. In his first speaking engagement, Frank reiterated the message that he had earlier stated during the 1929 tour and which he had repeated during each subsequent visit— that the two Americas needed to become one. At the same time, while carefully avoiding any mention of Castillo, he warned his audience that "a particular race of men, like a particular individual, may go down, despite man's high destiny, into darkness and death. Many are called; few are chosen. The Americas are called. And this is the sacrament of our lives: that in our hands, our humble hands and minds, is the choice. . . ."[64]

Several days after the banquet, Frank began encountering the first attempts at official harassment. Shortly before leaving to give his first public lecture in Buenos Aires, he was informed by the police that he had not been issued the special license needed to hold a meeting in which "public" matters were to be discussed. After over an hour's delay, an Argentine friend was able to convince the authorities that no license was needed since the lecture was to be academic, not political. Before giving final acceptance, however, the local authorities insisted that the academic purity of the lecture be maintained by deleting certain words and phrases: "In a few places I have named names: Hitler, Mussolini, Germany. Out they must go"; as Frank remembered, "and in their stead references any child can understand. When I say fascism, I must change to 'the philosophy . . . the theory . . . of fascism.' "[65] A second incident of official harassment occurred a few

days later in the port city of La Plata. There once again shortly before
Frank was to make a scheduled speech, this time on the radio, the
local officials interfered. Frank's talk, they feared, might touch on the
"world situation," and this might prove harmful to the formulation of
Argentina's foreign policy.[66] Even though the cancellation of the
broadcast disappointed him, Frank was more convinced than ever that
he was being heard, especially by his opponents.

While the government of Argentina seemed to try to hide its harassment of Frank behind the veneer of bureaucratic procedure, extremists
on both Left and Right were far less careful about their attacks on
him. Heading a list of anti-Frank publications was the scurrilous, pro-
Nazi, afternoon daily, El Pampero, which delighted in referring to
Frank as "the Yankee-Jew Frank," and which frequently characterized him in blatantly anti-Semitic cartoons. At the opposite end of
the political spectrum were the Argentine Communists who, like the
Castillo government, at first tried to ignore him. Eventually, however,
a prominent party member, perhaps still detecting a faint odor of
Trotskyism, distributed a pamphlet which suggested that Frank's belief
in intuition placed him on the philosophical fringes of fascism. Such
harassment from both official and unofficial sources left Frank un-
scathed. Driven by a messianic belief in the absolute necessity of his
mission, Frank waded through the almost daily abuse that he encountered more determined than ever to deliver his message.[67]

The first weeks Frank spent in Argentina were confined to Buenos
Aires. But past experience told him that the country's largest city did
not typify the rest of the nation, and he was anxious to travel more
widely through the provinces. While preparing to leave the city, he was
informed, much to his surprise, that he would be granted an interview
with President Castillo. The meeting between the two men was brief,
formal, and almost totally lacking in substance. No mention was made
of any of the issues Frank had been stressing in his lectures. The
interview convinced him that there was nothing more to be accomplished in Buenos Aires. Thus, from the middle of June until near the
end of July Frank visited most of the country's important provincial
cities, speaking in public lecture halls, classrooms, and even cinemas.

He first traveled north to Rosario, then on to Parana, Santa Fe, Cordoba, and Tucuman. The enthusiastic welcome he received everywhere brought back pleasant memories of a similar warm reception in 1929. It was only in Cordoba that he encountered any harassment, and then it was only through a series of unexplainable, but certainly far from accidental, incidents. At times, in fact, it seemed as though he had been set upon by legions of poltergeists who seemed determined to make each lecture in Cordoba more difficult to give than the last. During Frank's first two lectures, loudly tolling chapel bells made it impossible for the audience to hear him. Next, in the midst of the Argentine winter, he spoke in an auditorium in which the building's supervisors had "forgotten" to turn on the heat. Undaunted by the icy air, Frank launched into his speech only to find that all of the amplifiers were broken. At the end of the evening, he was tired, cold, and hoarse. He later admitted: "Before I had finished I had to keep on repeating to myself: 'You are a soldier.'"[68] Despite such adversity, Frank continued his tour through the provincial cities and then flew to Montevideo for several days of rest.

Refreshed by his stay in Montevideo, Frank made a final excursion deep into Patagonia to lecture and to inspect the living conditions of the workers in the dreary mining town of Rio Gallegos. Once back in Buenos Aires, he assessed the overall results of the tour and felt generally dissatisfied. Although he had traveled practically the entire length and breadth of Argentina pleading for hemispheric unity and warning of the fascist menace, he remained doubtful of how effective he had been. Expressing these doubts in his journal, he asked: "Am I sufficiently aware of my mission? Am I doing my whole job? I do not know. I know that I am sick at heart—sick, sick, unto death."[69] Although his lectures had been enthusiastically attended, Frank was still disturbed by the fact that the Castillo government had shown no intention to break its ties with the Nazis. Frank thus decided at the conclusion of the tour to court openly the hostility of the Castillo government. He may have seen this effort as a necessary, final defiant gesture or may simply have wanted to attract more attention to his presence in Argentina. Believing as he did that he was a soldier, he may have felt that he had not been forthright enough in delivering his message and had thus let down those who were depending on him. In any case, as his visit to Argentina drew to a close, he became more and more convinced that a final uncompromising gesture was needed to awaken the Argentine people once and for all to the dangers they were facing through the activities of the Castillo government. "What had to be said was unpleasant for Argentine ears;" he later wrote in describing why he decided to act as he did, "therefore *must* be said . . . not in Chile, not back home where it would be easy . . . but in Argentina. To leave it unsaid here, and to say it elsewhere would be to betray every motive and every word of my journey."[70]

It was in this frame of mind that Frank began to write his "Farewell to Argentina." He planned to release it to the press several days before departing Buenos Aires for Chile. On July 29, he showed the completed text to several friends, including fellow writer Eduardo Mallea. After making minor stylistic changes, his friends suggested that the statement be published the very next day. Although the morning newspapers rejected the "Farewell" because it was too controversial, the more sensational afternoon dailies eagerly published it in their July 30 editions. The "Farewell" was relatively long—approximately seventeen hundred words. Unfurling all of the techniques of a Fourth of July orator, Frank attempted to flatter, to anger, to shame, and ultimately to convince the Argentine people that their government's policy of "neutrality" was morally wrong and politically unsound. He favorably compared the moral integrity of George Washington and San Martín, and praised the "spiritual qualities" of such past Argentine statesmen as Domingo Faustino Sarmiento and Bartolomé Mitre. Then with the obvious intention of embarrassing the present government, Frank bluntly asked: "What would these leaders—and there are others—what would they feel, if they could witness the present moral condition of Argentina?—these leaders who have made Argentina great far beyond the actual weight of its wealth or population? What would they say if they could see the confusion, the blind egoism, the egoistic blindness of Argentina's present international position before the world and the Latin American nations?"[71]

The reaction to Frank's "Farewell" was both immediate and predictable. The July 31 edition of *El Pampero* led the attack by italicizing its front-page broadside, "Adios, Miserable Waldo Frank," and categorically stating that never again would he be allowed in Argentina.[72] As if to canonize such attacks, the next day the Castillo government declared that no longer was Frank *persona grata.* Later that same afternoon he began receiving anonymous phone calls to his hotel room. By early evening the calls had become so frequent and threatening that Frank asked the hotel porter—a trusted friend—not to let strangers come up to his room. Lying awake for most of the night, Frank decided to write in bed the next morning; he was doing so when the bell to his apartment rang. On cracking the door, he saw the porter and five other men who identified themselves as police officers and asked to see his passport. Frank let them in, and, as he was looking in a drawer for the passport, he was struck from behind with the butt of a pistol. Somehow managing to remain standing, he began screaming at the top of his voice while trying to ward off the blows of his four assailants—the fifth was holding a pistol on the astonished porter. Apparently unnerved by the resistance and the loud bellowing of their uncooperative victim, the five men suddenly bolted from the apartment, leaving Frank battered and frightened, but still very much alive.[73]

As a result of the beating, Frank was hospitalized for a severe concussion, multiple lacerations of the scalp, a cut on the hand, and numerous bruises on his shoulders and arms. Remarkably calm only a few hours after the incident, he issued a statement from his hospital bed in which he said: "I do not blame the Argentine people for what had happened, but rather the poison from foreign ideas brought into the country from abroad."[74] During the next week wires from all over Latin America poured in expressing shock and indignation at the attack. In marked contrast, the Castillo government showed little or no interest in world opinion, Frank's condition, or finding his assailants. Although one of the five men had left behind a hat, no arrests were made for almost three weeks. Even then the suspects were only briefly questioned and released. The Argentine police continued their investigations for two months; predictably, they never brought anyone to trial.[76]

Frank believed that the attack was motivated by more than the anger of the Castillo government. He was scheduled to lecture next in Chile, and he was convinced that his brush with death was meant to keep him from going there. Such thoughts only left Frank more determined to make the trip. He checked out of the hospital in Buenos Aires after less than a week, and by August 10 was flying over the Andes toward Santiago. Even though he anticipated trouble, to Frank's surprise, none developed. In fact, compared with his Argentine experience, the Chilean tour was anticlimactic. After giving four lectures in Santiago and visiting briefly in Peru, Frank stayed for some time in Brazil where he traveled, relaxed, and began mapping out his next book, *South American Journey*. It was only after returning to the United States that he learned more about the police investigation of the attack in Buenos Aires. The man whose hat had been left behind in the hotel room had eventually been questioned, but released because of a "lack of evidence."[76] In spite of no observable changes in the attitude of the Castillo government, Frank still felt that his South American tour had been a success. His justification of the trip is contained in a letter he wrote to the North American Newspaper Alliance, explaining his "Farewell to Argentina:"

> I knew that if I went away with a diplomatic farewell, something of supreme importance which the *people* expected of me would be left undone. The "i's" had to be dotted, the "t's" crossed. What I had to say no Argentine could say; his words would not be published, and no non-Argentine could say it effectively, his words would not be heard. I had won the Argentine public. They expected from me the final, clear utterance, not in the general terms of my lectures, but straight—of what was in their hearts. From the beginning I had made clear that this was a war in which national barriers did not count, so that if I were true to my own vision, I must not let national etiquette stop me. I said what had to be said.[77]

In saying what he felt had to be said, Frank showed great courage, and he suffered for his convictions. Yet he still returned to the United

States in a euphoric frame of mind. Frank was certain that, as in 1929, he had once again found the "great audience" which had always been his need. What made this trip even more important was his conviction that the South American people had also needed him and that he had been able to reach them despite the most difficult conditions.

In many ways Frank's trip to Latin America in 1942 was symbolic of his lifelong relationship with the Hispanic world. Just as he was attracted to America Hispania by its cultural uniqueness and a genuine like for its peoples, so too were Latin Americans drawn to Frank by qualities that they appreciated in his writing or found pleasing about his personality. This mutual attraction is worthy of closer examination. Unlike other writers and cultural ambassadors who had traveled in South America, Frank was willing to criticize his own country before offering critiques of the nations he visited. In a Jeffersonian lament, he suggested in *In The American Jungle*: "We Americans are weak—infinitely weaker than the peasants of China, America Hispania, or old Russia—in that intuitive connection with soil and self and human past, which makes a folk an effective medium for creative action."[78] Frank's brand of Pan Americanism called for an equal partnership in which Latin America's spiritual and cultural contributions were to be every bit as important as his own country's political and organizational ones. Even his criticism of America Hispania was constructive since, like Fenollosa's view of East and West, Frank was interested in a new synthesis in which the Americas would become whole by becoming one. Thus, in his view, new, revitalized leadership from the Americas was especially needed, for the world had become destructively fragmented through centuries of atomization.

Yet even the symbiotic nature of Frank's Pan Americanism does not fully explain why he was so highly regarded in much of the Hispanic world. Perhaps, as Arnold Chapman has suggested, Latin Americans listened to Frank because they thought of him as an outsider, as they also felt themselves to be. His Jewish origins and radicalism during the 1930s had forced him outside the mainstream of life in the United States; he could thus come to Hispanic America as a fellow sufferer, dedicated to the continuing struggle for social equality.[79] Moreover, his frequent praise of the cultural synthesis produced by the intermixing of Indian and Spaniard, his description of Brazil as the world leader in "racial democracy," and his sympathetic portrayal of blacks in much of his fiction must have been noticed and appreciated on a continent of such enormous heterogeneity.[80] Frank also won the affection of a large part of the Spanish-speaking intellectual community through his understanding and sincere appreciation of Hispanic culture. If *Virgin Spain* paved the way for a first visit in 1929, his ability to speak Spanish and his knowledge of the history and literature of the countries he visited ensured that he would be asked back again and again. In fact, it is quite possible that many South Americans regarded Frank as one of their own. It was Frank, after all, a Yankee, who was commissioned by the Venezuelan government in 1948 to write a biography of the national hero—Simón Bolívar.

Although he claimed to be in search of a "great audience," Frank directed most of his writing and lecturing in Latin America to fellow intellectuals. Frank was a man who was at ease with abstract thought, and his Latin American involvement was far more intellectually oriented than the activism abroad of most of the other writers discussed thus far. Certain by 1929 that too much dependence on rationalism and materialism had destroyed the organic unity of Europe, he believed that world salvation lay in the creation of a new hemispheric synthesis in the Americas. Throughout the 1920s and the greater part of the 1930s he thought that the United States was by far the most spiritually deficient regime of the Western Hemisphere and thus the most in need of help. However, the beginning of World War II and the spread of international fascism caused his viewpoint to change. He found in North American traditions and institutions much more to admire than to criticize. "To love is to see clear. See America clear," he wrote in an article in 1942, "in its body, its dream, in the eyes of its deep vision, and we will love America. We will know its promise to be *our* flesh and blood. No fear that we will betray it. The machines we make to destroy Hitler will be safe in our hands."[81] By the 1940s the hemispheric link which seemed most in need of repair was not the

United States, but Argentina. Frank feared that Castillo's policy of "neutrality" was pushing the nation ever closer to the fascist camp, and he was also convinced that the government was keeping this fact from the people. In the face of this official subterfuge, Frank feared, as he pointed out in a speech at Rosario in 1942, that the "Argentine people, despite the clarity of their democratic tradition, have lost their way; despite their extraordinary high culture, have forgotten how to say and to do what they mean."[82] Thus seeing his dream of hemispheric unity threatened by an external ideology that was in danger of becoming internalized, Frank believed it his personal mission to bring the truth about the world situation as well as about their own government to the attention of the Argentine people.

Yet there was also a very deeply personal side to Frank's Latin American commitment. Apart from any devotion to the people, their culture, the beauty of the land, the concept of an organic unity, and any number of other things, Frank was also drawn to Latin America because it was there that he was more fully appreciated and listened to than in any other place in the world. Such attention mattered greatly to Frank. Once when leaving a café in Buenos Aires, he was recognized by a number of its patrons who began to applaud. Obviously moved by the gesture, Frank later asked in *South American Journey*: "Where else is such warmth given, not to movie stars, pugilists, politicians, but to a mere man of letters?"[83] His Latin American reception stood in marked contrast to the reception offered him by his own country. After returning from a tour of the Midwest in the summer of 1941, Frank recorded his feelings of neglect: "Twenty-two years ago, I published 'Our America,' *and I have made no organic impression upon my countrymen*: for most *of course*, I do not exist."[84] Like all writers Frank wanted to be read, appreciated, and, perhaps most important of all, to be known—especially in his lifetime. In this respect, his literary popularity in South America helped to nourish a sizable ego which received scant sustenance in the United States. Frank's own words may shed some light on why he was recognized more in Latin America than in his own country. Recalling his reception in Argentina in 1929, he remembered:

When I first visited Argentina it was front page news—not only the first day, day after day I was played up in interviews, pictures, that was in 1929. The president offered me an airplane and a private car.

. . .

My position was like that of the writers of other times, close to a national leader, respected as an adviser. A position similar to what MacLeish has, I presume, in Washington.

Here in my own country, it has been hard, frankly. I have an audience here, and it grows. But the growth is slow. Of course, I have doubts of myself. But if the fault were wholly mine then how explain the success of my books in Latin America, in the Latin countries generally, and in Russia? May it not be the fault of the industrial revolution, of the exchange we effected that places temporary well-being above salvation, above the relationships of men to the infinite, which is the theme of all my books, every one of them, and which is understandable to people not too marked, too regimented, by industry, by the forces that have destroyed to so great an extent . . . the dignity, the divinity in man?[85]

Over the years several of Frank's closest friends were aware of how literary neglect in the United States was affecting him. In his introduction to Frank's posthumously published memoirs, Lewis Mumford recalled that his friend's ego and sense of commitment always seemed to be in perpetual turmoil: "the contrast between Frank's ego-dominated energies and his vision of social justice and personal love brought exacerbating inner conflicts, and those conflicts were never to be resolved, even in the period of self-criticism and personal humility that marked the last decade of his life."[86] Mumford may indeed be correct in his assessment, especially with respect to Frank's social activism in the United States. At the same time, through his activities in Argentina, Frank probably came as close as he ever would to reaching a kind of equilibrium between self-interest and social commitment. By going to Argentina in 1942 he was returning to a country where he was known, admired, and where—how could he ever forget—he had been publicly applauded like a movie star. But he also went to Argentina because of a commitment to a vision. Deeply fearing what fascism could do to that country, he was convinced that the people of Argentina would find both political and spiritual salvation in his message. Thus, his involvement in Argentina was based on reciprocal needs, but, as he had always stressed in his lectures on hemispheric unity—the very essence of any organic relationship is reciprocity.

8

Ezra Pound:
Commitment as Metaphor

> *. . . for we all of us, grave or light, get our*
> *thoughts entangled in metaphors, and act*
> *fatally on the strengths of them.*
>
> George Eliot
> *Middlemarch*

BY PEARL HARBOR DAY the American community in Rome had all but disappeared with the exception of the Consulate staff and a handful of journalists. Among those who still lingered in the imperial city were the Rome correspondent of the United Press, Reynolds Packard, and his wife Eleanor, and they too were preparing to leave. Their hasty packing, however, was interrupted by the unexpected visit of a friend and fellow countrymen, Ezra Pound. He had just made a speech over the Italian Broadcasting System in which he had warned that the United States was being drawn into a war to defend the British Empire. Inside the Packards' apartment, Pound continued his jeremiad, predicting that war between America and Italy was now inevitable. Still agitated by the broadcast, he declared his intention of remaining in Italy regardless of what happened. When Packard reminded him that such a decision might make him a traitor, Pound replied: "But I believe in Fascism. And I want to defend it. I don't see why Fascism is contrary to American philosophy. I consider myself a hundred percent American and a patriot. I am only against Roosevelt and the Jews who influenced him." Changing the subject slightly, Packard then asked Pound how much he was being paid for his radio broadcasts. Pound explained that he received the equivalent of ten dollars for each fifteen-minute talk: "it's not much," he said, "but you don't think I do it just for the money do you? I tell you I want to save the American people." As Packard later recalled, there was no use in arguing with Pound, for he had obviously made up his mind to stay in Italy.[1] Packard was probably correct in his assessment, for Pound was convinced of the rightness of his political vision and thoroughly astounded by what he considered to be the shortsightedness of his own country. Adding to his frustration was the fact that over the years few in the United States had been willing to listen to his political advice. He could never understand why his reputation in the areas of poetry and literature failed to guarantee him the same respect and authority in politics. For these reasons, Pound remained in Italy even after the United States entered the war. But he was not content with the role of wartime expatriate. Instead, Pound supported the fascists by making propaganda broadcasts from Rome which were intended to "save the American people."[2] Yet his intentions were viewed in a different light by those he proposed to "save." When United States troops finally entered northern Italy in 1945, Pound was seized and flown home to stand trial for treason.

An only child, Ezra Pound was born on October 30, 1885, in the little mining town of Hailey, Idaho, where his father, Homer, was recorder of the government land office. Unable to adjust to the altitude, Isabel Pound eventually took her eighteen-month-old son to live with grandparents in New York, and then two years later joined her husband in Philadelphia where he was employed as the assistant assayer of the United States Mint. The family lived in the comfortable, middle-class suburb of Wyncote where Pound received his early education. Later he went to Cheltenham Military Academy in Ogontz, Pennsylvania, and then attended Cheltenham High School in Elkins Park. A precocious boy, Pound entered the University of Pennsylvania in the fall of 1901, shortly before his sixteenth birthday. In spite of his age, he soon adjusted to campus life, dividing his time between academic interests in the classics and drama, fencing lessons, tennis, and ushering at university football games. It was during his first two years at the university that Pound met William Carlos Williams, who shared many of his younger friend's aesthetic interests even though Williams himself was preparing for a medical career. Although the friendship was to last a lifetime, Williams was always uneasy with Pound's flamboyant enthusiasm and with his tending to see himself an expert in all that he tried. While Williams considered him a "fine fellow," he also recognized that "not one person in a thousand likes him, and why? Because he is so darned full of conceits and affectation. He is really a brilliant talker and thinker but delights in making himself just exactly what he is not: a laughing boor."[3] Both the friendship and Pound's career at Pennsylvania were interrupted in 1902 when Homer Pound decided that his son's scholastic record might improve in the more tranquil atmosphere of Hamilton College in upstate New York. The choice of Hamilton was fortuitous, especially with regard to Pound's future literary career, for it was there that he began a thorough study of Dante and Provençal poetry under the guidance of medieval scholar William Pierce Shepard.[4] After Pound graduated from Hamilton in 1905 he returned to the University of Pennsylvania to work on a master's degree in Romance languages. Throughout his graduate career, Pound was convinced that his future lay in poetry. During this period of his life he lived in one of the university towers, wrote a sonnet a day (all of which he later destroyed), and in dress and mannerisms affected the lifestyle of a modern troubadour. Self-assured, vocal, enthusiastic, often loud, and always opinionated, he constantly bombarded William Carlos Williams and anyone else who would listen with his theories about literature or demanded that they read his latest poem while he offered to read anything they might have written.

In the midst of his creative endeavors and exaggerated lifestyle, Pound continued the study of Romantics. He was awarded a master of arts degree in the spring of 1906, and a fellowship of five hundred dollars for dissertation research in Europe on the Spanish dramatist and poet Lope de Vega. Pound spent the rest of the year in Spain,

France, Italy, and Germany, excited by the Provençal poets he was discovering, but gradually losing interest in an academic career. It was not that he disliked scholarship, but he had grown increasingly disenchanted with what he considered to be the narrow confines and specialized nature of academic research. A number of years later he precisely defined what he had found to be most distasteful about graduate work: "The graduate student is not taught to think of his own minute discoveries in relation to his subject as a whole. If that subject happened to be the history of an art he is scarce likely to have considered his work in relation to the life of that art." He added, "the usual doctor's thesis is dull, is badly written," and to make matters even worse, "the candidate usually has to pay for the printing of the required copies. . . ."[5]

Back in Philadelphia by January 1907, Pound told his parents that he was no longer interested in graduate school, but wanted instead to write poetry. With his usual self-confidence, he also let them know the kinds of poems that he planned to create: "I want to write before I die the greatest poems that have ever been written."[6] Yet dreams of literary acclaim had to be tempered by financial reality. In the fall of 1907 he accepted a teaching position at Wabash College in Crawfordsville, Indiana. This little town and the introductory French and Spanish course he taught provided scant nourishment for an aspiring young poet. Pound later compared the time spent in Crawfordsville to being "stranded in Devil's Island, Indiana."[7]

After only four months his first teaching effort came to an abrupt end. So often have the circumstances leading to his dismissal from Wabash College been retold that they have become a colorful if exaggerated part of the Pound legend. Supposedly upon meeting an abandoned, penniless actress, Pound took her to his room, gave her his bed, and, then in the socially accepted tradition of Crawfordsville, spent the night on the floor. Nonetheless, the next day after Pound had left for class, his landlady discovered the sleeping visitor, and immediately telephoned the president of the college. Pound soon found himself unemployed, bound for Philadelphia.[8] Within a few weeks he was on his way to Europe, having decided that the United States, and particularly the Midwest, was an unfit incubator for the development of a poet, especially one who was planning to write the greatest poems of his day.

Fortified with confidence and little else, Pound landed in Gibraltar in 1908 with only eighty dollars in his pocket. Several weeks later he was in Venice spending a part of these funds to publish a first book of poetry, *A Lume Spento*. Having to use his own money for publication, and to publish in a foreign country were two factors which deeply affected Pound, particularly as he believed that his predicament was not unique. He had gone to Europe with no definite plans, but he remained there as one of the century's first expatriates, a man convinced that there was no place in his own home for the serious artist, especially a young and innovative one.

Several months after arriving in Europe, Pound settled in Kensington, a suburb of London, and began meeting the artistic entourage which revolved about *The English Review* and its editor, Ford Maddox Hueffer. He was soon satisfied that he had found one of the few suitable locations for an aspiring poet. "London, dear old London, is the place for poetry," he wrote to Williams, and by way of an invitation added: "if you have saved any pennies during your stay in Nueva York, you'd better come across and broaden your mind. Besides, you'd much prefer to scrap with an intelligent person like myself than with a board of directing idiots . . ."[9] Over the next few years Pound continued to find London a stimulating place in which to write, and in 1909, he published two more small books of verse, *Personae* and *Exultations*. Both were well received. At the age of twenty-four he was on his way to literary recognition and a position of leadership in the newly emerging schools of English and American verse.

Pound's remarkable literary achievements over the next dozen years while living in London and Paris have been well explored by his biographers. During this most creative period of his life, he published twenty-five books of verse and prose, wrote over five hundred articles for magazines and newspapers, helped found new poetic schools such as Imagism and Vorticism, and began work on the *Cantos*.[10] He also painted, sculptured, composed, acted as editor and adviser for numerous small magazines, and served as William Butler Yeats's literary secretary during the winters of 1913 to 1916. Apart from personal accomplishments, Pound's most lasting contribution to the world of art during these years was the criticial and economic assistance he unselfishly gave to many young artists. Even while still a young man, Pound, with customary egotism, had come to believe that it was his mission to keep the arts alive, and what better way to do so than by aiding struggling but potential luminaries? Among those who received his help were T. E. Hulme, T. S. Eliot, James Joyce, Ernest Hemingway, Henri Gaudier-Brzeska, Robert Frost, Marianne Moore, Constantin Brancusi, Rabindranath Tagore, and George Antheil. Pound constantly pleaded with and badgered potential young artists to free themselves from the suffocating folds of tradition. Another patron of the young, Lincoln Steffens, recalled that Pound was every bit a "private, professional propagandist, as Gertrude Stein was. They both encouraged the young artists to despise the old forms and the old stuff, to rebel, break away and dare."[11] One of Pound's young beneficiaries was Ernest Hemingway who gratefully recalled near the end of his life that Pound was "the most generous writer I have ever known and the most disinterested. He helped poets, painters, sculptors and prose writers that he believed in and he would help anyone whether he believed in them or not if they were in trouble."[12]

Throughout his life Pound was especially sensitive to the problems of young American writers, for he believed that artistic integrity and innovative creativity had little hope of flourishing in the uncultivated American soil. "Hardly a week goes by but I meet or hear of someone who goes into voluntary exile—some reporter who throws up a steady job to 'come to Europe and breathe'; some professor from a freshwater college who comes away on scant savings," he bitterly wrote in 1912, perhaps remembering his own experiences in Crawfordsville. "Our artists are all over Europe. We do not come away strictly for pleasure. And we, constantly-railed-at 'expatriates' do not hear this with unconcern. We will not put up with it forever."[13] Despite his bitterness, Pound still differed from those expatriates who had left the United States convinced that it was doomed to a plodding mediocrity.

In fact, there was something noticeably paradoxical about his attitude, for even while denouncing the nation's stultifying superficiality, he never ceased believing in its artistic potential. Just how great a potential it was he outlined in *Patria Mia*; written almost four years after he arrived in Europe:

> I have declared my belief in the imminence of an American Risorgimento. I have no desire to flatter the country by pretending that we are at present enduring anything except the Dark Ages.
>
> A Risorgimento means an intellectual awakening. This will have its effect not only in the arts, but in life, in politics, and in economics. If I seem to lay undue stress upon the status of the arts, it is only because the arts respond to an intellectual movement more swiftly and more apparently than do institutions, and not because there is any better reason for discussing them first.
>
> A Risorgimento implies a whole volley of liberations; liberation from ideas, from stupidities, from conditions and from tyrannies of wealth or of army.[14]

This American renaissance would not begin through chance or any blind dialectical process. Instead, it could only originate through the efforts of those who recognized deficiencies in American life and who were willing and able to suggest how to eliminate them. Pound had already assumed the role of a Petrarch by 1915, for as he wrote to the editor of *Poetry*: "My problem is to keep alive a certain group of advancing poets, to set the arts in their rightful place as the acknowledged guide and lamp of civilization."[15] An individualist and an elitist by inclination, Pound was also convinced that most Americans were totally incapable of recognizing the need for a national revitalization. It was only the artist, and, only the superior artist, at that, who could correctly anticipate the country's intellectual needs. "It is true that the great artist has in the end," he had written in 1914, "always, his audience, for the Lord of the universe sends into this world in each generation a few intelligent spirits, and these ultimately manage the rest. But this rest—this rabble, this multitude—does not create the great artist. They are aimless and drifting without him."[16] Pound's belief bordered on the Messianic, for by his late twenties he was supremely confident that it was his duty, even his mission, to lead America out of its cultural wilderness. Years later he would still be trying to lead, having by then reshaped his cultural attitudes with economics.

Like the main character in a proletarian novel, Pound's interest in economic issues grew largely out of personal need. As his literary reputation soared, his financial condition declined. In fact, financial concerns persistently plagued Pound's early career.[17] During his first few years in London, his father had sent him a small monthly allowance of about ten dollars, but this had ended in 1911.[18] Pound had tried to supplement this income by writing articles for various small magazines and by lecturing on Romance and Medieval literature at the Regent Street Polytechnic during the winters of 1909 and 1910. It was while lecturing at the Institute that he fell in love with one of his students, Dorothy Shakespear, whom he eventually married in 1914. Although Dorothy brought to the marriage a small annuity of one hundred and fifty pounds, the newly wed couple were chronically poor. Even as Pound's list of publications grew, all they could afford was a small, poorly lighted two-room apartment in Kensington.

Despite his continuing financial difficulties, Pound still believed that he and other American artists could hope to support themselves best by living abroad. In 1939, he explained his absence of nearly thirty years from the United States: "You know damn well the country wouldn't feed me. The simple economic fact that if I had returned to America I shd. have starved, and that to maintain anything like the standard of living, or indeed to live, in America from 1918 onwards, I shd. have had to quadruple my earnings . . . it would have been impossible for me to devote any real time to my real work."[19] Pound firmly believed that if a cultural renaissance were to begin in America, the government must recognize the economic needs of artists. As he insisted in *Patria Mia*: "if America has any desire to be a center of artistic activity she must learn her one lesson from the Ptolemies. Art was lifted into Alexandria by subsidy, and by no other means will it be established in the United States."[20]

Even before World War I, Pound's thinking began to shift as he observed that the impoverished condition of the artist was far more universal than he had imagined. There were, in fact, numerous fellow artists (many of whom were friends) whose creativity was being thwarted by the difficult task of earning a living in an unappreciative world. There was James Joyce, unknown and practically starving in Trieste—and it was Pound who helped him obtain a subsidy from the Royal Literary Society, and who out of his own pocket anonymously gave the struggling genius twenty-five pounds. A few years later it was T. S. Eliot whom Pound rescued from a burdensome job in an English bank. Besides pledging ten pounds a year to speed Eliot's release from banking, Pound and several friends sent out a circular (which actually embarrassed Eliot more than it helped him) that they hoped would encourage other patrons to pledge themselves to support the then unknown poet.[21] Besides Joyce and Eliot there were many others whom Pound helped. As the translator and art critic John Cournos recalled, even though Pound was never totally free from financial worries, "he would raise heaven and earth to help any fellow artist in need."[22] While Pound unselfishly assisted fellow artists, he still maintained an elitist viewpoint. In a letter to Williams in the early 1920s, he warned that only a few individuals were concerned about the needs of artists because only a few saw the need for great art. "Only those of us who know what civilization is, only those of us who want better literature, not more literature, better art, not more art, can be expected to pay for it. No use waiting for masses to develop a finer taste, they aren't moving in that way."[23] Concerned about the overall state of the arts and angered by his poverty as well as that of friends and fellow artists, Pound's economic discontent continued to fester. Many years later, as Dorothy Pound recalled the financial hardships that she and her husband suffered, she reminded a young American poet: "If you only make 40 pounds a year, it impresses itself upon you that it's not enough, and you begin to wonder why?"[24]

Precisely when Pound's "wondering why" began to take a more systematic turn is difficult to pinpoint. It may have been in 1912—the year he started contributing literary and musical criticism to A. R. Orage's *The New Age*. While working on the magazine, Pound met such radical economic theorists as A. J. Penty, S. G. Hobson, and G. D. H. Cole, and their ideas may have influenced his own.[25] Another influence on Pound's thinking was Orage himself, who editorialized from the viewpoint of a guild socialist. It was Orage's view that self-governing associations or guilds made up of all the workers of an industry should eventually replace the traditional capitalistic managerial system. He introduced Pound to the guild ideal—an ideal which the poet, perhaps, later believed was put into practice by Mussolini's corporate state.[26]

Notwithstanding the influence of Orage and other theorists who clustered around *The New Age*, it was the horrors of World War I which intensified Pound's economic thinking more than anything else. After an initial burst of enthusiasm for the war and an unsuccessful attempt to enlist, Pound gradually came to view the conflict with a growing sense of contempt.[27] Whether writing in Yeats's cottage in Sussex or in his little Kensington apartment, he tried as best he could to remain aloof. But as the war's destructive tide rose to unimaginable heights his indifference became harder to sustain. In particular, the deaths of friends such as the poet T. E. Hulme, and the 24-year-old sculptor Henri Gaudier-Brzeska forced Pound to recognize the horror of the war.[28] When it was over he expressed his feelings in *Hugh Selwyn Mauberly*—one of the earliest condemnations of the conflict and the tawdry civilization that followed in its wake. Like the revisionist historians, Pound also began to question why war had occurred in the first place. Who or what was to blame? How could another catastrophe be prevented? Many years later, after a second great war had again shattered Western civilization, Pound was interviewed for the *Writers at Work* series about his views in World War I:

> *Interviewer:* I know you consider monetary reform the key to good government. I wonder by what process you moved from aesthetic problems towards governmental ones. Did the great war which slaughtered so many of your friends, do the moving?
>
> *Pound:* The great war came as a surprise, and certainly to see the Anglish—these people who have never done any-

> thing—get hold of themselves, fight it, was immensely
> impressive. But as soon as it was over they went dead,
> and then one spent the next twenty years trying to pre-
> vent the Second War. I can't say exactly where my
> study of government started. I think *The New Age*
> office helped me to see the war not as a separate event
> but a part of a system, one war after another.[29]

Ironically, in fleeing what he viewed as the botched civilization of his own country, Pound escaped into the horrors of war-torn Europe; by the end of the conflict he was more convinced than ever that something was devastatingly wrong with the overall structure of western civilization.

Still troubled by financial matters, and haunted by the causes of the war, by 1920 Pound was studying economics almost to the point of obsession. With the scholarly range of an Albertus Magnus and the intensity of a Marx, he examined the monetary systems of Britain, France, the United States and many other countries. The more widely he read the more certain he became that the impoverished condition of the arts and the artist, and the most basic causes of war were all parts of essentially the same question. The problem, as he understood it, centered on the basic question of who controlled the distribution of money in the world states. As Pound believed that he was unraveling the most serious economic question facing modern civilization, he became more personally dedicated to finding possible solutions. In searching for answers, he moved into the ranks of the Social Credit Movement and then into direct involvement in fascist Italy.

Even before World War I, Pound began to differentiate in his writing between those who created money through the actual production of goods and those who created it through manipulation of goods produced by others. Like artists, the first were creators who were valuable to society, while the latter were parasitic or, as Pound characterized them, usurers—manipulators of money or goods at someone else's expense. As early as 1912 he compared the producer and the nonproducing manipulator in terms similar to those of Thorstein

Veblen, although there is no evidence that Pound had read any of the works of the great debunker:[30]

> The type of man who built railways, cleared the forest, planned irrigation, is different from the type of man who can hold on to the profits of subsequent industry. Whereas the first man was a man of dreams, in a time when dreams paid, a man of adventure, careless— this latter is a close person, acquisitive, rapacious, tenacious. The first man had personality, and was, "God damn you" himself. . . . The present type is primarily a mask, his idea is the nickel-plated cash register, and toward the virtues thereof he doth continual strive and tend.[31]

As Pound's economic interests expanded during the interwar period, so too did his denunciation of all kinds of financial manipulation. The usurer was not only the creator of wars and depressions, but also the unmistakable *bête noire* of artists, or for that matter, of anyone else who tried to earn an honest living through honest labor. Indeed, the very course of history itself, as Pound understood it, was simply a "continuous struggle between producers and nonproducers, and those who try to make a living by inserting a false system of bookkeeping between the producers and their just recompense."[32]

In 1918, while he was still deciphering the world's economic ills, Pound was introduced by Orage to Major C. H. Douglas, the Scottish engineer who founded the Social Credit Movement. Douglas argued that wages or purchasing power would always amount to less than production costs—the final price charged for the finished product or manufactured good on the open market.[33] This gap between the price of goods and money available to purchase them would continue to grow even wider until the entire distributive process became so unbalanced that a depression, or at least economic stagnation, would result. In spite of these criticisms, however, Douglas did not call for an end to capitalism. He argued, in fact, that profit was a legitimate part of production costs even though it was responsible for widening the gap between price and purchasing power. Instead of advocating an end to capitalism, Douglas suggested that the way out of this economic morass was to have government subsidize profit. That is, the government should simply make up the difference between the selling price and the available purchasing power. This could be accomplished by circulating more money or by paying a subsidy to manufacturers who did not include profits in their production costs. If either of these two remedies were applied, Douglas claimed that the difference between selling price and purchasing power would disappear and there would be no further problems in the distributive processes.[34]

Soon after meeting Douglas, Pound became a convert to the Social Credit theory, and in the spring of 1920 he enthusiastically reviewed Douglas's *Economic Democracy* for the *Little Review*. Although he continued to rain abuse on the usurers, Pound had a more optimistic economic outlook after his conversion to Social Credit. For him everything had come into focus. As he later explained in *The ABC of Economics*: "Probably the only economic problem needing emergency solution in our time is the problem of distribution. There are enough goods, there is superabundance, why should anyone starve?"[35] Since monetary distribution was at the heart of most economic problems, it was clearly the duty of the state to guarantee that money circulated properly. This could be done, Pound argued, by governments seeing to it that "there is enough money in the hands of the whole people, and in adequately rapid EXCHANGE to effect distribution of all wealth produced and produceable."[36]

Apart from the question of distribution, Pound saw but one other major obstacle to maintaining a well-adjusted economy, and that, he emphasized, was the constant fluctuation in the value of money. Influenced not only by his reading of Douglas, but also by Alexander del Mar's *History of Monetary Policy* and, somewhat later, by Brooks Adams's *The Law of Civilization and Decay*, Pound believed that the fluctuating value of money was, like manipulated production costs, the direct result of financial juggling on the part of the ever-present usurer.[37] Since private bankers and financiers controlled a vast proportion of most countries' financial resources, they were obviously in the best position to manipulate and thus determine the value of money the world over. Needless to say, these speculating interests were far more concerned with personal gain than with public gain, and herein lay Pound's greatest objection. Why should private interests control something as vital to the public good as the value of money? While agreeing that banks could make loans and charge interest on their legitimate deposits, Pound, like Douglas, vehemently denied that they should have the right to create credit by making loans over and above their deposited resources.[38] Writing like a twentieth-century Jacksonian, Pound mistrusted broad, financial power in the hands of banks, for he believed that without exception "the credit of the nation belongs to the nation, and there is not the slightest reason why the nation should have to pay rent for its own credit. There is nothing to force it to hire credit from private interests."[39] Pound also argued that the state was obligated to maintain control over the country's enterprises and thereby over the value of money. If this were done, and if public credit were made more readily available, then, as he outlined in *The ABC of Economics,* all would be in proper perspective, for the state would be "conceived as the public convenience. Money conceived as a public convenience. Neither as a private bonanza."[40]

Just as Pound's absorption in economic matters increased during the 1920s, so too did his economic needs; by the end of the decade he was helping support two families. In 1922 he had met the concert violinist Olga Rudge, who bore his daughter Mary, in 1925. Arrangements were made for Mary to live for most of the year with a peasant family in the village of Gais in the Italian Tirol, with Pound contributing to her upkeep. Adding to the domestic complexity, the next year Dorothy Pound bore a son, Omar Shakespear, who was left in the care of his maternal grandmother in England. Pound lived with Dorothy most of the time, but when she visited their son in England, he would join Olga and Mary, usually in Venice or Gais.[41]

When the Depression began, Pound's interest in economics deepened. At first he was annoyed and then angered that the general public did not seem to share his concerns. Since he viewed the abuses perpetrated by the usurers and bankers as obvious, and the remedies to these abuses equally clear, he simply failed to understand why the masses and their representatives did not remove their blinders. Pound, a poet, had made the transition from literature to economics. Why could not others? "Contemporary economics goes over my desk NOW, just as the Joyce, Lewis, Eliot, etc/ went over it in 1917 and nobody will do any real work who refuses to look at it," he wrote to a friend in the mid 1930s.[42] Completely confident in his intellectual abilities, it seemed so logical to Pound that if he had been correct earlier in calling attention to neglected literary geniuses, he was equally correct in now calling attention to valid economic theories. Already viewing himself as an expert in the area of economic theory, he wrote in the pamphlet *Social Credit* (1935): "economics are like Euclid or like physics in that if you don't understand a few simple principles you will fall into error after error, but if you have a very few simple perceptions you can construct soundly without any very great learning."[43] Pound had no doubt whatsoever that he had grasped these few "simple perceptions," and just as he had earlier thought it his mission to lay the groundwork for the forthcoming American Renaissance, he now applied himself to awakening the United States, if not the entire world, to what he considered to be the critical economic questions of the day. Clearly, the task he had set for himself was large, but so too was his confidence in his intellectual abilities. Like Nietzsche's madman, he raged through the world's market places shouting his warning, offering nostrums, and finding his cries falling on deaf ears. Yet the more he was ignored the more certain he became that the masses were incapable of acting themselves and that in the end someone would have to act for them. In the 1920s, he believed that someone to be Benito Mussolini. The Duce was a man who got things done, and from Pound's specialized reading of history it was just this kind of person who time and again had led the attack against the age-old problem of usury.[44]

Like the ecclesiastical historians, Pound used history rather than studied it. He assessed the relative worth of individuals, institutions, and governments according to their attitude toward money and their stand against usury.[45] While finding the Middle Ages a particularly attractive period because of the insistence of the Church on a just price, he likewise concluded from his reading of American history that the young Republic combatted financial privilege and the would-be manipulators of the national money supply.[46] Believing that pre-Civil War America was an age of economic heroism, he included in his lexicon of monetary saints such statesmen as John Adams, Thomas Jefferson, John Quincy Adams, Andrew Jackson, Martin Van Buren, Thomas Hart Benton, and Abraham Lincoln. Pound insisted that all had fought against individuals and groups who tried to monopolize the Republic's financial system. But this effort to protect the American economy from monopoly was cut short by the Civil War. From that time on, various individuals and groups tried to impose monopolies, control the country's transportation systems, and to water stocks of numerous industrial enterprises.[47] The trend continued into the twentieth century. Pound claimed that none of the Presidents—Woodrow Wilson, especially—had paid enough attention to the question of money and its distribution. Neither had the public which seemed easy to fool: "Half mankind from myopia don't see, and when there is a gang of scoundrels, managing demos they learn to erect false dilemmas, camouflage, smoke-screens, political issues 'made' simple to divert the electorate and keep them from discovering the real issues."[48]

The New Deal seemed yet another political "smoke-screen," for Pound believed that the Roosevelt Administration was as ignorant of monetary policy as its predecessors.[49] Thus his attraction for fascist Italy is explained, for it was there, as Pound saw it, that the government was confronting the crucial economic issues.[50] Although there is no evidence that Mussolini built a unique Italian credit system, Pound's acceptance of the Duce's pronouncements was always somewhat like Kierkegaard's acceptance of God—a gigantic leap of blind faith: "Any thorough judgment of Mussolini will be in a measure an act of faith, it will depend on what you believe the man means, what you believe that he wants to accomplish."[51] In response to a speech given by the Italian leader, Pound observed: "On Oct. 6th of the year current (anno XII) . . . Mussolini speaking very clearly four or five words at a time . . . told 40 million Italians together with auditors in the U.S.A. and the Argentine that the problem of production was solved, and that they could turn their minds to distribution."[52] Perhaps recalling the putative harmony of the medieval guild system,

Pound was also impressed by Mussolini's efforts to enforce cooperation of employer and laborer through the creation of a corporate state.
No longer was there to be class strife or costly labor disputes, but
instead a new kind of enforced cooperation in which "A thousand
candles together blaze with intense brightness. No one candle's light
damages another's. So is the liberty of the individual in the ideal and
fascist state."[53]

By the early 1930s Pound's historicism and faith in Mussolini led
him to believe that the Duce was carrying on the same kind of fight
against usury and special privilege that was conducted years earlier in
the United States by Thomas Jefferson. There were more similarities
than differences between the two leaders, Pound argued in a pamphlet
written in 1933, *Jefferson and/or Mussolini*. Each man, he stressed,
showed an interest in agriculture, each, in his own way, possessed an
artist's temperament, and each initiated a new order in which privilege
and usury were checked. "The heritage of Jefferson, Quincy Adams,
old John Adams, Jackson, Van Buren is Here," Pound proclaimed,
"now *in the Italian peninsula* at the beginning of fascist decennio, not
in Massachusetts or Delaware."[54] While Pound observed the heritage
of the young Republic flourishing in Mussolini's Italy, he did not
believe that the fascist ideology could simply be transplanted to America: "This is not to say I 'advocate' fascism in and for America," he
wrote in *Jefferson and/or Mussolini*, "or that I think fascism is possible in America without Mussolini, any more than I or any enlight-
ened bolshevik thinks communism is possible in America without
Lenin." What was needed in the United States, therefore, was not so
much an ideology, but the same kind of dynamic leadership provided
by the Duce. As Pound concluded: "I think the American system *de
jure* is probably good enough, if there were only 500 men with guts
and sense to *use* it, or even with the capacity for answering letters or
printing a paper."[55]

Seeing himself as one of the stout-hearted five hundred, Pound
throughout the 1930s bombarded an immense variety of people with
letters in the hope of converting them to his economic views. Besides
fellow artists and friends, he wrote to heads of state (Roosevelt twice

in 1934), to representatives of Congress and members of the House of Commons, to ambassadors and cabinet officials like Henry A. Wallace, to professors and members of various monetary societies. He wrote to anyone who he thought might be in a position to help initiate monetary reforms or who could possibly assist in easing the growing tensions between Italy and the Western democracies.[56] The only head of state to respond to Pound was Mussolini, who granted the American poet an interview. The meeting was probably arranged because Pound was working at the time on a film scenario portraying the history of fascism.[57] Although the film was never completed, the meeting between Pound and the Italian dictator took place on January 30, 1935. In the course of their extremely short conversation, Mussolini apparently paid little or no attention to Pound's political and economic suggestions. When Pound read aloud several lines from *A Draft of XXX Cantos,* which he had given the dictator as a present, the Duce said that he found them to be *divertente* (entertaining). As Noel Stock has suggested, Pound took the Duce's statement as serious literary criticism, believing that he had understood in the *Cantos* what was still eluding many critics.[58] Despite the insignificance of this brief meeting, the very fact that it had occurred fed Pound's ravenous ego, especially in view of his failure to meet with other world leaders. As he so often did in his various intellectual pursuits, Pound undoubtedly read into the meeting exactly what he wanted to; there is some justification in the American novelist Phyllis Bottome's observation that Pound probably "accepted Fascism, largely I believe because he mistakenly but honestly thought that Mussolini agreed with him."[59]

Pound's attraction for Mussolini and fascist Italy sharpened his concern in the 1930s with the growing tensions between the Axis and Democratic powers. Still hoping to convince Americans of their political and economic needs, he ended his twenty-seven-year exile and returned to his native country in the spring of 1939. Although one of his major biographers believes that he did not anticipate the approaching conflict and had visited the United States to preach Social Credit, Pound later claimed that he had returned home to try and prevent war.[60] According to his daughter Mary he seemed driven by this objective and believed that he could justify Italy's position if American officials would only listen to him.[61] Failing to obtain a hearing with President Roosevelt, Pound did meet with other important leaders of government, including Senators Bankhead, Vandenberg, Borah, Byrd, and Taft, Congressmen Voorhis, Fish, Tinkman, and Dies, and Secretary of Agriculture Henry A. Wallace.[62] He also received an honorary degree at Hamilton College, published several of his books, and renewed a number of old friendships. In late June he returned to Italy, to the seaside resort town of Rapallo where he and Dorothy had been living since 1924. Pound was more bitter than ever. As he reviewed his visit to America, it seemed that not a single one of his ideas had taken hold.

Undaunted by the apparent failure of his American visit, Pound continued his voluminous correspondence, more convinced than ever that usurious economic practices and weak political leadership were carrying the United States to ruin. But a new shrillness permeated his correspondence. For example, in a letter to Congressman Voorhis, written soon after the invasion of Poland, he unabashedly praised Hitler: "You needn't take my word for it yet, but keep your minds open to the possibility that in another 20 years men may think Hitler a better friend of the plain man, and especially of the men who grow or would like to grow crops in England, than any government England has had in our times."[63] Later in October he again wrote to Voorhis, this time locating the blame for the war. "As far as I can make out, about 90% of right and justice are on the German side in the present shindy. AND it is impossible for anyone in America to judge Europe if they insist on neglecting the jewish problem. Only the jews want war. Only Russia and the jews stand to gain by European war and Russia has already had her slice."[64] As his support for Germany became widely known, Pound found himself increasingly cut off from old friends in England and the United States. A number of journals in which he had published for years refused his articles and he was forced to send most of his material to Italian and Japanese periodicals and newspapers.[65] Feeling increasingly isolated, Pound allowed an occasional note of despair to creep into his correspondence. In the spring of 1940 he wrote to E. E. Cummings: "Pitty my talentz is gittin so lorst to my native tongue. But still, I suppose the furriners profit."[66] A month later, however, his outlook seemed to change. In a letter to publisher James Angleton, Pound declared that he had not been "starved to the wall yet," and jauntily predicted that a new Europe was in the making. "All midwives to hand and ready. Greatest show since Napoleon and a number of Nap's errors listed as 'to be avoided.' "[67] From Pound's perspective it would be a Europe in which the lines were clearly drawn between those countries which opposed usury like Germany and Italy and those which sanctioned it and whose governments were "run by figureheads working for money lenders."[68] By early June, with the fall of France all but complete, it seemed critical that the United States continue its neutrality, and that the American public not be led into reckless decisions by its leaders. "As Roosevelt, Morgenthau and Bullitt are responsible for the war/along with shits like Churchill, Eden, Reynaud and other pimps it wd/be a crime to let the U.S. endorse their stinking politics/."[69] Convinced as he was that Germany and Italy were on the correct economic course, and believing it his mission to keep the United States neutral, it is not at all surprising that Pound began his broadcasts. The radio was but another means of communicating his views when they were most ignored, but also most needed. Broadcasts, he proclaimed on April 19, 1942, were necessary at a time "when the postal service with the Western Hemisphere is somewhat reduced. Result, so far as my private life is concerned, is that not bein' able to continue private correspondence by letter with the more lively American youth, gentry and professoriate, I had to stir round and git onto the air, only line [left] me."[70]

At a future time when Pound was suffering the consequences of the broadcasts, he told a friend that he had tried to express his views on the air for some two years before finally succeeding.[71] What had been impossible in peacetime became feasible once Italy entered the war, although it was not until late 1940 that Pound began his new activity. At first he wrote speeches that were read in English by other broadcasters over the Italian radio. In January 1941 he began reading his own material.[72] For the next year he made two and sometimes three broadcasts a week over the *Ente Italiano Audizione Radio-foniche*—the government broadcasting agency. Since the United States was still a neutral nation, these broadcasts were not monitored until October 2, 1941, and even then the monitoring was intermittent.[73]

The radio talks took a scatter-gun approach in the variety of topics covered. Pound praised the accomplishments of fascism, urged the United States to remain neutral; discussed economics and literature, blamed the conflict on the British, and frequently vilified Churchill, Roosevelt, Stalin, and Jews.[74] Recognizing that the talks had some propaganda value, the Italian Ministry of Popular Culture paid Pound about 750 lire per broadcast, but, as the poet later testified, this was a very small sum, hardly enough to cover hotel expenses and the cost of traveling between Rapallo and Rome.[75] Another American, Giorgio Nelson Page, the son of onetime American Ambassador to Italy, Thomas Nelson Page, was head of the Ministry for Popular Culture and in charge of all foreign broadcasts. Unlike Pound, however, Page had become an Italian citizen in 1935, and thereby escaped treason charges.[76]

On December 7, 1941, 6:24 p.m. Rome time (12:24 Eastern Standard time) Pound was on the air. After an introductory announcement of a talk by Ezra Pound entitled, "Those Parentheses," Pound began to speak using a folksy Midwestern drawl:

> Europe callin', Pound speakin'. And I think I am perhaps still speakin' a bit more TO England than to the United States of America but you folks may as well hear it. They say an Englishman's head's made of wood, and the American head made of watermelon. Easier to git something INTO the American head, but nigh impossible to make it stick there for ten minutes.

After reminding his audience that much of what he would be saying had already been said in the *Cantos*, Pound added:

> What I am gitting at is, a friend said to me the other day that he was glad I had the politics I have got, but that HE didn't understand how I, as a North American, United Stateser could have it.
> Well that looks simple to me. Things OFTEN DO look simple to

me. On the CONfucian system that if you start right, and then go on, start at the root and move upward, the pattern often is simple, whereas if you start constructin' from the twig downward, you get into a muddle.

Warming to his subject he proceeded in staccato harangues to denounce Jews, the Treaty of Versailles, and the merchants of war before adding:

> God knows I have loathed Woodie Wilson, and I don't want to see more evil done to humanity than was done by Woodrow codface. And the sooner all America and ALL England wake up to what the Warburgs and Roosevelt are up to, the better for the next generation and this one.
>
> . . .
>
> And in any case I do NOT want my compatriots from the ages of 20 to 40 to go git slaughtered to keep up the Sassoon and other British Jew rackets in Singapore and in Shanghai. That is not my idea of American patriotism.

Concluding, he waltzed over a number of other topics before finally settling on the ubiquitous question of money:

> Lord knows I don't SEE how America can have fascism without years of previous trainin'. Looks to me, even now as if the currency problem was the place to start savin' America. As I have been sayin' for some time back, call it ten years or call it twenty.

With the conclusion of the December 7 talk, Pound's broadcasting activities came to a temporary halt, and relatively little is known about his activities for the next few weeks. At some point during this period he apparently tried to return to the United States by attempting to board the last diplomatic train leaving Rome. Precisely what happened remains unclear. Possibly because of an argument with a consular official over Pound's political activities he was either refused permission to board, or because of the official's accusations he became angry and voluntarily decided not to.[77] Other reasons also possibly changed Pound's decision to leave. His parents, who had been living in Rapallo for some years were old and not well. At the same time, Italy was home to Pound, and as an admirer of Mussolini, he probably had political as well as personal reasons for staying. In any case, Pound not only remained in Italy, but also began broadcasting again on January 29, 1942. Immediately his activism took on a new dimension because now the United States was at war.

Over the next year and a half (January 29, 1942 to July 25, 1943) Pound made one hundred and twenty-five broadcasts, all of them monitored by the United States Federal Communications Commission. For reasons that remain unknown, he made no broadcasts between the end of July 1942 and February 1943. Most of the broadcasts were directed toward the United States although several were intended exclusively for Great Britain. All of the broadcasts were prerecorded, and Pound usually taped between ten and twenty per session while in Rome.[78] Each broadcast customarily began with Vivaldi recordings followed by an announcer who introduced Pound. Beginning with the new broadcasts on January 29, 1942, the announcer also read the following statement which had been composed by Pound:

> Rome Radio, acting in accordance with the fascist policy of intellectual freedom and free expression of opinion by those who are qualified to hold it, has offered Dr. Ezra Pound the use of the microphone twice a week. It is understood that he will not be asked to say anything whatsoever that goes against his conscience, or anything incompatible with his duties as a citizen of the United States of America.

Pound began the broadcast on January 29, 1942, by explaining his eight-week absence:

> On Arbour Day, Pearl Arbour Day, at 12 o'clock noon I retired from the capital of the old Roman Empire to Rapallo to seek wisdom from the ancients.
>
>   . . .
>
>   I spent a month trying to figure things out, well did I, perhaps I concluded sooner. At any rate I had a month clear to make up my mind about some things. I had Confucius and Mencius, both of whom had taken up against similar problems. Both of whom had seen empires fallin'. Both of whom had seen deeper into the causes of human confusion than most men even think of lookin'.

What ever else Pound's study of the ancients had taught him, he was certain that it was his duty to convince his fellow countrymen that they were misinformed. Even more important, there was a danger that the United States would become as isolated during this war as Britain had become during the wars of Napoleon:

> I began figurin' out that a COMPLETE severance of communication between the calm and sentient men is not to be desired.
>
> I have before now pointed out that England was CUT off from the current of European thought during and BY the Napoleonic Wars, and that she never got ketched up again, not during all the damned nasty and 19th century. Always laggin' behind.
>
> At any rate it is NO GOOD.
>
> The United States has been MISinformed. The United States has been led down the garden path, and may be down under the daises. ALL thru shuttin' out news.
>
> . . .
>
> I think the United States and even her British Allies might do well to keep more in touch with continental opinion.

By returning to the air Pound defined America's dilemma and his own mission.

With each new broadcast Pound warned, scolded, and pleaded with his audience. Testing the intellect if not the patience of the listeners, the broadcasts, like Pound's poetry, ranged widely over the language, literature, and history of world civilizations. Pound's unwillingness or perhaps his inability to stay with a single train of thought added even more confusion to the talks, and, at times, they appear to be the random impressions of a highly intellectualized but disjointed stream of consciousness. Those closest to Pound were troubled by his behavior; his daughter Mary recalled noticing drastic changes taking place in her father: "He was losing ground, I now see, losing grip on what most specifically he should have been able to control, his own *words*. . . . And perhaps he sensed it and the more strongly clung to the utterances of Confucius, because his own tongue was tricking him, running away with him leading him into excess, away from his pivot, into blind spots." She was puzzled by the brutal hostility which underlay so many of his talks. "I know no other explanation for some of his violent expressions—perhaps he felt the exasperation at not being able to get his real meaning across. The long hostility of his country must have weighed heavily upon him but he remained free from self-pity."[79] During the broadcasts Pound added little if anything new to what he had been saying over the past two decades, but as time passed his anger seemed to build and his denunciations became more abrasive. He vilified Roosevelt, claiming that the President, along with Morgenthau, Baruch, Churchill, and Stalin, was most responsible for the continuation of the war. As for the fascist leaders, Pound had nothing but praise. In a broadcast on May 28, 1942, he declared:

> Something has OCCURRED in old Europe. Even the cloistered apes of Oxford or the inventors of stink gas in Harvard ought by now to have heard that, at least that, something has happened IN EUROPE, and you do not know what has happened.
>
> You do not know what has HAPPENED. And the first thing to DO about it is to pull OUT of this war—a war that you never ought to have flopped into. Every hour that you go on with it is an hour lost to you and your children.
>
> And every sane act you commit is committed in HOMAGE to Mussolini and Hitler. Every reform, every lurch toward the just price, toward the control of the market is an act of HOMAGE to Mussolini and Hitler.
>
> They are your leaders, however much you are conducted by Roosevelt or sold up by Churchill. You FOLLOW Hitler and Mussolini in EVERY CONSTRUCTIVE act of your governments.

As the war continued Pound became increasingly irritated by ties between the United States, Britain, and the Soviet Union. Claiming the alliance to be against American self-interest, he asked his countrymen to re-examine their beliefs. In a broadcast aired on March 2, 1942, he asked:

> DO you believe in the homestead or in communal ownership? If you believe in the Homestead, WHY fight FOR the abolition of ALL private ownership?

In taking sides in a quarrel do at least try to find out what's fighting WHICH.

Three months later, June 19, 1942, he repeated his warning:

England and the United States OUGHT to be on the Axis side
AGAINST the Red terror. And every Englishman and American
knows that.

A little less than a year later, after failing to bring about a shift in the
wartime alliances, Pound took a slightly different approach. He now
began to speculate about the dangers of a powerful, unchecked Russia
set loose in the postwar world. In a broadcast made on April 20,
1943, he chided his fellow Americans:

The supreme betrayal of Europe is inherent in the alliance of
Anglo-Jewry with Moscow. Debts rise. That is one part of the war.
It is a contest between STOPPING the war and going on with
it. And only one side does any fighting. Namely the party that
STARTED the war. They are for its continuance. Who are they?
BUT they are also for starting the next one. They openly proclaim that AFTER (that is IF) America finishes with Japan, she will
have to fight Russia. IF Russia should break into Europe.
Only blindness and deafness can keep you unaware of these proclamations. The U.S. must protect the world? Why? Does the world
want it? The U.S., once this war is over, must be strong enough to
beat Russia.

One of the most distressing aspects of Pound's broadcasts was his
ever-increasing anti-Semitism. For years he had depicted Jews as
usurers; the House of Rothschild was one of his devils and was most
thoroughly maligned. But Pound's scurrility reached new depths in the
broadcasts, and seemed to grow more malevolent as the war went on.[80]
On April 9, 1942, he proclaimed:

The danger to the United States as a system of government is
NOT from Japan, but from Jewry, and whether that invasion has
been absolutely SUCCESSFUL, having been gradual since 1863,
but accelerated since Taft was eased out of the White House.

By March 21, 1943, he was proclaiming a worldwide Jewish threat:

> The Jews have ruin'd every country they have got hold of. The Jews
> have worked out a system, very neat system, for the ruin of the rest
> of mankind, one nation after another. Now many Americans are igno-
> rant of this fact, and *The Economist* does its periodical bit to main-
> tain that ignorance; but YOU like the ignorance. I do not think the
> normal American likes his ignorance. That may produce a funda-
> mental dichotomy.

Though most of the time Pound sounded like an ill-tempered, befud-
dled old man who repeatedly used the word *Jew* as an epithet of
abuse, his language, as his daughter suggested, could indeed run away
with him as happened in a broadcast on April 30, 1942:

> Don't start a pogrom. That is, not an old style killing of small
> Jews. That system is no good whatsoever. Of course if some man had
> a stroke of genius and could start a pogrom UP AT THE top, there
> might be something to say for it.
>
> But on the whole legal measures are preferable. The sixty Kikes
> who started this war might be sent to St. Helena as a measure of
> world prophylaxis. And some hyper-kike, or non-Jewish kikes along
> with 'em. I shall be content if I contribute my buffalo nickel to arouse
> a little sane CURIOSITY, a little healthy inquiry as to what causes
> the whichness.

The great tragedy of Ezra Pound is that the same man who wrote the
Cantos could engage in such deplorable nonsense. Yet the broadcasts
continued and so too did Pound's invective.

There is no way of measuring how many Americans heard Pound's
broadcasts. Those who did, however, generally agreed that Pound's
talks were ineffective as propaganda and not much better as enter-
tainment. As early as March 1941, *Newsweek* reported that Pound
could be heard twice weekly on Radio Rome's nightly, "American
Hour of Music and Cultural Talks." No reference was made to the size
of his American audience.[81] Two years later the New York *Times*
dismissed one of his broadcasts as part of the same "old rigmarole
with which he had bored the international air a hundred times."[82]

Writing in *Poetry*, Eunice Tietjens claimed that the broadcasts made Pound sound "like a disgruntled squirrel," while fellow writer Malcolm Cowley suggested that Pound "may have wished to be a dangerous traitor, but he was too incoherent to succeed."[83] Critic Paul Rosenfeld added, after enduring several minutes of Pound's incoherent ramblings that he felt as though he were being spoken to in the cryptic language of Joyce's *Finnegans Wake*.[84] It was not Americans alone who were puzzled by the talks. Supposedly, at first, even the Italian Government was perplexed by the bizarre rhetoric of the American poet and wondered if he might not be sending coded messages to the Allies.[85] Many of Pound's friends were frankly embarrassed by the broadcasts. William Carlos Williams, who had never heard a single one, was questioned by an FBI agent because Pound had used his name during one of his rambling discourses.[86]

Despite the ineffectiveness of the broadcasts, Pound was indicted for treason on July 26, 1943. When he learned of the indictment, Pound immediately registered a written protest with the Swiss legation, which was in charge of the American Embassy in Rome. Several days later he also wrote to Attorney General Francis Biddle, arguing his innocence: "I do not believe that the simple fact of speaking over the radio, wherever placed, can in itself constitute treason. I think this must depend on what is said, and on the motives for speaking." His motives, he added, were not intended to be treasonous:

> I have not spoken with regard to *this* war, but in protest against a system which creates one war after an other, in series and in system. I have not spoken to the troops, and have not suggested that the troops should mutiny or revolt. The whole basis of democratic or majority government assumes that the citizen should be informed of the facts which are an essential part of the total that should be known to the people.

In concluding he showed the same sense of mission that was apparent in his writing during the interwar period:

> At any rate a man's duties increase with his knowledge. A war between the U.S. and Italy is monstrous and should not have occurred.

And a peace without justice is no peace but merely a prelude to future wars. Someone must take count of these things. And having
taken count must act on his knowledge; and his judgement subject
to error.[87]

In matters of poetry, economics, and finally in matters of war, Pound
always assumed that his knowledge was superior to that of almost
everyone else. By acting on this knowledge he became involved in
Italy, but, as he tried to convince the Attorney General, his involvement there was to aid the United States by showing Americans,
through the broadcasts, where their real interests lay.

On July 25, the day before Pound was indicted, Mussolini and his
cabinet were forced to resign in favor of a provisional government
headed by Marshall Pietro Badoglio. The transfer of power caused
Pound and thousands of others to flee Rome. In a state of semi-shock,
Pound eventually made his way to Gais and his daughter Mary. There
he stayed, restless but exhausted, until mid-September, when he
learned of Mussolini's spectacular liberation by German paratroopers.
Excited by this turn of events, Pound decided to return to Rapallo to
offer his services to the reinstated dictator. In Rapallo he enthusiastically supported the Salo Republic, the German puppet state created in
northern Italy. According to one of his most recent biographers,
Pound, on at least one occasion in late 1943, began speaking over a
German supervised radio station in Milan, and wrote scripts for the
station over the next eighteen months.[88] There is no evidence, however, that any of these broadcasts were heard in the United States.[89]
In the spring of 1944, when the Germans began to fortify the water-
front at Rapallo, the Pounds were forced to leave their apartment.
They then went to live with Olga Rudge in the hills above the city. It
was here that Pound was found by Italian partisans on April 29, 1945.
With only enough time to grab a copy of Confucius and a Chinese
dictionary, he was handcuffed and driven away to be turned over to
the American army.

Pound's descent into Purgatory thus began. After imprisoning him
for several weeks in Genoa, the United States government sent him in
late May 1945 to the Army Disciplinary Training Center outside of

Pisa. Here the army's most dangerous criminals were incarcerated. Pound, the only civilian prisoner, was kept in solitary confinement in an outdoor wire cage. After weeks of such treatment, he suffered a physical and mental breakdown. He was removed from the cage to a tent and given medical treatment, and finally on October 3, saw his wife for the first time. A little over a month later he was flown to Washington, D.C., to stand trial for treason.

Before the trial, four psychiatrists examined Pound and declared him insane.[90] On February 13, 1945, the jury at a sanity hearing accepted the testimony of the psychiatrists, determining that Pound, being unsound of mind, was unfit to stand trial. The court then committed him to Saint Elizabeth's Hospital for the Insane, in Washington, D.C., where he remained for the next twelve years. Finally, on April 18, 1958, the government formally dropped all charges on the grounds that he would never be mentally competent to stand trial and that his release into the custody of his wife would not endanger the safety of others. Seventy-three years old at the time of his discharge, Pound immediately returned to Italy with his wife. There, as one friend wrote, he continued to "sing and scold by the Latin Sea."[91] He died on November 1, 1972, only two days after his eighty-seventh birthday.

While Pound eventually regained his freedom, the question of his sanity lingers. Was he truly insane or was insanity used by the government to avoid a death penalty? Should the testimony of the four psychiatrists be judged in strict medical terms or must other motives be considered in their conclusions? Was Pound's supposed insanity a result of the Pisan experience, or was he mentally unstable during the 1920s and 1930s? These questions, of course, can probably never be answered.[92] But whatever Pound's mental state was, there is an obvious continuity in his life, thought, and activities abroad which cannot be dismissed by reason of eccentricity or mental illness.

Throughout his life Ezra Pound believed that to be a writer in the fullest sense one also had to be a social activist. "Literature does not exist in a vacuum," he wrote in the *ABC of Reading*. "Writers as such have a definite social function exactly proportioned to their ability AS WRITERS. This is their main use. All other uses are relative, and temporary, and can be estimated only in relation to the view of a particular estimator."[93] The great writers, moreover, were to be the leaders of society, the oracles whose advice everyone followed. Because of exceptional insights and other unique creative abilities, the great writer was, therefore, an intellectual jack-of-all-trades, capable of understanding the most complex issues whether they were artistic, economic, or political. From this elitist perspective, Pound believed that it was always the duty of the few to lead the many, especially since the great mass of humanity seemed incapable of making its own good judgments. Such leadership by the capable should be the basis for all governments, for as he explained in yet another of his pedagogic ABC books: "The preconception of democracy, let us say at its best, is that the best men, kaliokagathoi, etc. *Will Take the Trouble* to place their ideas and policies before the majority with such clarity and persuasiveness that the majority will accept their guidance, i.e., 'be right.' "[94]

But herein lay the rub. Time after time he had taken the trouble to explain his views, to offer his leadership, to provide advice, and time after time he was snubbed. It was exasperating, at times debilitating, and he could not understand why people paid avid attention to some things he said and totally ignored others. Had he not opened the eyes of the literary world with his poetry, by founding new poetic schools, and by discovering brilliant new writers? Why then could he not open the eyes of the rest of the world on matters of economic and political importance? It possibly never occurred to him that his literary judgments were more skillful than his economic predictions. Yet Pound did not stand alone in confusing personal creative ideals with public political movements during the interwar period. Such confusion was prevalent on both Left and Right according to another poet, Stephen Spender, who tried to explain the phenomenon:

> The temptation for the poet is to take over the rhetoric of political will and action and translate it into the rhetoric of poetry without confronting the public rhetoric of politics with the private values of poetry. If there is a sin common to poetry such as Auden's *Spain*, the anti-Semitic passages in Eliot's Sweeney poems, the political passages

in Pound's cantos, Wyndham Lewis' adulation of what he calls "the party of genius" (meaning Michelangelo and Wynham Lewis), Lawrence's worship of the dynamic will of nature's aristocrats (in *The Plumed Serpent*), certain of my own lines, it is that the poet has—if only for a few moments—allowed his scrupulous poet's rhetoric of the study of "minute particulars" to be overwhelmed by his secret yearning for a heroic public rhetoric.[95]

If Spender's secret yearnings were momentary, Pound's delusion was lifelong. He never saw any difference between the private world of his own vision and the public world of politics, for Pound was a man totally confident in what he believed were his unique intellectual abilities. As his old friend William Carlos Williams suggested more than once, Pound felt that he could become an expert on anything and everything, and, could do so in a single sagacious bound.[96] Williams recalled this aspect of his personality from an incident during their youth: Pound "could never learn to play the piano though his mother tried to teach him. But he 'played' for all that. I remember, my mother's astonishment when he sat down at the keyboard and let fly for us . . . seriously. He took mastership at one leap; played Listz, Chopin,—or anyone else you could name—up and down the scales, coherently to his own mind, any old sequence. It was part of his confidence in himself."[97] Throughout his life Pound showed this same confidence in instantaneous mastery of an amazing variety of activities (fencing, tennis, languages, opera, economics, history, politics to name a few), and, like most self-styled experts, he expected to be taken seriously when he expressed his views. In many respects, Pound resembled the civic boosters so often satirized by Sinclair Lewis in that he approached practically every problem with the certainty that he could quickly understand and solve it. Pound, however, believed that the solution lay less within the civic spirit of the community than within the range of his own insights and abilities. This in part explains the hundreds of letters he sent to people of influence warning against the dangers of usury while praising Social Credit and Italian fascism.[98] To Pound it all seemed so clear, the solutions so simple, that he could never understand why his advice was ignored. The problems of fellow artists, of the United States and Europe, of civilization itself, could easily be remedied if only the masses and their leaders would realize that a "proper" understanding of economics was the universal key as he declared in a broadcast on February 23, 1943:

> I may have been late myself, but not quite as tardy as most of you. Twenty years ago I had got onto the money racket. Mebbe I have learned something since then, movin' round on the continent.
>
> Your economics professors are driftin' behind. Lot 'em were behind, oh, SOMEWHAT, when I was last in America, but it ain't enough for 'em to just get to where I was in '39. EUROPE has been a movin'.

Even when Pound was brought to Washington to stand trial for treason, his sense of mission was as strong as ever. One of his first requests was for a Georgian dictionary because he believed that he might be asked to explain his economic views to Stalin. Anticipating a meeting with the Soviet dictator, he also sought a discussion of economic issues with President Truman.[99] Perhaps these expectations were a sign of Pound's mental confusion at the time, but for years he had expressed similar grandiose plans. It was, in fact, his desire to be known as a political and economic thinker as well as a great poet that had led him to a commitment in fascist Italy. During the 1920s he grew exasperated with world leaders who failed to move in the right direction, especially since he was available to advise them. At the same time he also became enamored of the few world leaders who seemed to express their beliefs and act upon them. By the 1930s the willingness to act was half the battle; as Pound wrote in *What Is Money For?*: "Mussolini and Hitler wasted little time PROPOSING. They started and DO distribute BOTH tickets and actual goods on various graduated scales according to the virtues and activities of Italians and Germans."[100]

Like the dictators he so admired, Pound believed that he too was an activist, a man who got things done. Thus he became involved in Italy. Convinced as he was by the mid-1930s that Mussolini and Hitler truly understood the dangers of usury and were trying to implement monetary reform, he declared time and again in his broadcasts that war was a "monstrous" intrusion at a time when economic salvation was imminent. Absolutely certain that wars were waged by usurers, Pound desperately tried to warn Americans that they were fighting the very world leaders who were doing the most to oppose the usurers. Pound never lost faith in the ability of his country to awaken to its folly. In this respect his activism in Italy was Janus-faced. Hoping to convince his fellow countrymen that they were fighting on the wrong side, he tried to sway them by defending the virtues of fascism. If the war were stopped, if more attention were paid to monetary distribution, if the usurers were driven from the temple, the Republic could then return to the halcyon days of Adams and Jefferson. Such were the dreams of Ezra Pound. That they led to a point where means and ends were lost in a self-righteous blur of dogmatism helps to explain his attachment to Social Credit, his anti-Semitism, his infatuation with fascism, and his activism abroad. Ironically, his literary achievements will long outlive his involvement with Italian fascism, although Pound never viewed his art and social views in a different light. His legacy is perhaps best explained in a Chinese proverb he enjoyed quoting: " 'A man's character apparent in every one of his brush strokes.' "[101] So it is and must be with Ezra Pound.

9

Retrospect and Prospect

> For what is it that we Americans are seeking always on this earth? Why is it we have crossed the stormy seas so many times alone, lain in a thousand alien rooms at night hearing the sounds of time, dark time, and thought until heart, brain, flesh and spirit were sick and weary with the thought of it; "Where shall I go now? What shall I do?"..
>
> Thomas Wolfe
> *Of Time and the River*

DURING THE FIRST HALF of the twentieth century American writers were in the vanguard of social activism, participating in the monumental events of their time. The causes they supported were as different as the countries in which they acted. Their activities abroad ranged from the well-publicized to the little known, from the spectacular to the prosaic. These writer activists could be remarkably perceptive about their causes, as well as woefully naïve. Their participation in foreign causes, however, often placed them far ahead of their countrymen in recognizing the importance of world events.

Lea and Fenollosa, for example, were among the few visionaries of their time to proclaim the strategic, economic, and artistic importance of the Far East. Despite his tendency to romanticize soldiering, Seeger recognized the profound impact of World War I on the course of history. Even as he was thoroughly demoralized by World War I, Reed grasped the immense importance of the revolution in Russia which it spawned. He eagerly supported the Bolsheviks, but also argued that their blueprint for revolution would fail in his own country unless altered to the dimensions of the American experience. He seemed to know almost intuitively what the American Left would require years to learn.

Others were visionaries in different ways. Many of the New Left of the 1960s would denounce virtually the same kind of overorganization that Dos Passos feared all of his life. And, similarly, the interest of Dos Passos and Frank in the mystical and symbiotic lifestyles of Hispanic culture anticipated many of the interests of a future counterculture. Internationalism was a well-developed concept in Fischer's mind long before Wendell Willkie's idea of "One World" became fashionable.

Prophetic vision and political insight were not the only qualities brought by these eleven writers to their activities abroad. They could be oblivious to the inconsistencies in the causes that attracted them, and often dogmatic in their attitudes. During most of his stay in Japan, for example, Fenollosa strove to remove all traces of Western art, regardless of merit, from the schools and museums of the country. Wharton never wavered from her belief that there was but one side to World War I. Reed and Fischer were often blinded by their enthusiasm for the Soviet experiment. Although he opposed censorship of any kind, Hemingway accepted Republican excesses during the Spanish Civil War, and rationalized the death of José Robles as simply a byproduct of war. Pound's lapses were even more noticeable, for his broadcasts from Rome were often prejudicial to the point of absurdity.

Some writers abroad did question the causes they were serving. Seeger, for example, never believed that his side during World War I represented ultimate good, and he was more than willing to imagine a German victory. The doubts held by Dos Passos and Fischer about means and ends were also, in part, responsible for the termination of their commitment. If most of these writers, at one time or another, lent uncritical support to their cause, they were, perhaps, much like other activists who find it difficult to evaluate events in which they are involved. Evaluation was even more troublesome for those writers not familiar with the language of the country in which they were actively engaged. Fenollosa faced the complex task of learning the Japanese language at the same time he studied Japanese art. Lea also went twice to China lacking any real familiarity with the native language. And Reed became involved in the Russian Revolution before being able to say little more in Russian than "Ya Americanski Sotsialist." Finally, by the time Fischer arrived in Spain he could speak Russian comfortably, but not Spanish, and ultimately had to deal with a dictatorial brigade commander who was French. Thus, added to the isolating experience of being an American writer, was the difficulty of serving a foreign cause while living a metaphorical existence.

All of the writers in this study showed a desire to act as well as to write. All experienced, both personally and professionally, the difficulties of being writers in America. From these common needs and hardships emerged, in large part, their motivation to become active in a foreign cause. Wharton, Seeger, and Pound left the United States in search of the proper literary atmosphere. Originally expatriates, all three were to become directly involved in the affairs of the countries in which they chose to live. Although never permanently abandoning the United States, Hemingway, Dos Passos, and Frank were equally dissatisfied with the creative atmosphere of their native country. While searching for alternatives to the business-oriented ethos of interwar America, Hemingway and Dos Passos discovered Spain. There they became committed during the Civil War. Frank's dissatisfaction was always more personal, for he not only disliked America's creative environment, but also the poor reception accorded his writing. In Latin America, and particularly Argentina, during a triumphant lecture tour in 1929, he found a lifestyle that he liked and intellectuals who praised his work. Emotionally and intellectually committed to Argentina long before World War II, he eagerly returned there in 1942 to help prevent the spread of fascism.

Frank was not the only writer abroad who felt unappreciated at home. When Lea and Pound saw their warnings about dangers to the national good ignored, each responded by becoming active in a foreign cause. Hoping that a militarily strong China might help counter a militant Japan, Lea donated his services to K'ang Yu-wei and Sun Yat-sen. Pound used Italian radio to persuade Americans that they were fighting on the wrong side during World War II. Both writers wanted to shape the world to their convictions; direct involvement abroad came only after years of frustrated attempts to awaken slumbering countrymen with their writing.

Unlike most of the other writers in this study, Fenollosa, Cowley, and Fischer were at the threshold of their careers when they became active in foreign causes. Thus, their involvement in foreign causes is more directly related to career opportunities and literary ambitions. When Fenollosa graduated from Harvard, he felt stigmatized as a second generation American until he took a teaching job in Japan. There he found social acceptance and the cause that would dominate his life. Cowley also attended Harvard, but when he found the educational atmosphere oppressive, he chose a different kind of classroom. He rushed off to France and World War I where he hoped not just to read about life, but experience it. Unlike Fenollosa and Cowley, Fischer never graduated from college, and was vague about career directions when he left for Palestine in 1918. He was, however, certain of one thing: he wanted to escape from the ghetto where he had spent his youth. When Zionism failed to fulfill his needs, he returned to the United States and decided to become a writer. But doubts about the origins of World War I and the dull normalcy of the Harding years led him to see Europe rather than his homeland as his training ground. Once on the Continent, Fischer found a single country that welcomed social change. For the next fourteen years he honed his writing skills while praising Soviet achievements.

While Fischer concluded from observation that the United States was barren ground for social reform, Reed and Pound knew so from personal experience. In fact, much of their enthusiasm for foreign causes sprang from their failures to carry out social change at home. Reed's guilt about the financial disaster of the Paterson Pageant and his disgust at America's entry into the war made him all the more willing to devote himself to a cause which promised the Russian workers peace, bread, and land—all the things denied workers in the rest of the world. During the 1930s, Pound's economic advice was, from his perspective, considered in Italy, but ignored at home. His unsuccessful trip home in 1939, and his failure to obtain an interview with President Roosevelt, further convinced him that America rejected his call for sweeping monetary reform.

Whether they experienced the problems of being writers in America or failed to effect meaningful social change, all the writers in this study firmly believed in the worthiness of their involvement in a foreign cause. In their most idealistic moments, they believed they were moving toward a more perfect social and political order. Reed thought he had found the workers' paradise in Russia. Frank visualized the creation of the "whole person" through the organic union of North and South America, while Fenollosa was certain that a superior civilization was forming in the artistic meeting of East and West. And just as Pound saw salvation for the world through monetary reform, Fischer found it in internationalism, and Dos Passos in the simple lifestyle and individual freedom of a Spanish village. That the dreams of these writers were unfulfilled, that their Utopia never materialized, reflects not so much their own inabilities, but human failure itself—in short, the tragic limitations of the human condition.

The subjects of this study also mixed with their idealism feelings of guilt about the activities of their own country. The resolve of Edith Wharton, for example, to aid France during World War I emerged, in part, from the guilt she felt over her own country's inactivity. Her activity in France was her own way of atoning for America's failure to act. By her example she would lay the groundwork for American participation in the war. Twenty years later, Hemingway, Dos Passos, and Fischer hoped that their involvement in the Spanish Civil War might awaken America and shame it into changing her neutral stance.

Apart from their differing motivations, all of these writers, in a sense, were acting in place of America and, at the same time, many were also acting for the good of America. Lea persistently argued that his activities were closely tied to the interests of his own country. Concerned about the lack of a martial spirit in the United States, he believed that the nation's security could best be ensured by a Chinese state powerful enough to challenge Japan. It was not enough to write books about the dangers ahead. Lea had to participate in the Chinese Revolution to create an American ally.

Reed did not so much want to save the United States as change it. To do so he helped form an American Communist Party, and tried to keep its ideology in line with the realities of America. When in Moscow his thoughts still turned to his own country. He defended the Wobblies against opposition because he believed their philosophy and tactics would accomplish social change in the United States. By 1919 he was willing to face a trial and possible imprisonment to return home to publicize his revolutionary ideas, and only his arrest in Finland prevented him from doing so. Well before his old friend Lincoln Steffens ever visited the Soviet Union, Reed believed that he had seen there the workings of the future. Nonetheless, he wanted communism to work beyond the borders of Russia. Reed may have died a Party member, but it was an American communist who was buried beneath the Kremlin walls.

Fischer, Dos Passos, and Hemingway feared the spread of fascism throughout the world. They strongly believed that unless fascism was contained in Spain, it would inevitably appear elsewhere. If their activity in Spain was intended to aid the Spanish Republic, it was also meant to awaken their own country to a potentially powerful foe. Frank too was alarmed by the spread of fascism, especially in Argentina. There his hatred of fascism underlay his involvement. He also sought to establish a hemispheric unity which he believed essential to the survival of the Americas. Before World War II he argued that the United States had much to teach Hispanic America but much to learn from it as well. By 1942, the opposite seemed to be true. He feared that fascism in Argentina and its spread throughout Latin America would not only destroy the future of hemispheric unity, but also damage the development of the non-materialistic side of his own country's personality. From Frank's perspective the needs of the United States were so closely tied to the needs of Latin America that the two could not be separated.

With respect to fascism, Ezra Pound's position was poles apart from that of all other writers. Instead of rejecting fascism, Pound believed that no one was closer than the fascist leaders to solving the monetary problems of the world. Although he never advocated that America follow the Italian example, he was adamant in his conviction that his country should avoid involvement in World War II. If American financial difficulties were ever to be confronted, if the Republic was ever to return to the common-sense monetary policies of the founding fathers, if the American Risorgimento was ever to occur, Pound argued that only a new American leadership could accomplish it. The new leaders would understand the nature and power of money. They would be attentive to advice of the financial experts, one of whom was Pound himself. So sure was he of his knowledge of monetary matters that even after his arrest for treason Pound still believed his counsel would be sought. Such certainty might be the delusion of a confused mind, but, confused or not, Pound was determined to revive the American dream by leading his country back on the proper financial course.

Although some writers came to foreign involvement with the monism of the hedgehog and others showed the pluralism of the fox, only Reed and Pound were ever tied to a specific ideology. Reed's loyalty to the Russian Revolution, however, did not keep him from sharply questioning Party policy. Even though his writing became increasingly propagandistic, he never blindly followed an ideological line. Apart from Pound's single-minded support of fascism, many of the elements he found in its doctrine were little more than reflections of his own theories. Fischer, involved in the Zionist movement, was motivated less by political beliefs than by the influence of his own background. While in Russia during the 1920s and 1930s, he never considered joining the Communist Party. Both Frank and Dos Passos eagerly supported the communists during much of the 1920s and 1930s, but each later became disillusioned.

That ideological commitment played such a minor role in the activities abroad of most of these writers may, in part, be explained by the absence of an ideological tradition in the United States. Moreover, the pragmatic cast of their idealism and the uniquely personal nature of their commitment may also have diminished their attraction to foreign ideologies. Never renouncing their citizenship, they were more comfortable with the vague idealism of the American dream than with a more specific blueprint for change. Lacking a strong ideological commitment, writers like Wharton, Hemingway, and even Fischer engaged only in the "shining emergent causes," and were never actively involved in specific causes again. Ideological commitment, then, was not a fundamental part of their involvement in foreign causes, for their commitment was as individually oriented and inner-directed as were the personalities of the writers themselves.

In the final analysis, any effort to understand fully the motives and the depth of commitment of the writers in this study ultimately returns to how their activism related to their lives and personal needs. Whether it was the desire for a military career or literary recognition, or even the simple need to be taken seriously, all of the writers were significantly motivated by personal needs and ambitions. It is within this mixture of self-interest and disillusionment, idealism and guilt, that lies the essence of their motivation.

None of the eleven writers better demonstrates the merging of self-interest and idealism than Fenollosa. When he left the United States for Japan, he had no intention of becoming actively involved. Instead he was searching for social acceptance and a career. Once in Japan he fell into a commitment that made him a recognized authority on Asian painting, a curator in a prestigious American museum, and a popular lecturer on the Chautauqua circuit. None of these achievements was planned, but rather emerged from the dovetailing of opportunities, abilities, and personal ambitions. In many ways, Homer Lea followed a similar pattern. Determined to pursue a military career in the face of overwhelming handicaps, Lea first made himself a military theoretician and then ingeniously found a revolutionary group willing to accept him. If his rank of general was a creation of his own fantasy, his activities with the Pao-huang-hui and the T'ung-meng-hui were real. His career at times reads like a shabby melodrama, and his ambitions seem grandiose if not absurd. But the fact that he had a military career at all is astonishing. Lea's activism abroad, then, was nurtured by monumental determination and will.

Personal aspirations also affected the activities of Seeger and Cowley, for both of these young Americans were intent—at times almost self-consciously so—upon becoming writers. But before they could write about life, they would have to live it intensely. For them, World War I filled the void of their inexperience and gave them a unique, spectacular subject for their pens. In the case of both Seeger and Cowley, their activities in France intertwined with their literary ambitions. Wharton's case, however, was different. By 1914, her career and interests were already well-established. But there was also a very personal side to her involvement in France. In her own way she saw an attack on France as an attack on herself. She had fled the crass materialism of America to live in a world which better fit her needs. Although she never became a French citizen, Wharton's expatriation went much deeper than that of the other writers in this study. Thus the threatened destruction of France and the civilization she loved was unthinkable. Wharton defended herself by defending France.

Whereas Wharton's involvement in a foreign cause was tied to World War I and ended with it, Reed spent many years searching for a cause in which he could both serve and believe. Reed's love of travel and adventure as well as his impetuosity led to his involvement in the Russian Revolution, but so too did his concern for the working classes and his disgust with World War I. Riding with Pancho Villa, reporting on the workers' plight at Ludlow, and traveling through war-torn Europe were adventures enough for a lifetime. But by the time he was thirty Reed found himself floundering. To fulfill his life, to add meaning to his being, he needed a cause that would demand all his commitment, all his energy, and all his belief. That cause he found in Russia.

Neither Fischer nor Dos Passos were ever comfortable with the kind of total commitment that so appealed to Reed. Their commitments abroad were less intense and of shorter duration. Fischer unsuccessfully tried to maintain his sense of individualism and journalistic professionalism while involved abroad. He found that in Palestine, Russia, and Spain his activities restricted his personal needs and he never remained an active participant for very long. Unwilling to accept the discipline of others, and disliking any form of censorship, he gradually decided to abandon his involvement in foreign causes and devote his life to journalism. Dos Passos also found it difficult to sustain a foreign commitment, although he spent much of the interwar period supporting radical causes at home. Firmly believing that any large social organization smothered the individual, he went to Spain an avid anti-communist. But the mysterious death of one friend and the unwavering commitment of another led him to believe that perhaps he was better at writing about foreign causes than serving them. Thus, the activities abroad of both Fischer and Dos Passos were closely tied to their discomfort with organizations and causes which restricted individual freedom. For them, participation in a foreign cause was brief and, quite often, disillusioning.

While the American writers studied are in many ways vastly different individuals, perhaps the strongest common features can be found in Hemingway, Frank, and Pound. For all three, their writing and their activism were one and the same. Hemingway, for example, loathed fascism as much as he loved Spain, but what attracted him most in 1937 was the war—a fabulous subject for his writing. Once Hemingway was in Spain, his commitment deepened, perhaps demonstrating the validity of Cowley's belief that "you become committed to a cause by serving a cause."[1] It was only after driving across the Guadalajara battlefield and seeing the bodies of "volunteers" from fascist Italy that Hemingway could relate personally to what was happening. The political ramifications were not as important as the fact that Loyalist and international soldiers were heroically defending the Republic against fascist troops. This was something that Hemingway could understand, and for him the battling in Spain was not just another war.

Frank, like Hemingway, also had monumental literary ambitions. Hoping to be a great writer, he settled for a literary reputation in the Hispanic world. When fascism emerged and Argentina drifted toward the Right in the 1940s, Frank saw a potential threat to his goal of hemispheric unity and to the only society that admired him. Neglected at home and facing the loss of recognition abroad, it is little wonder that Frank became involved in Argentina. Nationalistic impulses and theoretical ambitions may well have influenced his actions, but personal needs meant more.

Literary neglect also troubled Pound during much of his early career, but by the 1930s it was the lack of interest in his political and economic views which caused him the most concern. Pound believed that great poets were also great thinkers. They were as capable in the realm of politics as in literature. Failing to acknowledge that few people shared this belief, Pound could not understand why Mussolini listened to his economic theories, and Roosevelt did not. If Italy respected his opinions, why did his own country reject them? By the 1940s, Pound's need for attention and respect obsessed him and became an intricate part of his activism in Italy.

Although the foreign commitments and literary careers of Hemingway, Frank and Pound were more closely interrelated than those of other writers in this study, all wrote about their experiences while they supported a foreign cause. A few wrote the most enduring works of their careers as a direct result of their activities abroad: Fenollosa's *Epochs of Chinese and Japanese Art*, Seeger's "I Have a Rendezvous with Death," and Reed's *Ten Days That Shook The World*. While imprisoned in an army stockade in Italy, Pound composed *The Pisan Cantos*, which received the Library of Congress Bollingen Prize in 1948. Dos Passos was not so fortunate. His novel of the Spanish Civil War, *The Adventures of a Young Man*, marked the beginning of his drift toward the Right, and reflected his declining creative abilities. While all writer-activists drew upon their foreign experiences in their writings, none became involved in a foreign cause solely for literary or professional reasons. In fact, their activities abroad often caused their writing to suffer, and some even paid a greater price.

If participating in foreign causes adversely affected the careers of some writers, there is little doubt, however, that most writers found it easier to become committed because of their professions. As writers, most had a degree of career flexibility and personal mobility unknown in other professions. While participating in a foreign cause, they did not have to obtain institutional permission, follow guidelines, or justify actions. Some writers like Reed and Fischer used professional writing skills first to reach countries in which they would later become involved. These same writers also used their journalistic abilities to support themselves while serving a foreign cause. Others, like Wharton, Hemingway, Dos Passos, and, to some extent Fischer and Pound, used some of their royalties while active abroad. Thus, writing for a living could aid as well as handicap these writers in search of a foreign cause.

From a somewhat different perspective, the fact that ten of these eleven writers came from middle-class backgrounds may also have influenced their initial foreign commitments. Unlike Fischer, who became active in a foreign cause to escape his background of poverty, most of the other writers were led to foreign involvement, in part, by their middle-class origins. Fenollosa, Reed, Frank, and Pound might have had little opportunity to become involved abroad had it not been for their educational advantages. Wharton, Frank, Seeger, and Dos Passos all enjoyed the luxury of travel while still young, and all but Frank later became involved in areas they had visited. The Harvard backgrounds of Cowley and Dos Passos helped them obtain positions in Ivy League-dominated volunteer organizations during World War I. And although Hemingway entered the same war via the newspaper rather than collegiate world, his middle-class credentials probably enhanced his acceptance by the Red Cross.

Apart from how and why these writers became involved in foreign causes, one quality which a number shared was a practical bent, a willingness to engage in the most physically mundane activities. The American love of efficiency and for pitching in to get the job done is reflected in their efforts. Their willingness to dirty their hands contained none of the patronizing *noblesse oblige* of media celebrities who lend their names to a cause.[2] While Seeger led the monotonous life of a common soldier, Wharton organized workshops in Paris, and Cowley wearily drove ammunition trucks to the front. Once in Spain, Fischer undertook perhaps the most thankless task of all and provided for the material needs of the International Brigade. But for some, along with the dirt and drudgery of such activities was also the glamor and recognition. Nearly all the subjects of this study effectively used their literary ability to aid their causes, whether through radio or film, the political pamphlet, the newspaper, or the lectern.

For most of the writers examined here, participation in a foreign cause did not appreciably change their political or philosophical outlooks. Only Dos Passos and Fischer noticeably altered their political beliefs as a direct result of their activities abroad, and in both cases their disillusionment with communism developed years before their involvement in the Spanish Civil War. Cowley's feeling of deracination was intensified by his participation in World War I, while Reed's attitude toward the Communist Party scarcely differed from that which he expressed earlier in his writings for *The Masses*. Fenollosa, Wharton, and Hemingway were no more socially concerned after their ventures than they had been before, and their activism ended with their cause. In summary, while diversity remains the essence of writer-activism abroad, all writers studied here still shared a number of characteristics. All were affected by the difficulties of being writers in America. All became participants in foreign causes in the belief that they could make their own lives and their causes meaningful. All were disillusioned with their native land and many felt guilty about what their country was doing, but none relinquished their citizenship, and none lost hope in the fulfillment of the American ideal.

While the number of writer-activists abroad may fluctuate from one generation to another, the difficult position of being a writer and artist in America will probably change little. Echoing the words of Ezra Pound, Russell Lynes declared in 1970 that creative artists still lacked support in the United States. Perhaps they were more financially secure and more socially accepted, but their overall position was much the same as it had been years earlier. Lynes argued, in fact, that with the exception of a few prominent artists, the scale of living of the vast majority was closer to that of the "unskilled laborer than that of the craftsman—nearer to the carwasher than to the electrician or brick-layer or plumber."[3] Such gloomy remarks seem appropriate also to the 1980s with a new administration projecting cuts in funding for the arts. There seems little doubt, then, that questions of economic need and social status will continue to play a significant role in the continu-ing disillusionment of the writer in America. While such disillusion-ment can lead to expatriatism or bitterness, it can also lead writers to seek recognition or fulfillment by serving a cause in a country other than their own.

In spite of the continuing disillusionment of modern American writers, it is still difficult to predict how strong their impulse to act abroad will be. Few writer-activists emerged during the post-World War II period; few exist today. One such rare figure is journalist and freelance writer Shirley Graham Dubois, a woman who helped run the radio station of the Nkrumah government in Ghana. Another is novel-ist Richard Gibson, a worker for the Algerian Bureau of Information and Communications under the Ben Bella regime.[4] With continuing interest in Black Nationalism, there will be other Afro-American writ-ers who believe in the emergence of powerful African states as a stimulus for significant racial advancement in this country. Some will, perhaps, become involved in the affairs of these states to hasten the process.

For other would-be writer activists, critical problems at home may make protest there seem far more important than activism abroad. In addition, the innumerable issues and conflicts of the contemporary world may make choosing a good cause a more complicated matter. The very fact that the United States has become vastly more involved abroad than at any other time in its history may discourage involve-ment by individuals. In recent days, we find that dissident American writers demonstrate their views in Washington rather than in Moscow or Tel Aviv. At the same time, America's activities abroad have be-come so extensive that commitment by Americans might be seen by foreigners as yet another example of the Pax Americana. In other words, suspicions about the intentions of all Americans have grown with the expansion of American power and influence. On the other extreme, it is quite possible that if writers were involved in foreign causes concerned with social change, they might find themselves pitted against the interests of their own government. In *America and the World Revolution*, Arnold Toynbee argues that the United States no longer leads the world in efforts to improve human existence. Viewing such a goal as hopeless, Americans today seem embarrassed for having thought it could ever be achieved. During the twentieth century, the United States gradually discarded its original mission, replacing it with the somber responsibilities and imagined duties of a world power. In the process America has become as anti-revolutionary in outlook as Imperial Rome. The Pax Romana and the Pax Americana, in Toynbee's view, bear similarities as striking as they are disturbing.

> Rome consistently supported the rich against the poor in all foreign communities that fell under her sway; and, since the poor, so far, have always everywhere been far more numerous than the rich, Rome's policy made for inequality, for injustice, and for the least happiness of the greatest number. America's decision to adopt Rome's role has been deliberate, if I have gauged it right. It has always been deliberate, yet, in the spirit that animates this recent American movement in reverse, I miss the enthusiasm and the confidence that made the old revolutionary America irresistible. Lafayette pays a high psychological price when he transforms himself into Metternich.[5]

Toynbee further observes that a nation which seeks largely to protect its wealth or interests risks isolation from the rest of the world. "It is a fearful thing to be isolated from the majority of one's fellow creatures," he concludes, "and this will continue to be the social and moral price of wealth so long as poverty continues to be the normal condition of the world's ordinary men and women."[6]

Sharing with their countrymen this sense of isolation from the great mass of humanity, writers may be even more profoundly affected. As Americans they feel isolated from society. Some resist isolation by losing themselves in their work or burying themselves in aesthetic values. Others adopt an Erasmian approach by trying to change their country from within. Still others, as this study suggests, attempt to combat their dual sense of isolation by immersing themselves in a foreign cause. Thus, for some American writers involvement in a foreign cause will forever be an attempt either to ignore the maladies of their own country or to atone for them by participating in the cause of another. By donning the mantle of a Byron or Lafayette, they fulfill America's humanitarian mission in the world. Their activism abroad is the product of two conflicting values: selfishness and idealism. Reflecting deeply felt personal needs, writer-activism of the future may assume new and varied forms, and may seek in more direct ways to reawaken the conscience of America. No matter how it changes over time, however, the essential impulse of the writer-activist will always remain the same—that is, the inclination, indeed, the need, for individuals to aid their fellow human beings.

Notes

PREFACE

1. Lord Byron to Thomas Moore, Genoa, May 12, 1823, *The Works of Lord Byron*, ed. Rowland E. Prothero (13 vols., 1904), VI, p. 206.

CHAPTER 1: MOTIVATION AND INSPIRATION

1. Using Richard Hofstadter's definition of an intellectual in *Anti-Intellectualism in American Life* (New York, 1962), 26–29, as a person who lives for ideas, I have deliberately shied away from labeling the writers in this study with that term because a number simply do not fulfill the requirements of such a rubric.

2. Stanley Weintraub, *The Last Great Cause: The Intellectuals and the Spanish Civil War* (New York, 1968), p. 309.

3. Van Wyck Brooks, *Days of the Phoenix* (New York, 1957), p. 172.

4. David M. Potter, "Reflections on American Society," in *History and American Society: Essays of David M. Potter*, ed. Don E. Fehrenbacher (New York, 1973), p. 365.

5. Josephine Herbst, "Yesterday's Road," *New American Review*, III (1968), p. 85.

6. Lincoln Steffens, *The Autobiography of Lincoln Steffens* (New York, 1937), p. 702.

7. Merle Curti, *American Philanthropy Abroad* (New Brunswick, 1963), p. viii.

8. *Ibid.*, pp. 621–24.

9. Henry Miller, *The Air-Conditioned Nightmare* (New York, 1945), *passim*.

10. Alfred Kazin, *On Native Grounds: An Interpretation of Modern American Prose Literature* (New York, 1942), p. 14.

11. D. W. Brogan, *The American Character* (New York, 1954), pp. 85, 94.

12. Kenneth Kenniston, *The Uncommitted: Alienated Youth in American Society* (New York, 1960), p. 412.

13. Walt Whitman, "Democratic Vistas," in *Whitman: Leaves of Grass and Selected Prose*, ed. Sculley Bradley (New York, 1962), p. 496.

14. Alexis de Tocqueville, *Democracy in America*, trans. by George Lawrence, eds. J. P. Mayer and Max Lerner (New York, 1962), p. 443.

15. Hofstadter, *Anti-Intellectualism in American Life*, p. 3.

16. Eric F. Goldman, in *The Tragedy of Lyndon Johnson* (New York, 1969), pp. 495–563, discusses the role that he played in initiating this festival and the attitudes toward it of a number of the participants.

17. Christopher Lasch, *The New Radicalism in America 1889–1963: The Intellectual as a Social Type* (New York, 1965), and Richard H. Pells, *Radical Visions and American Dreams: Cultural and Social Thought in the Depression Years* (New York, 1973), have poignantly dealt with the tensions found in many writers and intellectuals concerning the decision to withdraw from or participate in the social arena.

18. Reinhold Niebuhr, *The Irony of American History* (New York, 1952), p. 62.

19. Max Eastman, *Love and Revolution* (New York, 1964), p. 49.

20. Daniel J. Boorstin, *The Genius of American Politics* (Chicago, 1953), p. 179.

21. David Riesman is one such critic, and in *The Lonely Crowd* (abridged edition, New Haven, 1950), p. 297, writes that as a nation we must realize that "each life is an emergency, which only happens once, and the "saving" of which, in terms of character, justifies care and effort. Then, perhaps, we will not need to run to a war or a fire because the daily grist of life is not felt as sufficiently challenging, or because external threats and demands can narcotize for us our anxiety about the quality and meaning of individual existence."

22. T. B. Bottomore, *Critics of Society: Radical Thought in North America* (New York, 1968), pp. 12–15, 80–81, 104–5.

23. Steven Spender, "Writers and Politics," *Partisan Review* (Summer 1967), p. 375.

24. Historian Christopher Lasch, *The New Radicalism in America 1889–1963*, has demonstrated that numerous American intellectuals have often shown similar inclinations.

25. Lasch in *The New Radicalism, passim*, and *The Agony of the*

American Left (New York, 1969), pp. 63–114, and Pells, *Radical Visions and American Dreams,* pp. 346–64, discuss this tendency on the part of American writers and intellectuals.

26. Henry Steele Commager, *The American Mind: An Interpretation of American Thought and Character Since the 1880's* (New Haven, 1950), pp. 95–98, 410–11; Henry F. May, *The End of American Innocence: A Study of the First Years of Our Own Time, 1912–1917* (Chicago, 1959), p. 14; Kenniston, *The Uncommitted,* pp. 343–53, 444–47.

27. William James, *Collected Essays and Reviews* (New York, 1920), p. 67. Arthur Schlesinger, Jr., in his essay, "The One Against the Many," in *Paths of American Thought,* eds. A. M. Schlesinger, Jr., and Morton White (Boston, 1963), p. 538, labels practitioners of this kind of practical idealism as "free men"—individuals who understand the frailty of all human effort, but strive just the same.

28. Weintraub, *The Last Great Cause,* p. 309.

29. *Ibid.*

30. Sacvan Bercovitch, *The Puritan Origins of the American Self* (New Haven and London, 1975), pp. 136–86; Stephen Spender, *Love-Hate Relations: English and American Sensibilities* (New York, 1974), pp. 261–318.

31. Perry Miller, *Errand into the Wilderness* (Cambridge, Mass., 1956), pp. 1–15.

32. David Potter, *People of Plenty: Economic Abundance and the American Character* (Chicago, 1954), pp. 97–98. Because of the significant role that disillusionment plays in shaping the motivations of these writer activists as well as the individualistic nature of their commitment, their activities cannot be regarded as merely another manifestation of American mission which has most often been defined as some variation of a national willingness to go to the defense of democracy in Europe. See, for example, Frederick Merk, *Manifest Destiny and Mission in American History* (New York, 1963), and Edward McNall Burns, *The American Idea of Mission: Concepts of National Purpose and Destiny* (New Brunswick, 1957), for in-depth discussions of this idea.

33. Granville Hicks, "The American Writer Faces the Future," in *The Writer in a Changing World,* ed. Henry Hart (New York, 1937), p. 190.

34. Spender, "Writers and Politics," p. 369.

35. André Malraux, *The Walnut Trees of Altenburg* (London, 1952), p. 74.

CHAPTER 2: THE CHRYSANTHEMUM AND THE SWORD

1. Lawrence W. Chisolm, *Fenollosa: The Far East and American Culture* (New Haven, 1963), pp. 158–59.

2. *Ibid.*, chapter 9, *passim.*

3. Nathan Haskell Dole in *Ninth Report of the Class Secretary of the Class of 1874 of Harvard College.* Harvard Archives (Cambridge, Mass.), p. 40.

4. Chisolm, *Fenollosa*, 28, believes that Harvard's well-known art historian Charles Eliot Norton influenced Fenollosa's turning from philosophy to art.

5. Dorothy G. Wayman, *Edward Sylvester Morse: A Biography* (Cambridge, 1942), pp. 238–39.

6. *Ibid.*, p. 286.

7. Chisolm, *Fenollosa*, pp. 17, 31.

8. Edwin O. Reischauer, *Japan: The Story of a Nation* (New York, 1970), p. 135; Marius B. Jansen, "Changing Japanese Attitudes Toward Modernization," in *Changing Japanese Attitudes Toward Modernization*, ed. Marius B. Jansen (Princeton, 1965), pp. 59–62.

9. Robert S. Schwantes, *Japanese and Americans: A Century of Cultural Relations* (New York, 1955), p. 152, claims that between 1860 and 1912 there were 234 Americans employed as full-time teachers in various Japanese educational institutions.

10. *Third Report of the Secretary of the Class of 1874 of Harvard College*, July 1874–June 1880. Harvard Archives (Cambridge, Mass., 1880), p. 20.

11. *Ibid.*

12. *Ibid.*

13. Taro Kotakane, "Ernest Fenollosa, His Activities and Influence on Modern Japanese Art," *Bulletin of Eastern Art*, no. 16 (April 1941), p. 21; Taro Odakane, "Ernest F. Fenollosa's Activities in the Field of Art," 3 parts, *Bijutsu Kenkyu*, no. 110 (February 1941), p. 50. For translation of this article I am indebted to Mieko Osho, instructor of Japanese at Ohio State University.

14. S. Miyoshi, "Ernest Fenollosa," *Japan Magazine*, V, no. 11 (October 1920), p. 205.

15. Kotakane, "Ernest Fenollosa, His Activities and Influence," p. 22.

16. *Seventh Report . . . of Harvard College*, June 1874–June 1899, Harvard Archives (Boston, 1889), p. 46. Ernest F. Fenollosa, *Epochs of Chinese and Japanese Art*, 2 vols. (New York, 1921), II, p. 70, later recalled the feeling of bliss that he felt while traveling through Japan at this time in search of paintings: "In those sweet days of the early eighties, and accompanied by Kano Tomonobu and Sumiyoshi Hirokata, with either my student, Mr. Okakura, or the now famous Mr. Miyaoka of the diplomatic service for

interpreter, I felt like an unworthy, degenerate Noami privileged to revisit the very treasures that had delighted his eyes 450 years before."

17. *Seventh Report . . . of Harvard College*, p. 22.

18. Wayman, *Morse*, p. 282.

19. Ernest F. Fenollosa, "Contemporary Japanese Art," *The Century*, XL (1893), p. 577.

20. Uyeno Naoteru, "The Cultural Background of Meiji Art, With an Outline of Painting" in *Japanese Arts and Crafts in the Meiji Era*, ed. Uyeno Naoteru, English adaptation by Richard Lane (Tokyo, 1958), pp. 16–17.

21. Foster Rhea Dulles, *Yankees and Samurai* (New York, 1965), p. 217.

22. Hisatomi Mitsugu, "Ernest F. Fenollosa and Japanese Art," *Japan Quarterly*, V (1958), pp. 309–10.

23. Naoteru, "Cultural Background of Meiji Art," p. 19; Mitsugu Hisatomi, *Fenollosa* (Tokyo, 1957), p. 119. For translation of the Hisatomi biography I am indebted to Mrs. Fumika Harada of Columbus, Ohio.

24. Ernest F. Fenollosa to Edward S. Morse, April 26, 1884, quoted in Wayman, *Morse*, p. 289.

25. *Ibid.*, pp. 288–89.

26. Ernest Fenollosa, "History of Kangwakai," typescript, n.d., 2, in Ernest Fenollosa Papers, Houghton Library, Cambridge, Massachusetts.

27. William Sturgis Bigelow, "Awakened Public Interest Both Popular and Official," Boston *Evening Transcript*, December 24, 1920, in Quinquennial Folder, Harvard Archives. Cambridge, Massachusetts.

28. Fenollosa, "History of Kangwakai," pp. 2–3, Fenollosa Papers.

29. Hisatomi, "Fenollosa and Japanese Art," p. 311.

30. Ernest F. Fenollosa to Edward S. Morse, September 27, 1884, quoted in Wayman, *Morse*, p. 291.

31. Ernest F. Fenollosa, *Review of the Chapter on Painting in Gonse's "L'Art Japonais"* (Boston, 1885), p. 44.

32. Naoteru, "The Cultural Background of Meiji Art," pp. 20, 27–28; Hisatomi, *Fenollosa*, p. 121.

33. Ernest F. Fenollosa, "Advantages and Disadvantages of Introducing Japanese Drawing into Schools," typescript, n.d., pp. 2–3, Fenollosa Papers.

34. Ernest Fenollosa, "The Fine Arts Commission to Europe and America," *circa* 1888, p. 1, Fenollosa Papers.

35. Miyoshi, "Ernest Fenollosa," p. 283.

36. Ernest Fenollosa, [address] delivered at Ibumuraro, typescript, September 19, 1886, p. 3, Fenollosa Papers.

37. Salem *Gazette*, October 19, 1886.

38. Naoteru, "Cultural Background of Meiji Art," p. 26; Odakane, "Fenollosa's Activities in the Field of Art," no. 111 (March 1941), pp. 93–94.

39. *Ibid.*, no. 11 (April 1941), p. 113.

40. Ernest Fenollosa, "Report of Fine Arts Commissions," typescript, *circa* 1887, p. 8, Fenollosa Papers.

41. Ernest Fenollosa, "Relation of Paintings to Art-Industries," typescript, n.d., pp. 3–4, Fenollosa Papers.

42. Ernest Fenollosa to Kentaro Kaneko, Tokyo, *circa* 1888, Fenollosa Papers.

43. Taro Kotakane, "Fenollosa, Activities and Influences on Modern Japanese Art," p. 25.

44. Ernest Fenollosa, "The Prospect of Japanese Art," typescript, *circa* 1889, p. 8, Fenollosa Papers.

45. Ernest Fenollosa to Arinori Mori, n.p., *circa* 1888, Fenollosa Papers.

46. Delmer M. Brown, *Nationalism in Japan: An Introductory Historical Analysis* (Berkeley, 1955), p. 167.

47. Fenollosa's taking his collection with him might be viewed as exploitative, and not in keeping with his activities in Japan. Quite possibly he may have rationalized taking the collection on the grounds that only by doing so could he hope to demonstrate to the West the splendors of the Eastern tradition.

48. *Sixth Report of the Secretary of the Class of 1874 of Harvard College*, June 1889–June 1894, Harvard Archives (Boston, 1894), p. 25.

49. Frederick L. Chapin, "Homer Lea and the Chinese Revolution," unpublished A.B. Honors Thesis, Harvard University, 1950, p. 5. Chapin is working on a longer biography of Lea and has been most generous in allowing me to read the unfinished manuscript. He has also been of great assistance in answering questions pertaining to Lea's life and activities.

50. Marshall Stimson, "A Great American Who Saw It Coming," *Christian Science Monitor Magazine* 8 (March 7, 1942), p. 6.

51. David Starr Jordan, *The Days of a Man*, 2 vols. (New York, 1922), II, pp. 32, 34.

52. San Francisco *Call*, April 22, 1900.

53. *Ibid.*

54. *Ibid.*

55. *Ibid.*, June 23, 1900.

56. New York *Herald*, June 24, 1900.

57. According to Harold Z. Schiffrin, *Sun Yat-sen and the Origins of the Chinese Revolution* (Berkeley, 1970), pp. 229–30, the great value to Chinese revolutionaries in having "foreign confederates" lay in the foreigners'

ability to move in and out of China without being bothered by the Chinese constabulary.

58. *Ibid.*, pp. 206–7. Although there is no evidence that he knew Sun Yat-sen at the time, Lea was interested in joining together the revolutionary forces of Sun with those of the Pao-huang-hui, but was overruled in this matter by K'ang Yu-wei.

59. Amos P. Wilder (American Consul-General in Shanghai) to Department of State, December 30, 1911. Enclosure on *China Press*, December 28, 1911. State Department Records Relating to the Internal Affairs of China 1910–1929. Microfilm 8652 (Washington: National Archives, 1963), 893.00/1008; unsigned, untitled article, *Bookman*, XXVII (April 1908), p. 131.

60. Whereas Chapin, "Homer Lea and the Chinese Revolution," pp. 23–24, believes that Lea was present at the battle of Po Lo in southern China, neither Schriffrin, *Sun Yat-sen*, n. 207, nor Marius B. Jansen, *The Japanese and Sun Yat-sen* (Cambridge, 1954), p. 247, have found any Chinese or Japanese sources that in any way verify or suggest his presence.

61. Jordan, *Days of Man*, II, p. 32.

62. K. Oishi to Homer Lea, January 11, 1901, Tokyo, in Joshua B. Powers Collection, Hoover-Institute, Stanford, California; Jansen, *The Japanese and Sun Yat-sen*, p. 53.

63. When Lea returned to China in 1911 the following exchange took place between him and a reporter from the *China Press*:

"Where did you get your title of General?"

"I was commander of four divisions, organized by myself for the rescue of the Emperor Kwang Su eleven years ago."

"Where was the army organized?"

"Chiefly in the South and commanded by American officers. I was later commander of Chinese troops in America."

Found in Amos P. Wilder to Department of State, December 30, 1911. Enclosure on *China Press*, December 28, 1911. State Department Records, 893.00.1008.

64. Chapin, "Homer Lea and the Chinese Revolution," and Doris Sloan Egbert, "Homer Lea: A Military Leader," unpublished M.A. Thesis, University of South Dakota, 1967, have dealt in depth with the origins and development of these military academies.

65. Carl Glick, *Double Ten: Captain O'Banion's Story of the Chinese Revolution* (New York, 1945), pp. 23, 59–60. Glick's book is an undocumented study written some thirty-five years after the events discussed, and it is filled with numerous unsubstantiated exaggerations and factual errors.

66. Adjutant-General J. B. Lauck to Mr. Roger S. Page, Secretary,

Western Military Academy, December 18, 1904, Sacramento, California, Powers Collection.

67. K'ang Yu-wei to General Homer Lea, October 10, 1904, London, Powers Collection.

68. Philadelphia *Inquirer*, June 25, 1905; New York *Daily Tribune*, June 28, 1905.

69. New York *Sun*, June 28, 1905.

70. New York *Tribune*, July 5, 1905.

71. For a short period it apeared to Lea that K'ang Yu-wei was trying to ease him out as head of the Pao-huang-hui military academies in the United States. Although the dispute was settled in Lea's favor, the seeds of mistrust lingered. For a full discussion of this dispute see Chapin, "Homer Lea and the Chinese Revolution," pp. 55–72; Glick, *O'Banion*, pp. 136–44. There is also a statement in the Powers Collection issued by K'ang Yu-wei on April 7, 1905, proclaiming Lea as the proper head of the academies.

72. Los Angeles *Times*, October 13, 1966. This still confusing issue is discussed although not adequately explained in *K'ang Yu-wei: A Biography and A Symposium*, ed. and translated by Jung-Pang Lo (Tucson, 1967), pp. 205–12.

73. Homer Lea to C. B. Boothe, September 21, 1908, Long Beach, California, Laurence Boothe Collection, Hoover Institute, Stanford, California.

74. Dr. Yung Wing to C. B. Boothe, October 9, 1908, Hartford, Connecticut; Yung Wing to Homer Lea, December 4, 1908, Hartford Connecticut.

75. W. W. Allen to C. B. Boothe, January 29, 1909, New York, Boothe Collection.

76. Homer Lea to C. B. Boothe, April 7, 1908, Laguna Beach, California; C. B. Boothe to K'ang Yu-wei, June 14, 1909, Los Angeles, Boothe Collection.

77. Yung Wing to Charles B. Boothe, January 16, 1909, New York, Boothe Collection.

78. W. W. Allen to C. B. Boothe, January 21, 1909, New York, Boothe Collection.

79. C. B. Boothe to Dr. Yung Wing, December 23, 1909, Los Angeles, Boothe Collection.

80. Harold Z. Schiffrin, "The Enigma of Sun Yat-sen," in *China in Revolution: The First Phase, 1900–1913*, ed. Mary Clabaugh Wright (New Haven, 1971), p. 468; *Sun Yat-sen*, p. 337.

81. C. B. Boothe to W. W. Allen, July 19, 1910, Los Angeles; Sun Yat-sen to Homer Lea, Penang, September 5, 1910; Sun Yat-sen to Charles

B. Boothe, November 8, 1910, Penang, Boothe Collection. A statement by Sun Yat-sen concerning the appointment of Boothe as foreign financial agent for the Federal Association of China made on March 14, 1910, is in the Boothe Collection.

82. W. W. Allen to C. B. Boothe, February 6, 1909, New York, Boothe Collection. Apparently Allen tried to interest J. P. Morgan in the plan although there is no evidence that Morgan ever responded to Allen's inquiries. W. W. Allen to C. B. Boothe, February 13, 1910, New York, Boothe Collection.

83. W. W. Allen to C. B. Boothe, January 12, 1909, New York, Boothe Collection.

84. Yung Wing wrote to Boothe a last time in November 1910 and obliquely expressed his disapproval of Sun Yat-sen by suggesting that ultimately China would have to settle for a limited monarchy. Dr. Yung Wing to Charles B. Boothe, November 10, 1910, Hartford, Connecticut, Boothe Collection.

85. Sun Yat-sen to C. B. Boothe, September 4, 1910, Penang, Boothe Collection.

86. Sun Yat-sen to C. B. Boothe, November 8, 1910, Penang, Boothe Collection.

87. Schiffrin, *Sun Yat-sen*, pp. 206–7, and Lyon Sharman, *Sun Yat-sen: His Life and Its Meaning* (Hamden, Connecticut, 1965), p. 126, claim that a meeting between the two did not occur until sometime in 1909. Jordan, *Days of Man*, II, p. 33; Glick, *Double Ten*, p. 159, and Chapin, "Homer Lea and the Chinese Revolution," pp. 90–91, all suggest an earlier meeting around the time of Lea's first trip to China in 1900. Regardless of when the first encounter took place, there is no evidence that Lea and Sun Yat-sen began their collaboration before 1910.

88. Sun Yat-sen, "My Reminiscences," *The Strand Magazine* (March, 1912), p. 304.

89. Homer Lea, *The Valor of Ignorance* (New York, 1943), p. 100.

90. Lea argues in *The Day of the Saxon* (New York, 1942), pp. 87–89, that Japan's victory in the Russo-Japanese War not only consolidated her position in the Pacific but also had channelled Russian aggression toward the British Empire in India.

91. John P. Mallan, "Roosevelt, Brooks Adams, and Lea: The Warrior Critique of the Business Civilization," *American Quarterly*, VIII (Fall 1956), pp. 226–29.

92. New York *Tribune*, July 5, 1905.

93. Sun Yat-sen to Homer Lea, February 24, 1910, San Francisco,

Boothe Collection; *ibid.*, September 5, 1910, Penang, Boothe Collection.

94. Sun Yat-sen to Homer Lea, September 5, 1910, Penang, Boothe Collection.

95. Telegram from Sun Yat-sen to Homer Lea, October 31, 1911, n.p., Powers Collection.

96. There are several letters in the Powers Collection showing that Lea attempted to establish contacts with various London bankers in order to obtain loans for Sun Yat-sen.

97. Shelley Hsien Cheng, "The T'ung-meng-hui: Its Organization, Leadership and Finances, 1905–1912," unpublished dissertation, University of Washington, 1962, pp. 182–83; Harold Z. Schiffrin, "The Enigma of Sun Yat-sen," in *China in Revolution*, p. 471, explains that the contact with Grey came through Sir Trevor Dawson of Vickers, Sons and Maxim Company, who obviously hoped that the revolutionaries would repay this kindness through ordering arms and munitions by way of his firm. Dawson also wrote to Grey asking him to assist Sun Yat-sen in gaining permission to enter Hong Kong, where he had been barred some years earlier. A. Trevor Dawson to Sir Edward Grey, November 15, 1911, Powers Collection.

98. New York *Times*, November 21, 1911.

99. David M. Figart (American Vice-Consul-General in Singapore) to Department of State, December 18, 1911. Enclosure on Penang *Gazette*, December 14, 1911. State Department Records 893.00/984.

100. Untitled, undated typescript written by Homer Lea describing the journey towards China in December, 1911, Powers Collection.

101. David M. Figart to Department of State, December 20, 1911. Enclosure on Singapore *Free Press*, Dec. 18, 1911. State Department Records 893.00/984.

102. Schiffrin, *Sun Yat-sen*, p. 364.

103. Cable from George E. Anderson (American Consul-General in Hong Kong) to Department of State, December 22, 1911. State Department Records, 893.00/1016.

104. Cable from George E. Anderson to Department of State, December 21, 1911. State Department Records, 893.00/801. Lea tried to persuade Elihu Root to act as an adviser to Sun Yat-sen as a way of gaining unofficial support for the revolution within the United States. Only two days before issuing the above statement, Lea received a letter from Root turning down the offered advisory role. "You know how I feel regarding the assertion by the Chinese of their right of self-government," Root declared, "but the fact that I am a member of the Senate and of the Committee on Foreign Relations, and therefore one of the constitutional advisors of the President in regard to foreign affairs, would make it impossible for me to act as advisor

for any other governmental body." Elihu Root to General Homer Lea, December 19, 1911, Washington, Powers Collection.

105. Amos P. Wilder (American Consul-General in Shanghai) to Department of State, December 30, 1911. Enclosure on *China Press*, December 28, 1911. State Department Records, 893.00/1008.

106. *Ibid.*

107. Herbert H. Gowen and Josef W. Hall, *An Outline History of China* (New York, 1927), p. 352. Several English-speaking observers in China at the time like Carl Crow, *China Takes Her Place* (New York, 1944), p. 60; Earl Albert Selle, *Donald of China* (New York, 1948), pp. 108–10; and Frederick McCormick, *Flowery Republic* (New York, 1913), p. 273, all claim that Lea's presence in China and his association with Sun Yat-sen appeared to cause ill feelings among some of the other revolutionaries. In this respect, Lea was encountering some of the same kind of anti-Western feeling that Fenollosa experienced earlier in Japan.

108. General Homer Lea to Sun Yat-sen, July 27, 1912, Ocean Park, California, Powers Collection.

109. *Pacific Stars and Stripes*, April 20, 1969, Powers Collection.

110. Ernest Fenollosa, "The Difference Between Eastern and Western Art," typescript, n.d., 2, Fenollosa Papers.

111. Hisatomi, "Fenollosa and Japanese Art," p. 312.

112. Fenollosa, *Epochs of Chinese and Japanese Art*, I, p. 2.

113. Homer Lea, "The Legacy of Commodore Perry," *North American Review*, CX (June 1913), p. 743.

114. John Higham, *Strangers in the Land: Patterns of American Nationalism 1860–1925* (New York, 1965), n. 366.

115. W. H. McNeill, *The Rise of the West* (Chicago, 1963), pp. 796–97.

116. Geoffrey Barraclough, *An Introduction to Contemporary History* (London, 1967), pp. 10–42.

CHAPTER 3: THE MAELSTROM OF WAR

1. Henry James, *The American Volunteer Motor-Ambulance Corps in France* (London, 1914), pp. 10–11.

2. Henry James to Henry James, Junior, July 20, 1915, in *The Letters of Henry James*, ed. Percy Lubbock, 2 vols. (New York, 1920), II, p. 491.

3. In scanning voluntary participation of American writers in the war, Henry F. May, *The End of American Innocence*, p. 378, claims that no

American writer left the United States to join the Central Powers although poet George Sylvester Viereck and critic and novelist Willard Huntington Wright strongly supported the German cause at home.

4. F. Scott Fitzgerald, *This Side of Paradise* (New York, 1948), p. 55.

5. For a discussion of the prewar intellectual temper of the country, see May, *The End of American Innocence.*

6. The newest and one of the most penetrating analysis of Edith Wharton's life and literary career is Cynthia Griffin Wolff, *A Feast of Words: The Triumph of Edith Wharton* (New York, 1977), pp. 10–24.

7. Both R. W. B. Lewis, *Edith Wharton: A Biography* (New York, 1975), pp. 74–76, 99, 297–98, and Wolff, *A Feast of Words,* pp. 42–48, 75–91, have discussed the identity crisis which Wharton suffered before shedding some of the intellectually limiting social and sexual stereotypes of her milieu.

8. Kazin, *Native Grounds,* p. 75.

9. Edith Wharton, untitled and undated typescript dealing with Mrs. Wharton's Wartime Activities 1914–1917, p. 2, in Edith Wharton Papers, Beinecke Library, Yale University, New Haven. Hereafter cited as Wharton Papers.

10. Edith Wharton, *A Backward Glance* (New York, 1933), p. 341.

11. Edith Wharton to Elizabeth Gaskell Norton, 1 February 1915, Paris, in Edith Wharton Papers, Houghton Library, Harvard University, Cambridge.

12. Wharton, typescript dealing with Mrs. Wharton's Wartime Activities 1914–17, pp. 5–6, Wharton Papers.

13. *Ibid.*

14. Lewis, *Edith Wharton,* p. 370.

15. Wharton, typescript dealing with Mrs. Wharton's Wartime Activities 1914–17, pp. 8–9, Wharton Papers.

16. *Ibid.,* pp. 11–13; Edith Wharton, typescript, The Children of Flanders Rescue Committee, Wharton Papers.

17. Edith Wharton to Minnie Cadwalader Jones, March 9, 1916, Paris, Wharton Papers.

18. Edith Wharton to Mrs. Bayard Thayer, November 16th, 1917, n.p., Wharton Papers.

19. Edith Wharton to Frederic Mathews, June 4th, 1917, n.p., Wharton Papers.

20. Wharton, *Blackward Glance,* p. 352.

21. Typical of these articles are: "In Argonne," *Scribner's Magazine,* LVII (June 1915), pp. 651–60; "In Lorraine and the Vosges," *ibid.,* LVIII (October 1915), pp. 430–42; "In the North," *ibid.,* LVIII (November

1915), pp. 610–11. All of these articles dealing with her trips to the front were later collected in *Fighting France* (New York, 1918).

22. *The Book of the Homeless,* ed. Edith Wharton (New York, 1916).

23. Edith Wharton to Miss K. E. Turnbill, 17 November 1919, n.p., Wharton Papers.

24. Edith Wharton to Miss Power-Schroeder, September 1, 1919, n.p., Wharton Papers.

25. There is but one, relatively brief, biography of Alan Seeger. Irving Weststein, *Sound No Trumpet: The Life and Death of Alan Seeger* (New York, 1967).

26. Alan Seeger, *Letters and Diary* (New York, 1917), p. 184.

27. Alan Seeger to Friedrick Dellschaft, Cambridge, 31 October 1908, Alan Seeger Papers, Houghton Library, Harvard University, Cambridge. Hereafter cited as Seeger Papers.

28. *Ibid.*

29. *Ibid.*

30. Alan Seeger to Charles Louis Seeger, Cambridge, 6 June 1909, Seeger Papers.

31. John Reed, *The Day in Bohemia—or Life Among the Artists* (Riverside, Conn., 1913), p. 42.

32. Alan Seeger, "As a Soldier Thinks of War," *New Republic,* III (May 22, 1915), p. 68.

33. Alan Seeger to Mrs. Charles L. Seeger, 19 September 1912, Paris, Seeger Papers.

34. Seeger, "As a Soldier Thinks of War," p. 66.

35. Seeger, *Letters and Diary,* pp. 2–3.

36. *Ibid.,* p. 86.

37. Alan Seeger to Charles Louis Seeger, 11 December 1914 [France], Seeger Papers.

38. Seeger, *Letters and Diary,* p. 49

39. *Ibid.* The article which disturbed Seeger is, "England's Poet-Soldier," *The Literary Digest,* L (May 29, 1915), pp. 1276–77.

40. Seeger, *Letters and Diary,* p. 117.

41. *Ibid.,* p. 170.

42. *Ibid.,* p. 211.

43. David M. Kennedy, *Over Here: The First World War and American Society* (New York, 1980), pp. 181–82.

44. Matthew Josephson, *Life Among the Surrealists* (New York, 1962), p. 36.

45. Cowley, *Exile's Return* (New York, 1934), p. 22.

46. Henry F. May has suggested in *The End of American Innocence,*

that nearly every intellectual phenomenon associated with the 1920s was present in the country before the First World War.

47. Cowley, *Exile's Return*, p. 30. Matthew Josephson, *Life Among the Surrealists*, p. 52, was even more explicit in describing the way in which the books his generation read had little to do with the urban environment in which they lived: "Perhaps we literary novices of that time, lived too much in our books, as compared with the youth of the 1940's and 1950's. But when we looked up from those books, we saw no enchanted woods or lakes, no crenelated castles such as we read of in our Victorian poets, but only the dreary urban landscape of the Brooklyns of the world, and the Pittsburghs and Clevelands, with their gridiron streets and their new made slums."

48. Cowley, *Exile's Return*, pp. 30–31, 34.

49. *Ibid.*, p. 36.

50. A predecessor of Cowley's at Harvard, Harold E. Stearns, "The Confessions of a Harvard Man," *Forum*, L (December 1913), p. 820, found life there during the prewar years to be as depressing as he would later find the entire country to be in the 1920s. In the process of becoming "educated" he argued that most of his fellow classmates rapidly lost far more of their early ideals than were ever replaced through academic exposure. See also May, *End of American Innocence*, pp. 35–37, 56–62, 298–300, 303. Whereas May focuses primarily on Harvard and Columbia, Stanley Cooperman, *World War I and The American Novel* (Baltimore, 1967), p. 6, generalizes about the overall inadequacies of what he calls "liberal arts culture" in the face of the new economic realities of prewar American society.

51. *History of the American Field Service in France*, 3 vols. (Boston, 1920), III, p. 171.

52. *Ibid.*, pp. 17–20.

53. *Ibid.*, p. 20.

54. *Ibid.*, p. 10.

55. Cowley, *Exile's Return*, p. 41.

56. Alan Seeger to Mrs. [Charles L. Seeger], 3 July 1915, France, Seeger Papers.

57. Lewis, *Edith Wharton*, pp. 351–54.

58. Edith Wharton to Robert Grant, August 31, 1914, Wharton Papers.

59. Cooperman, *World War I and the American Novel* (Baltimore, 1967), p. 71.

60. Malcolm Cowley, "Aprés la guerre finie," *Horizon*, X (Winter 1968), p. 115.

61. Alan Seeger to Mrs. C. L. Seeger, 17 February 1915, France, Seeger Papers.

62. Wharton, *Fighting France*, p. 53.

63. *Ibid.*, p. 54.

64. *Ibid.*, p. 238.

65. Charles A. Fenton, "Ambulance Drivers in France and Italy: 1914-1918," *American Quarterly*, III (Winter 1951), p. 334. Fenton takes issue with John W. Aldridge's assertion in *After the Lost Generation: A Critical Study of the Writers of Two Wars* (New York, 1951), p. 4, that most American volunteers had "committed themselves to hardship and danger with the recklessness of big game hunters and with as little compulsion beyond the thrills they expected to encounter along the way." Fenton believes that Aldridge has confused cause with effect and thus failed to give adequate credit to the idealistic involvement of many of the participants. See, for example, the passionately idealistic letters of Victor Chapman, *Letters of Victor Chapman*, ed. John J. Chapman (New York, 1917), who believed that flying for the Lafayette Escadrille was the most meaningful thing that he had done in his entire life.

66. Edith Wharton, *The Marne* (New York, 1918), pp. 58–59.

67. Edith Wharton to Robert Grant, August 31, 1914; *ibid.*, February 13, 1915, Paris; Edith Wharton to Sally Norton, September 27, 1914, Wharton Papers.

68. Wolff, *A Feast of Words*, pp. 261–63.

69. *Ibid.*, pp. 263–67.

70. Wharton, *Fighting France*, p. 157.

71. *Ibid.*, pp. 219–38.

72. *Ibid.*, p. 230.

73. Edith Wharton to Robert Grant, August 31, 1914, Wharton Papers.

74. *Ibid.*, September 7, 1915, Paris, Wharton Papers.

75. Edith Wharton to Sarah Norton, May 5th, 1917, Wharton Papers.

76. Alan Seeger to Elsie A. Seeger, 29 December 1914 [France], Seeger Papers.

77. Seeger, *Letters and Diary*, p. 141.

78. E. E. Cummings, *The Enormous Room* (New York, 1946), p. 19.

79. Alan Seeger to Mrs. Charles L. Seeger, 17 February 1915, France, Seeger Papers.

80. *Ibid.*, 3 July 1915, Seeger Papers.

81. Seeger, *Letters and Diary*, p. 144.

82. Alan Seeger to Elsie A. Seeger, 26 February 1916 [France], Seeger Papers.

83. Seeger, *Letters and Diary*, p. 144.

84. Cowley, *Exile's Return*, pp. 41–42.

85. *Ibid.*, p. 40.

86. *American Field Service*, III, pp. 9–10.

87. Malcolm Cowley, "The Dead of the Next War," *New Republic*, LXXVI (October 4, 1933), p. 216.

88. Cowley, *Exile's Return*, p. 39.

89. Floyd Dell, *Intellectual Vagabondage* (New York, 1926), pp. 235–61.

90. Cowley, *Exile's Return*, p. 46.

CHAPTER 4: JOHN REED

1. Clare Sheridan, the English sculptress who had gone to Russia to do busts of the revolutionary leaders, offers the best and most complete description of Reed's funeral in *Mayfair to Moscow* (New York, 1921), pp. 160–63.

2. *Ibid.*, p. 162.

3. Lincoln Steffens to Mrs. C. J. Reed, May 25, 1932, in *The Letters of Lincoln Steffens*, eds. Ella Winter and Granville Hicks, 2 vols. (New York, 1938), II, pp. 921–22.

4. John Reed, "Almost Thirty," in *Adventures of a Young Man* (San Francisco, 1975), pp. 125–26.

5. *Ibid.*, pp. 132–33.

6. Bertram D. Wolfe, "The Harvard Man in the Kremlin Wall," *American Heritage*, XI (February 1960), pp. 6–9.

7. Reed, "Almost Thirty," pp. 134–35.

8. *Ibid.*, p. 129.

9. Devoted to the training of young writers, Copeland neglected his own scholarship in order to devote his time and energies to students. He paid the price for such devotion by remaining an instructor for a number of years, and was regarded by many of his colleagues as an eccentric.

10. Granville Hicks, *John Reed: The Making of a Revolutionary* (New York, 1936), p. 48.

11. Robert Rosenstone, *Romantic Revolutionary: A Biography of John Reed* (New York, 1975), p. 78.

12. Reed, "Almost Thirty," p. 138.

13. *Ibid.*, p. 140.

14. Max Eastman, *Enjoyment of Living* (New York, 1948), pp. 406–7.

15. Rosenstone, *Romantic Revolutionary*, p. 111. Theodore Draper in *The Roots of American Communism* (New York, 1957), p. 118, argues that *The Masses* did not provide Reed with an all encompassing ideology since it did not have one itself. It did, however, provide him with a radical political climate which also tolerated his bohemianism.

16. John Reed, "War in Paterson," *The Masses*, IV (June 1913), reprinted in *Echoes of Revolt: The Masses 1911–1917*, ed. William L. O'Neill (Chicago, 1966), p. 43.

17. Mabel Dodge Luhan, *Movers and Shakers* (New York, 1936), p. 188.

18. Albert Rhys Williams, *Journey into Revolution: Petrograd, 1917–1918* (Chicago, 1969), p. 41.

19. Hutchins Hapgood, *A Victorian in the Modern World* (New York, 1939), p. 353.

20. *Ibid.*

21. Luhan, *Movers and Shakers*, p. 295.

22. Reed, "Almost Thirty," p. 143.

23. John Reed, "What About Mexico?" *The Masses*, V (June 1914), p. 11.

24. John Reed, *Insurgent Mexico* (New York, 1969), p. 77.

25. John Reed, "The Colorado War," *Metropolitan*, XL (July 1914), p. 12.

26. Rosenstone, *Romantic Revolutionary*, p. 182.

27. John Reed, "The Trader's War," *The Masses*, V (September 1914), pp. 16–17.

28. Reed, "Almost Thirty," p. 143.

29. Max Eastman, *Heroes I Have Known* (New York, 1942), p. 213.

30. John Reed, "At the Throat of the Republic," *The Masses*, VIII (July 1916), p. 7.

31. John Reed, "Whose War?" *The Masses*, IX (April 1917), p. 11.

32. Hearings before the Committee on Military Affairs (House of Representatives, 65 Congress, 1st sess.), April 14, 1917.

33. John Reed, "An Heroic Pacifist," *The Masses*, IX (November 1916), p. 10.

34. John Reed, "One Solid Month of Liberty," *The Masses*, IX (September 1917), p. 50.

35. Reed, "Almost Thirty," p. 143.

36. Max Eastman, *Love and Revolution: My Journey Through an Epoch* (New York, 1964), p. 63.

37. Barbara Gelb, *So Short a Time: A Biography of John Reed and Louise Bryant* (New York, 1973), p. 144.

38. Stanley Kauffmann, "Ya Americanski Socialist," *New Republic*, CLVII (November 4, 1967), p. 30. Emma Goldman later wrote, in *My Disillusionment in Russia* (New York, 1923), pp. 143–44, that Reed's lack of familiarity with Russian was largely responsible for his taking far too much for granted about the Soviet system.

39. Williams, *Journey into Revolution*, pp. 29, 46–49.

40. John Reed, *Ten Days That Shook The World* (New York, 1919), pp. 132–33.

41. Hicks, *John Reed*, pp. 261, 290–91.

42. Louise Bryant, *Six Red Months in Russia* (New York, 1918), p. 202.

43. Albert Rhys Williams, *Through the Russian Revolution* (New York, 1921), p. 171.

44. Williams, *Journey into Revolution*, pp. 201–202.

45. *Ibid.*; Edgar Sisson, *One Hundred Red Days* (New Haven, 1931), p. 258. George Kennan in *Russia Leaves the War* (Princeton, 1956), p. 407, quotes from a report made by Ambassador David R. Francis to the State Department in which the ambassador writes: "These two [Reed and Reinstein] together with Albert Williams, all Americans, stood guard at the Soviet Foreign Office one night at least, when attack was expected . . . no attack was made." Francis does not mention the incident in his memoirs, *Russia from the American Embassy* (New York, 1921), and p. 168, merely writes that he regarded Reed as a suspicious character he kept under surveillance.

46. Kennan, *Russia Leaves the War*, pp. 407–8.

47. Rosenstone, *Romantic Revolutionary*, p. 314.

48. Williams, *Journey into Revolution*, pp. 119–227, has discussed this incident in detail including his belief that not all of the material given to Lenin by Gumberg was written by Reed.

49. Eastman, *Heroes I Have Known*, p. 221.

50. John Reed, "Why Political Democracy Must Go," *The New York Communist*, I (May 8, 1919), p. 4.

51. John Reed, *The Sisson Documents* (New York, 1918), John Reed Collection, Houghton Library, Harvard University, Cambridge. The best analysis of these forged documents is in Kennan, *Russia Leaves the War*, pp. 413–20, 441–54.

52. Draper, *Roots of American Communism*, pp. 176–96; James Weinstein, *The Decline of Socialism in America* (New York, 1969), pp. 177–233.

53. Angelica Balabanova, *John Reed—Poet and Revolutionist*, undated pamphlet, Reed Collection.

54. Benjamin Gitlow, *The Whole of Their Lives* (New York, 1948), p. 30; Eadmonn MacAlpine, Account of Finnish Arrest, Written for Louise Bryant (1934), typescript, Reed Collection. MacAlpine was a friend of Reed's in Russia at the time of his arrest.

55. MacAlpine, Account of Finnish Arrest, Written for Louise Bryant (1934), Reed Collection.

56. *Ibid.* After Reed's release, MacAlpine claims that "Lenin told him [Reed] in my presence that the Finns had made a bad bargain as he would have exchanged a whole jail full of Finns—not merely three professors for Jack."

57. Emma Goldman, *My Further Disillusionment in Russia* (New York, 1924), pp. 26–27.

58. John Reed, "Soviet Russia Now," *Liberator*, III (December 1920; January 1921), p. 17.

59. Rosenstone, *Romantic Revolutionary*, pp. 372–73.

60. Gitlow, *Whole of Their Lives*, p. 31.

61. Rosenstone, *Romantic Revolutionary*, pp. 375–76.

62. John Reed, "The I.W.W. and Bolshevism," *The New York Communist*, I (May 31, 1919), p. 3.

63. Gitlow, *Whole of Their Lives*, pp. 31–32.

64. John Reed, "The World Congress of the Communist International," *The Communist*, No. 10 (1920), p. 2.

65. John Reed to Louise Bryant, February 11, 1916, Reed Collection.

66. Quoted in Hicks, *John Reed*, p. 392.

67. Rosenstone, *Romantic Revolutionary*, p. 377.

68. Gitlow, *Whole of Their Lives*, pp. 34–35; Angelica Balabanova, *My Life as a Rebel* (New York, 1938), p. 291.

69. Draper, *Roots of American Communism*, pp. 284–85, 287–90.

70. Louise Bryant, "Last Days with John Reed," *Liberator*, IV (February 1921), p. 11.

71. Emma Goldman, *Living My Life*, 2 vols. (New York, 1931), II, pp. 850–51; *My Further Dissillusionment in Russia*, pp. 26–28; Balabanova, *My Life as a Rebel*, p. 291; Marguerite E. Harrison, *Marooned in Moscow* (New York, 1921), p. 222; Jacob H. Rubin, *I Live To Tell: The Russian Adventures of an American Socialist* (New York, 1934), p. 218.

72. One of Louise Bryant's versions of Reed's last days was told to Benjamin Gitlow, *Whole of Their Lives*, pp. 33–36, while she was visiting him at Sing Sing Prison. See also Draper, *Roots of American Communism*, pp. 287, 284–93; Eastman, *Heroes I Have Known*, pp. 230–37.

73. Williams, *Journey into Revolution*, p. 320.

74. Hicks, *John Reed*, pp. 387–402; *ibid.*, "Playboy Poet to Revolutionary," *Saturday Review*, L (November 4, 1967), pp. 29–30.

75. Richard O'Connor and Dale L. Walker, *The Lost Revolutionary: A Biography of John Reed* (New York, 1967), pp. 292–306.

76. Draper, *Roots of American Communism*, pp. 291–92.

77. Rosenstone, *Romantic Revolutionary*, p. 379.

78. Eastman, *Heroes I Have Known*, p. 223.

79. The branding of Reed as a kind of revolutionary playboy had one of its earliest expressions in an article written by Walter Lippmann, "Legenary John Reed," *New Republic*, I (December 26, 1914), p. 15, in which he described Reed as "a person who enjoys himself. Revolution, literature, poetry, they are only things which hold him at times, incidents merely of his living."

80. Williams, *Journey into Revolution*, p. 50.

81. Notebook dated 1919–1920, Reed Collection.

82. Graham Taylor, "From Harvard to Moscow," *Saturday Review*, XIII (April 25, 1936), p. 10.

CHAPTER 5: INDIVIDUALISM, PROFESSIONALISM, AND LOUIS FISCHER'S SEARCH FOR ONE WORLD

1. Edwin Rolfe, *The Lincoln Battalion* (New York, 1939), pp. 306–8; Arthur H. Landis, *The Abraham Lincoln Brigade* (New York, 1968), p. xviii; Hugh Thomas, *The Spanish Civil War* (New York, 1961), pp. 637–38. Thomas estimates that there were about 40,000 foreigners who fought in the International Brigades. He also claims that no American actively participated on the side of the Nationalists.

2. Louis Fischer, *Men and Politics: Europe Between the Two World Wars* (New York, 1941), p. 576.

3. Personal Interview with Louis Fischer, December 17, 1968, Princeton, New Jersey.

4. Living in New York rather than Philadelphia, Vivian Gornick, *The Romance of American Communism* (New York, 1977), pp. 3–27, discusses how the ideas of socialism and Zionism were all-pervasive in her childhood environment as well.

5. Louis Fischer, "Why I Changed My Mind About Soviet Russia," typescript, n.d., p. 38, Louis Fischer Papers, Princeton University Library.

6. Isaiah Friedman, *The Question of Palestine, 1914–1918: British-Jewish-Arab Relations* (New York, 1973), pp. 44–47, 135–36, 139–40, 259–61.

7. Norman Bentwich, *England in Palestine* (London, 1932), p. 23; "Jews Are on Their Way to Fight for the Holy Land," *Literary Digest*, LVII (April 13, 1918), pp. 62–64; "The Jewish Legion of Honor," *ibid.*, LVIII (July 13, 1918), p. 30; New York *Times*, March 20, August 24, 1918.

8. Fischer Interview.

9. Fischer, *Men and Politics*, p. 241.

10. *Ibid.*

11. *Ibid.*

12. Louis Fischer, *This Is Our World* (New York, 1956), p. 280.

13. Fischer, *Men and Politics*, p. 242.

14. *Ibid.*

15. Fischer, *This Is Our World*, p. 280.

16. Fischer Interview.

17. *Ibid.*

18. *Ibid.*

19. Louis Fischer et al., *The God That Failed* (New York, 1949), p. 183.

20. Fischer Interview; *This Is Our World*, p. 359.

21. Fischer, *The God That Failed*, p. 180.

22. Fischer, *Men and Politics*, pp. 48–49.

23. *Ibid.*, p. 160; See also Markoosha Fischer, *My Lives in Russia* (New York, 1944).

24. Fischer Interview.

25. For a cross section of these reviews see: "Review of Louis Fischer's *The Soviets in World Affairs*," *Foreign Affairs*, IX (January 1931), p. 362; Simeon Strunsky, "Review of Louis Fischer's *The Soviets in World Affairs*," *New York Times*, October 26, 1930; Leonard Wolf, "Soviet Foreign Policy," *Nation and the Athenaeum*, XLVII (October 18, 1930), p. 109; V. M. Dean, "Soviet Foreign Policy," *New Republic*, LXIV (November 12, 1930), p. 355.

26. Alexander Berkman to Louis Fischer, Berlin, June 3, 1925; Louis Fischer to Alexander Berkman, Berlin, June 4, 1925, Fischer Papers.

27. Louis Fischer to Mr. Bloom, New York, March 5, 1927, Fischer Papers.

28. Frank A. Warren, *Liberals and Communism* (Bloomington, 1966), pp. 70–76.

29. Fischer, *Men and Politics*, p. 161.

30. Peter G. Filene, *Americans and the Soviet Experiment, 1917–1933* (Cambridge, 1967), pp. 268–76.

31. Fischer, *The God That Failed*, p. 183.

32. Louis Fischer, "Notes Re Soviet Union 1937," Typescript, n.d., Fischer Papers; *The God That Failed*, pp. 182–92.

33. Fischer, *Men and Politics*, p. 53.

34. John S. Reshetar, Jr., *A Concise History of the Communist Party of the Soviet Union* (New York, 1960), p. 221.

35. Fischer, *The God That Failed*, p. 189.

36. Fischer, "Notes Re Soviet Union 1937"; *The God That Failed*, p. 190.

37. Fischer, *The God That Failed*, p. 195.

38. Louis Fischer to Freda Kirchwey, Moscow, September 21, 1934, Fischer Papers.

39. *Ibid.*, May 25, 1936.

40. Several of these lists are to be found in the Fischer Papers. For example, see "Purge 1936," typescript, n.d., 6 pp., Fischer Papers.

41. Louis Fischer to Max Lerner, Paris, September 12, 1936, Fischer Papers.

42. Fischer, *Men and Politics*, p. 350.

43. *Ibid.*, p. 359.

44. *Ibid.*, p. 385.

45. *Ibid.*, p. 386.

46. Frederick R. Benson, *Writers in Arms: The Literary Impact of the Spanish Civil War* (New York, 1967), p. 7.

47. Thomas, *Spanish Civil War*, pp. 294–300.

48. *Ibid.*, p. 637.

49. Vincent Brome, *The International Brigades: Spain 1936–1939* (New York, 1966), pp. 47–48; Fischer, *Men and Politics*, pp. 386–401.

50. Fischer, *Men and Politics*, p. 387; Louis Fischer, "Testimony: Regarding Spanish Civil War, 1949—International Brigade," typescript, n.d., Fischer Papers, pp. 3–4. Fischer testified before the U.S. Immigration and Naturalization Service in 1949 concerning one of the refugees he had supposedly helped during the Civil War in Spain. He kept a record of his testimony.

51. Fischer, *Men and Politics*, p. 387. Although not giving a specific date, Hugh Thomas, *Spanish Civil War*, p. 432n, claims that Fischer from his Paris "headquarters at the Lutetia Hotel, near the Sèvres-Babylone Metro station directed an elaborate organization for the purpose of arms and the diffusion of pro-Republican propaganda." In an interview Fischer maintained that although he would have been more than happy to have purchased arms for the Republic, he was never engaged in any operations as those described by Thomas. He suggested, however, because he had access to key men in the Republic's government and was even allowed to attend several important cabinet meetings, Thomas and others took this to mean that he was directly involved in the purchasing of arms. Fischer describes in *Men and Politics*, pp. 391, 451, 382, most of the interviews and one of the cabinet meetings he attended.

52. Thomas, *Spanish Civil War*, p. 301.

53. Gustav Regler, *The Owl of Minerva*, trans. Norman Nenny (New York, 1959), pp. 277–78.

54. Fischer Interview.

55. Fischer, *Men and Politics*, pp. 389–90, 394, 400–401.

56. *Ibid.*, p. 401.

57. Louis Fischer to Freda Kirchwey, Paris, April 30, 1938, Fischer Papers.

58. Alan Campbell to Louis Fischer, New York City, 1937, Fischer Papers.

59. Louis Fischer to Eleanor Roosevelt, March 12, 1938, Fischer Papers. Mrs. Roosevelt answered Fischer by stating that since the majority of the American people supported the neutrality acts at the time believing that they would keep the country out of war, there was little chance that the acts would be repealed in the near future. Eleanor Roosevelt to Louis Fischer, February 28, 1938.

60. Typical of the many articles about the Civil War that Fischer wrote during the period 1937–39 are: "Spain's 'Red' Foreign Legion," *Nation*, CXLIV (January 9, 1937), pp. 36–38; "Franco Cannot Win," *ibid.*, CXLV (August 7, 1937), pp. 148–50; "What Can Save Spain?" *ibid.*, pp. 374–75; "Thirty Months of War in Spain," *ibid.*, CXVIII (January 7, 1939), pp. 28–30. He also wrote two books dealing with essentially the same subject: *The War in Spain* (New York, 1937); *Why Spain Fights On* (London, 1938).

61. Fischer, "Testimony: Regarding Spanish Civil War, 1949—International Brigade," Typescript, Fischer Papers, pp. 7–12.

62. Louis Fischer to Francisco Castillo Najera, Mexican Embassy, Washington, D.C., New York, March 18, 1941, Fischer Papers.

63. Fischer, *The God That Failed*, p. 199.

64. *Ibid.*, p. 201.

65. Fischer, *Men and Politics*, p. 47.

66. Fischer, *The Great Challenge* (New York, 1946), pp. 150–51.

67. Louis Fischer to Jacob Billikopf, New York, March 28, 1932, Fischer Papers.

68. Fischer, *The Great Challenge*, p. 213.

69. Fischer Interview; "The Idealist to Whom Wisdom Came Late," *Saturday Review*, LXIV (April 16, 1960), p. 23.

70. Louis Fischer to Freda Kirchwey, December 16, 1936, Paris, Fischer Papers.

71. Fischer, *The God That Failed*, p. 206.

72. Fischer, *Men and Politics*, p. 160.
73. *Ibid.*, p. 208.
74. *Ibid.*, p. 160.

CHAPTER 6: SWORDS AND PLOUGHSHARES

1. John Dos Passos, *The Best Times* (New York, 1966), p. 159.
2. *Ibid.*, pp. 37–38.
3. John Dos Passos to Rumsey Marvin, April 10, 1917, New York, in *The Fourteenth Chronicle: Letters and Diaries of John Dos Passos*, ed. Townsend Ludington (Boston, 1973), pp. 70–71.
4. Carlos Baker, *Ernest Hemingway: A Life Story* (New York, 1969), p. 36.
5. Dos Passos, *The Best Times*, p. 65.
6. John Dos Passos to Rumsey Marvin, August 23, 1917, near Verdun, *Fourteenth Chronicle*, p. 92. On the voyage home in 1918 Dos Passos wrote his first novel, *One Man's Initiation 1917* (London, 1920), which was eventually reissued as *First Encounter* (New York, 1945). In the novel, pp. 97–106, Dos Passos describes the effect that a similar gas attack has upon two young American ambulance drivers.
7. Dos Passos, *Diary*, August 26, 1917, in *Fourteenth Chronicle*, p. 95.
8. Dos Passos to Rumsey Marvin, August 27, 1917, near Verdun, *ibid.*, p. 98; *The Best Times*, p. 75.
9. Dos Passos, *The Best Times*, p. 75.
10. John Dos Passos to Mrs. Edward E. Cummings, December 16, 1917, Milan, John Dos Passos Papers, Manuscript Division, University of Virginia Library, Charlottesville, Virginia. Hereafter cited as Dos Passos Papers.
11. Dos Passos, *The Best Times*, p. 82. Dos Passos wrote in the letter that brought him to the attention of the authorities, John Dos Passos to José Giner Pantoja, February-March 1918, Bassano, in *Fourteenth Chronicle*, p. 152, "It's up to you, who can make revolutions either quietly or violently, who are trying vainly, perhaps, to evolve a purpose for the life of our times, it is up to you to safeguard all the finest human beings, while the rest of us struggle on brutally with suicidal madness. Why? For lies, even for some truths, for greedy nations in a world drunk on commercialism.
12. Quoted in Charles Fenton, *The Apprenticeship of Ernest Hemingway: The Early Years* (New York, 1954), p. 61.
13. *Ibid.*

14. Baker, *Hemingway*, pp. 43–44.

15. *Ibid.*, p. 45. Baker cites a 1944 letter which Hemingway wrote to Malcolm Cowley in which he affirmed the autobiographical authenticity of the wounding of Frederick Henry in *A Farewell to Arms*.

16. Philip Young, *Ernest Hemingway: A Reconsideration* (University Park, Pa., 1966), pp. 164–71.

17. John Dos Passos, *The Theme Is Freedom* (New York, 1956), pp. 1–2.

18. Dos Passos, *Diary*, July 21, 1918; October 1, 1918, in *Fourteenth Chronicle*, pp. 193, 213. For an incisive discussion of Dos Passos's abhorrence of the overorganizing powers of the state, see John P. Diggins, *Up from Communism: Conservative Odysseys in American Intellectual History* (New York, 1975), pp. 74–117.

19. John Dos Passos, *One Man's Initiation 1917* (Ithaca, 1969), p. 165.

20. Robert O. Stephens suggests in *Hemingway's Nonfiction: The Public Voice* (Chapel Hill, 1968), pp. 180–203, that during the 1920s and 1930s Hemingway's political writing centered on three fundamental premises: 1) the world's readiness for revolution; 2) the idea that permanent peace would not come to any portion of the world where one people held the land of another; and 3) all politicians, with only a few exceptions, were to be distrusted. Other scholars have been far less certain of Hemingway's interest in and knowledge of politics. Carlos Baker, for example, *Hemingway*, p. 231, writes: "The political world beyond his happy hunting-and-fishing ground seemed more than ever inimical. He said that he liked the yowling of the coyotes in the hills far better than the mounting clamor of the Hoover-Roosevelt campaign speeches that came from his portable radio." Agreeing with Baker, David Sanders likewise concludes in "Ernest Hemingway's Spanish Civil War Experiences," *American Quarterly*, XII (Spring 1960), p. 134, that Hemingway was "belligerently nonpolitical" in most of his attitudes and that he best fit the role of a literary expatriate.

21. Ernest Hemingway, *By-Line: Selected Articles and Dispatches of Four Decades*, ed. William White (New York, 1967), p. 25.

22. *Ibid.*, p. 56.

23. Ernest Hemingway, to John Dos Passos, October 14, 1932, Cooke, Montana, Dos Passos Papers.

24. In several letters to Dos Passos during the 1930s, Hemingway stressed his conviction that no unit larger than a village could effectively engage in self-government. Ernest Hemingway to John Dos Passos, March 26, 1932, Key West; *ibid.*, May 30, 1932, Havana, Dos Passos Papers.

25. Leicester Hemingway, *My Brother Ernest Hemingway* (New York, 1961), p. 170.

26. Dos Passos, *Theme Is Freedom*, p. 2. John P. Diggins, *Up from Communism*, pp. 94–95, argues that Dos Passos's youthful attraction to socialism was basically a psychological reaction to his father's successful corporate image.

27. Dos Passos, *Theme Is Freedom*, p. 68.

28. Granville Hicks, "The Politics of Dos Passos," *The Antioch Review*, X (Spring 1950), p. 90.

29. Dos Passos, *Theme Is Freedom*, pp. 86–87.

30. John Dos Passos to John Howard Lawson, October (?), 1934, [Havana], *Fourteenth Chronicle*, p. 447.

31. John Dos Passos to Edmund Wilson, December 23, 1934, Key West, *ibid.*, p. 459.

32. Matthew Josephson, *Infidel in the Temple: A Memoir of the Nineteen-Thirties* (New York, 1967), p. 432.

33. Ernest Hemingway to John Dos Passos, May 30, 1932, Havana, Dos Passos Papers.

34. John Dos Passos to Kate Smith Dos Passos, October 31, 1930, Painter, Wyoming, *ibid.*

35. Ernest Hemingway to John Dos Passos, [1927], Key West, *ibid*; Baker, *Hemingway*, p. 159.

36. Ernest Hemingway to John Dos Passos, 1928, Key West, Dos Passos Papers.

37. John Dos Passos to Ernest Hemingway, January 1933, New York, *ibid.*

38. John Dos Passos to Ernest Hemingway, October 24, 1929, Provincetown, *ibid.*

39. Ernest Hemingway to John Dos Passos, March 26, 1932, Key West, *ibid.*

40. Ernest Hemingway to John Dos Passos, [1927], Key West, *ibid.*

41. Ernest Hemingway to John Dos Passos, March 26, 1932, Key West, *ibid.*

42. John Dos Passos to Ernest Hemingway, Brookline, New York, January 14, 1932, *ibid.*

43. Ernest Hemingway to John Dos Passos, May 30, 1932, Havana, *ibid.*

44. John Dos Passos to Malcolm Cowley, December 1, 1934, Key West, *Fourteenth Chronicle*, p. 456.

45. John Dos Passos to Rumsey Marvin, December 4, 1916, *ibid.*, pp. 56–57.

46. John Dos Passos, "It's almost thirty years since I first knew Spain," undated typescript, p. 1, Dos Passos Papers.

47. John Dos Passos, *Rosinante to the Road Again* (New York, 1922), p. 28.

48. Ernest Hemingway, *Death in the Afternoon* (New York, 1932), p. 91.

49. Ernest Hemingway to John Dos Passos, 1933, Key West, Dos Passos Papers.

50. L. Hemingway, *My Brother*, pp. 132–40; John Dos Passos to Malcolm Cowley, November 13, 1934, Key West, *Fourteenth Chronicle*, p. 450.

51. Dos Passos, *Theme Is Freedom*, p. 115.

52. Baker, Hemingway, pp. 300, 296–97, maintains that as late as January 1937, Hemingway's approach to the Spanish Civil War was essentially humanitarian rather than political.

53. New York *Times*, January 12, 1937.

54. *Ibid.*, January 30, 1937; "Spain in Flames," *Nation*, CXXXX (March 27, 1937), pp. 340–41; Baker, *Hemingway*, pp. 299–300.

55. A belated review of *Spain in Flames* claims that the dialogue for the film was jointly written by John Dos Passos and Archibald MacLeish. If this is correct, it was their original script which Hemingway discarded. "Spain in Flames," *Nation*, CXXXX (March 27, 1937), pp. 340–41.

56. John Dos Passos to E. E. Cummings, n.d., On the Volga River in the Soviet Union, Dos Passos Papers.

57. There is some confusion as to who originated the idea of making the film. Lillian Hellman, *An Unfinished Woman* (Boston, 1969), p. 66, fails to mention Dos Passos and gives all of the credit to MacLeish. Dos Passos, on the other hand, claims that Hellman "butted into the committee," and suggests that several people thought up the idea of the film collectively. Personal interview with John Dos Passos, May 27, 1969, Westmoreland, Virginia.

58. Joris Ivens was born in 1898 in the town of Nkimgen into a family which had been in the photography business for some years. He attended Rotterdam College of Economics for several semesters, but eventually transferred to the University of Charlottenburg in the suburbs of Berlin, where he studied photochemical techniques. He independently produced a first film, *The Bridge*, in 1928. Three years later, sponsored by the Soviet Union, he made *Komsomol*, which showed the sacrifices and heroism of the young Komsomol workers at the Magnitogorsk plant in the Ural Mountains. In 1934 his most highly acclaimed film, *New Earth*, was completed. It was a documentary of the way in which the Zuider Zee area in the Netherlands had been restored through a mammoth collective effort. Joris Ivens, "Ap-

prentice to Films," *Theatre Arts*, XXX (March-April 1946), pp. 178–80, 244–51; Robert Stebbins and Jay Leyda, "Joris Ivens: Artist in Documentary," *Magazine of Art*, XXXI (July 1938), pp. 392–99, 436–38; Erik Barnouw, *Documentary: A History of the Non-Fiction Film* (New York, 1977), pp. 77–80, 131–39.

59. Baker, *Hemingway*, p. 300.

60. Stebbins and Leyda, "Joris Ivens," p. 438; Dos Passos Interview. Lillian Hellman maintains in *An Unfinished Woman*, pp. 66, 104; that she was planning to meet Ivens in Spain, but had to postpone her plans due to illness. Eight months later when she finally reached Madrid, the film was completed.

61. Dos Passos, Personal Interview, recalled that Ivens was primarily interested in demonstrating through the film that as a result of the Civil War a new society was being molded out of the ruins of a feudal one. Since, however, the film was to be seen primarily by American audiences, he was persuaded to mute his ideology.

62. John Dos Passos, "Spanish Tragedy," typescript, n.d., pp. 7–8, Dos Passos Papers.

63. Fischer, *Men and Politics*, p. 429.

64. John Dos Passos, "The Death of José Robles," *New Republic*, XCIX (July 19, 1939), pp. 308–9.

65. John Dos Passos, Untitled handwritten manuscript, n.d., p. 4, Dos Passos Papers.

66. Interview with Dos Passos.

67. Josephine Herbst, "The Starched Blue Sky of Spain," *Noble Savage*, I (March 1960), p. 96.

68. *Ibid.*, p. 99. There will probably never be any way of determining whether Robles was innocent or guilty or, for that matter, what happened to him. Dos Passos writes in *The Theme Is Freedom* (p. 129) that the Russians "had him [Robles] put out of the way because he knew too much about the negotiations between the War Ministry and the Kremlin and was not, from their very special point of view, politically reliable." Louis Fischer, however (*Men and Politics*, p. 429), remembers that "whispers said he had talked too much and revealed military secrets in Madrid cafés. If that could have been proved it might have warranted turning him over to the Spanish government for trial, but not taking him for a ride." The issue was further debated in the *New Republic*, with Malcolm Cowley "Disillusionment," *New Republic*, CXIX (June 14, 1939), p. 153) differing with Dos Passos and defending the Spanish authorities because "people who ought to know tell me that the evidence against him was absolutely damning." Later, joining the fray, Matthew Josephson (*Infidel in the Temple*, p. 433) wrote

that some of his Loyalist friends told him that the Robles execution was a mistake, and that he had been guilty only of some indiscretions.

69. Baker, *Hemingway*, p. 312.

70. Dos Passos Interview.

71. Barnouw, *Documentary*, pp. 135–36, Baker, *Hemingway*, p. 315. Other, financial contributors were Dashiell Hammett, Lillian Hellman, Ralph Ingersoll, Archibald MacLeish, Gerald Murphy, Dorothy Parker, Herman Shumlin, and the North American Committee for Spain. *Ibid.*, p. 315n.

72. John T. McManus, "Realism Invades Gotham," New York *Times*, August 22, 1937; Otis Ferguson, "And There Were Giants in the Earth," *New Republic*, XCII (September 1, 1937), pp. 103–4. While generally favorable toward the film, another reviewer suggested that since *The Spanish Earth* was openly pro-Loyalist, it should have packed a more decidedly Loyalist punch. Donita Ferguson, "The Spanish Earth," *Literary Digest*, CXXIV (September 11, 1937), p. 33.

73. Ernest Hemingway, "The Writer and War," in Henry Hart, ed., *The Writer in a Changing World* (New York, 1937), p. 69.

74. Barnouw, *Documentary*, p. 136.

75. New York *Times*, September 25, November 8, 1937.

76. Vincent Sheean, *Not Peace But a Sword* (New York, 1939), pp. 248–49; New York *Times*, April 25, 1938.

77. Baker, *Hemingway*, p. 339.

78. In addition to making the film, Hemingway was often seen giving both encouragement and whisky from his pocket-flask to Loyalist soldiers. The German novelist, Gustav Regler, *The Owl of Minerva*, p. 297, remembered seeing him giving instructions to a young recruit on how to operate his weapon. Yet in spite of all of these other activities, *The Spanish Earth* remains Hemingway's most significant contribution to the Loyalist cause.

79. Ernest Hemingway to John Dos Passos, 1938, n.p., Dos Passos Papers.

80. Coco Robles to John Dos Passos, January 26, 1947, Versailles, Mexico; H. C. Lancaster to John Dos Passos, December 24, 1946, Baltimore, Dos Passos Papers. Among other things, Dos Passos tried to assist Robles's son in getting a scholarship to Johns Hopkins.

81. Guttman, *Wound in the Heart*, pp. 167–95.

82. Josephson, *Infidel in the Temple*, p. 425.

83. Virginia Cowles, *Looking for Trouble* (New York, 1941), p. 31.

84. Dos Passos Interview; Ernest Hemingway to John Dos Passos, June 26, 1931, Madrid, Spain, Dos Passos Papers.

85. Ilya Ehrenburg, *Memoirs: 1921–1941* (New York, 1941), p. 31.

86. After observing Hemingway in action around the Hotel Florida, Josie Herbst later wrote, "Starched Blue Sky of Spain," p. 93, that she believed "Hemingway was entering into some areas that were better known to people like Dos Passos, or even myself. He seemed to be naïvely embracing on the simpler levels the current ideologies at the very moment when Dos Passos was urgently questioning them." For a similar viewpoint see Herbert Solow, "Substitution, At Left Tackle: Hemingway and Dos Passos," *Partisan Review*, IV (April 1938), pp. 62–64.

87. Joseph North, *No Men Are Strangers* (New York, 1958), p. 143.

88. Hemingway, *Green Hills of Africa*, p. 70.

89. Ernest Hemingway, "Treachery in Aragon," *Ken*, I (June 30, 1938), p. 26.

90. Herbst, "Starched Blue Sky of Spain," pp. 80–81.

91. Dos Passos Interview.

92. Herbst, "Starched Blue Sky of Spain," p. 194.

93. Hemingway, "Treachery in Aragon," p. 620.

94. John Dos Passos, "Farewell to Europe," *Common Sense*, II (July 1937), p. 10.

95. John Dos Passos to E. E. Cummings, August 25, 1937, n.p., John Dos Passos Papers, Houghton Library, Harvard University, Cambridge, Massachusetts.

96. Edmund Wilson to John Dos Passos, November 26, 1966, Cape Cod, Dos Passos Papers.

97. Dos Passos, *The Best Times*, p. 232.

98. Ernest Hemingway to John Dos Passos, 1938, n.p., Dos Passos Papers.

99. Ernest Hemingway to John Dos Passos, October 30, 1951, San Francisco de Paula, Cuba, Dos Passos Papers.

CHAPTER 7: WALDO FRANK

1. "Obituary [Waldo Frank]," *Nation*, CCIV (January 23, 1967), p. 101.

2. Lewis Mumford, "Introduction," in Waldo Frank, *Memoirs of Waldo Frank*, ed. Alan Trachtenberg (University of Massachusetts Press, 1973), p. xvi.

3. *Ibid.*, p. xix.

4. Waldo Frank, *In the American Jungle* (New York, 1937), p. 6.

5. Frank, *Memoirs*, pp. 27–29.

6. Frank, *American Jungle*, p. 7.

7. Frank, *Memoirs*, p. 44.

8. Frank, *American Jungle*, p. 8.

9. *Ibid.*, p. 11.

10. Exuding the kind of optimism and excitement that Henry F. May claims characterized the years before World War I, James Oppenheim, "The Story of the Seven Arts," *American Mercury*, XX (June 1930), p. 156, recalls at the time he believed the United States to be the "lost soul" among nations. But he also believed that it could be regenerated through art. "I even had a definite idea as to how America was to become more human. It was the dream so many have had: a magazine, *the* magazine which should evoke and mobilize all our native talent, both creative and critical, give it freedom of expression and so scatter broadcast the new Americanism which would naturally have the response of America."

11. *Ibid.*, p. 158.

12. Van Wyck Brooks, "An American Oblomov," *Dial*, LXII (March 22, 1917), p. 245.

13. Frank, *Memoirs*, p. 99.

14. Van Wyck Brooks, *Days of the Phoenix* (New York, 1957), p. 26; Mumford, "Introduction," *Memoirs of Waldo Frank*, pp. xxvii-xxviii.

15. For a discussion of Freud's influence on Frank's thinking, see Frederick J. Hoffman, *Freudianism and the Literary Mind* (Baton Rouge, 1945), pp. 256–76.

16. Waldo Frank, *The Re-Discovery of America* (New York, 1929), p. 306. See also William Bittner, *The Novels of Waldo Frank* (Philadelphia, 1955), p. 16, for a brief discussion of Frank's views on universal unity.

17. Paul J. Carter, *Waldo Frank* (New York, 1967), preface. For a provocative analysis of Frank's cultural philosophy in comparison with other "Liberal Traditionalists," like Lewis Mumford and Archibald MacLeish, see R. Alan Lawson, *The Failure of Independent Liberalism 1930–1941* (New York, 1971), pp. 133–68.

18. Frank, *Re-Discovery of America*, p. 19.

19. Frank, *American Jungle*, p. 250.

20. Frank, *Re-Discovery of America*, pp. 11–66.

21. *Ibid.*, p. 16.

22. Waldo Frank, *Our American* (New York, 1919), pp. 148–49.

23. *Ibid.*, pp. 18–22.

24. *Ibid.*, p. 63; *American Jungle*, pp. 153–57.

25. Frank, *Our America*, p. 229.

26. *Ibid.*, pp. 94–95.

27. Waldo Frank, *South American Journey* (New York, 1943), p. 379.

28. Frank, *Memoirs*, p. 111.

29. Waldo Frank, *Virgin Spain: The Drama of a Great People* (New York, 1942), p. 162.

30. *Ibid.*, p. 130.

31. Allen Guttman, *Wound in the Heart*, p. 134, argues that writers like Brooks, Mumford, Frank, and others were naïve in their optimistic descriptions of an organic society that they found in Spain prior to and during the Civil War. Spanish society was rent with social tensions and was less, rather than more, unified than America. On the other hand, Guttman suggests that primitive conditions in Spain did insulate much of the population from the most oppressive aspects of industrialism. It was this latter aspect that was so appealing to many American writers and intellectuals.

32. Frank, *Virgin Spain*, p. 323.

33. Ernest Peixotto, "The Sound of Spain," *Saturday Review*, II (April 17, 1926), p. 720, found the book "vivid, clean-cut, and at times as baffling as a modernistic picture," whereas Gorham B. Munson, "Symphonic History," *New Republic*, XLVIII (May 26, 1926), p. 39, was most impressed with the author's aesthetic approach which unified the study. On the other hand, Muna Less, "Speaking of Spain, Here Is Waldo Frank," *New York Times*, April 18, 1926, lamented the fact that "where Mr. Frank might enchant he prefers to astound with willful flamboyance."

34. Arnold Chapman, "Waldo Frank in Spanish America: Between Journeys, 1924–1929," *Hispania*, XLVII (September 1964), p. 518.

35. *Ibid.*, p. 519.

36. *Ibid.*

37. *Ibid.*, pp. 520–21.

38. Robert Cahen Salaberry, "North America Looks South," *Living Age*, CCCXXXVIII (June 1, 1930), p. 424. A sampling of the lectures that Frank gave on this tour is found in the Waldo Frank Collection, Charles Patterson Van Pelt Library, University of Pennsylvania.

39. Waldo Frank, "What Is Hispano-America to Us?" *Scribner's Magazine*, LXXXVII (June 1930), p. 586.

40. Frank, *Memoirs*, pp. 160–61.

41. M. J. Benardette, ed., *Waldo Frank in America Hispaña* (New York, 1930), pp. 41, 223–25.

42. *Ibid.*, pp. 50–51, 127.

43. Frank, *Memoirs*, p. 166.

44. There is a scrapbook in the Frank Collection containing the South American newspaper and periodical reaction to his 1929 tour.

45. Waldo Frank, *Dawn in Russia: The Record of a Journey* (New York, 1932), pp. 246, 265.

46. Frank, *Memoirs*, p. 178.

47. Malcolm Cowley, "Kentucky Coal Town," *New Republic*, LXX (March 2, 1932), pp. 67–70.

48. Frank, *Memoirs*, p. 196.

49. Aaron, *Writers on the Left*, pp. 301–2, 321–22.

50. New York *Times*, December 27, 1936.

51. Waldo Frank, "Moscow Trials," *New Republic*, XCI (May 12, 1937), pp. 19–20.

52. Carter, *Waldo Frank*, p. 118; New York *Times*, August 16, 1938.

53. Waldo Frank, "Spain in War," *New Republic*, XCV (July 13, 20, 27, 1938), pp. 269–72, 298–301, 325–27.

54. New York *Times*, June 6, 1940.

55. Carter, *Waldo Frank*, p. 152.

56. Notebook XV, Frank Collection.

57. "Waldo Frank Attacked in Argentina," *Publisher's Weekly*, CXLII (August 8, 1942), pp. 375–76.

58. New York *Times*, August 2, 1942. For the financial arrangements of the trip, see C. Halliwell Duell to Max Putzel, March 19, 1942, Frank Collection.

59. Two interesting discussions of the Popular Front mentality in the United States are Pells, *Radical Visions and American Dreams*, pp. 292–329, and Lawson, *The Failure of Independent Liberalism 1930–41*, pp. 133–79.

60. Frank, *South American Journey*, p. 80.

61. Hubert Herring, *A History of Latin America* (New York, 1962), pp. 674–76.

62. Frank, *South American Journey*, p. 207.

63. *Ibid.*, p. 76.

64. *Ibid.*, p. 384.

65. *Ibid.*, p. 82.

66. Notebook XVI, Frank Collection; *South American Journey*, p. 83.

67. Frank, *South American Journey*, pp. 85, 90, 199.

68. *Ibid.*, p. 129.

69. Notebook XVI, Frank Collection.

70. Frank, *South American Journey*, p. 205.

71. *Ibid.*, p. 387.

72. *Ibid.*, p. 212.

73. *Ibid.*, pp. 214–17.

74. New York *Times*, August 3, 1942.

75. H. B. Murkland, "The Waldo Frank Affair," *Current History*, III (October 1942); New York *Times*, August 22, 1942.

76. *Ibid.*, October 30, 1942.

77. Waldo Frank to the North American Newspaper Alliance, Buenos Aires, August 4, 1942, Frank Collection.

78. Frank, *American Jungle*, p. 273.

79. Arnold Chapman, "Waldo Frank in the Hispanic World: The First Phase," *Hispania*, XLIV (December 1961), p. 632.

80. Frank, *Our America*, p. 96; *South American Journey*, pp. 336–37.

81. Waldo Frank, "Our America: 1942," *American Mercury*, LIV (January 1942), p. 72.

82. Typescript, Box 33, Frank Collection.

83. Frank, *South American Journey*, p. 87.

84. Notebook XV, Frank Collection.

85. Robert Van Gelder, "An Interview with Mr. Waldo Frank," New York *Times*, April 19, 1942.

86. Mumford, "Introduction," *Memoirs of Waldo Frank*, p. xxii.

CHAPTER 8: EZRA POUND

1. Reynolds and Eleanor Packard, *Balcony Empire* (New York, 1942), p. 250.

2. Walter Laquer, "Literature and the Historian," in *Literature and Politics in the Twentieth Century*, ed. Walter Laquer and George L. Mosse (New York, 1967), p. 14. Laquer suggests that there is a danger among writers, theologians, scientists, and television personalities as well as other "experts" in a given field to believe that their expertise in one area automatically carries over into other areas—especially into the realm of politics.

3. William Carlos Williams to his mother, March 30, 1904, U. of P. Dorms, in *The Selected Letters of William Carlos Williams*, ed. John S. Thirlwall (New York, 1957), p. 6.

4. Ezra Pound, *The Spirit of Romance* (New York, 1968), p. 7.

5. Ezra Pound, *Patria Mia* (London, 1962), pp. 68–69.

6. Quoted in Charles Norman, *Ezra Pound* (New York, 1960), p. 21.

7. Ezra Pound, "Where Is American Culture?" *Nation*, CXXVI (April 18, 1928), pp. 443–44.

8. Charles Norman, in *Pound*, pp. 23, 24, suggests that Pound's dismissal from Wabash was a major turning-point in his life. In spite of his affinity for European life, Pound also might have remained in the United States had the University of Pennsylvania offered him a position. Norman believes that had it not been for these two failures Pound might have been both a great teacher and a great poet.

9. Ezra Pound to William Carlos Williams, February 3, 1909, *The*

Letters of Ezra Pound 1907–1941, ed. D. D. Paige (New York, 1950), p. 7.

10. Noel Stock, ed. *Ezra Pound: Perspectives* (Chicago, 1965), p. viii; also see Donald Gallup, *Bibliography of Ezra Pound* (London, 1963).

11. Steffens, *Autobiography*, p. 833.

12. Ernest Hemingway, *A Moveable Feast* (New York, 1964), p. 110.

13. Pound, *Patria Mia*, pp. 61–62.

14. *Ibid.*, pp. 26–27. The Harvard-educated poet Michael Reck writes in *Ezra Pound: A Close Up* (New York, 1967), pp. 116–27, that not since Whitman has there been a poet who believed so wholeheartedly in the possibility of the American Dream being fulfilled.

15. Ezra Pound to Harriet Monroe, January 1915, *Letters*, p. 48. Pound never ceased believing that he was personally responsible for keeping the arts alive and assisting fellow-American artists. In another letter, Ezra Pound to Felix E. Schelling, April 1934, *ibid.*, p. 256, he explained: "What little life has been kept in American letters has been largely due to a few men getting out of the muck and keeping the poor devils who couldn't at least informed."

16. Ezra Pound, *Poetry*, V (October 1914), p. 30.

17. Several of Pound's biographers feel that early financial difficulties had much to do with shaping many of his later economic viewpoints. C. David Heymann, *Ezra Pound: The Last Rower* (New York, 1976), p. 34; William M. Chace, *The Political Identities of Ezra Pound and T. S. Eliot* (Stanford, 1973), p. 18; Noel Stock, *The Life of Ezra Pound* (New York, 1970), pp. 1–35.

18. Patricia Hutchins, *Ezra Pound's Kensington: An Exploration 1885–1913* (London, 1965), p. 48.

19. Ezra Pound to Felix E. Schelling, April, 1934, *Letters*, p. 256. Pound continued to be obsessed with the fact that he could not support himself in the United States, and pointed out to a literary acquaintance (Ezra Pound to Douglas McPherson, September, 1939, *ibid.*, p. 325), "America does not pay me 500 dollars a year and I imagine Williams and Cummings get even less for their writings."

20. Pound, *Patria Mia*, p. 42.

21. Ezra Pound Papers, Beinecke Library, Yale University. Hereafter cited as Pound Papers (Y).

22. John Cournos, *Autobiography* (New York, 1935), p. 236.

23. Ezra Pound to William Carlos Williams, March 18, 1922, *Letters*, p. 172.

24. Quoted in Reck, *Ezra Pound: A Close Up*, p. 35. Pound believed that he could speak from personal experience about the financial difficulties of being an artist, for, as he wrote (*ABC of Economics* (London, 1933), p.

56), "I am an expert. I have lived nearly all my life, at any rate all my adult life, among the unemployed. All the arts have been unemployed in my time."

25. Earle Davis, *Vision Fugitive, Ezra Pound and Economics* (Lawrence, Kansas, 1968), pp. 49–50.

26. *Ibid.*, pp. 50–51. Davis offers an interesting and plausible explanation for Pound's transition from Guild Socialism to the corporate state by comparing similarities of the two theories, especially the projected partnership between labor and management.

27. Stock, *The Life of Ezra Pound*, p. 184.

28. Ezra Pound, *Gaudier-Brzeska: A Memoir* (New York, 1970), p. 17.

29. Donald Hall, "Ezra Pound," in *Writers at Work: The Paris Review Interviews*, 2nd series, ed. Malcolm Cowley (New York, 1963), p. 51.

30. Davis, *Vision Fugitive*, pp. 51–52.

31. Pound, *Patria Mia*, p. 21.

32. Ezra Pound, *Impact: Essays on Ignorance and the Decline of American Civilization*, ed. Noel Stock (Chicago, 1960), p. 33.

33. Davis suggests in *Vision Fugitive*, p. 71, that both Major Douglas and Pound were deeply indebted to Marx's theory of surplus value.

34. *Ibid.*, pp. 69–75.

35. Pound, *ABC of Economics*, pp. 17–18.

36. Pound, *What Is Money For?* (London, 1951), p. 7.

37. Davis, *Vision Fugitive*, p. 76.

38. *Ibid.*, p. 79. Pound never strayed from the capitalistic system in his economic thinking. Although he did not want business to be taken over by the government, he did believe that banks and the monetary privileges that they possessed should be more tightly controlled by the government.

39. Ezra Pound, *A Visiting Card* (London, 1952), p. 27.

40. Pound, *ABC of Economics*, p. 93.

41. Pound's daughter, May de Rachewiltz, describes her unconventional life in *Discretions* (Boston, 1971).

42. Ezra Pound to Morton Dauwen Zabel, Rapallo, November 25, 1934, in Morton Dauwen Zabel Papers, Joseph Regenstein Library, University of Chicago.

43. Ezra Pound, *Social Credit: An Impact* (London, 1951), p. 15.

44. Ezra Pound, *Jefferson and/or Mussolini* (New York, 1935), *passim*.

45. Noel Stock, *Poet in Exile* (Manchester, Eng., 1964), p. 209.

46. Two excellent discussions of Pound's interpretation of American history are: Davis: *Vision Fugitive*, pp. 115–45; Stock, *Poet in Exile*, pp. 210-19.

47. Davis, *Vision Fugitive*, p. 213.

48. Pound, *Jefferson and/or Mussolini*, p. 120.

49. Pound, *Social Credit*, pp. 6–7.

50. Pound, *Jefferson and/or Mussolini*, pp. 94, 108, 127.

51. *Ibid.*, p. 33. Davis, *Vision Fugitive*, pp. 156–57, claims that the Italian economic theorist and minor fascist official Odon Por had an important influence on Pound shortly before the beginning of the war by convincing him of the good intentions and proper direction of Mussolini's economic programs.

52. Pound, *Jefferson and/or Mussolini*, p. vii.

53. Pound, *A Visiting Card*, p. 7.

54. Pound, *Jefferson and/or Mussolini*, p. 12.

55. *Ibid.*, p. 98.

56. Stock, *The Life of Ezra Pound*, p. 325, claims that beginning in the 1930s both the direction and intent of Pound's correspondence began to take on nightmarish aspects.

57. Louis Simpson, *Three on the Tower: The Lives and Works of Ezra Pound, T. S. Eliot and William Carlos Williams* (New York, 1975), p. 75.

58. Stock, *The Life of Ezra Pound*, pp. 306–7.

59. Phyllis Bottome, *From the Life* (London, 1946), p. 80.

60. Charles Norman, *The Case of Ezra Pound* (New York, 1968), p. 37; William Van O'Connor and Edward Stone, *A Casebook on Ezra Pound* (Cornwall, N. Y., 1959), p. 147.

61. Mary de Rachewiltz, *Discretions*, p. 118.

62. Heyman, *Last Rower*, pp. 84–86.

63. Ezra Pound to J. H. Voorhis, September 15, 1939, Pound Papers (Y).

64. *Ibid.*, October 24, 1939, Rapallo.

65. Heymann, *Last Rower*, pp. 95–99.

66. Ezra Pound to E. E. Cummings, 5 or 6 maggio, Rapallo, Ezra Pound Papers, Houghton Library, Harvard University. Hereafter cited as Pound Papers (H).

67. Ezra Pound to James Angleton, 7 June [1940], Rapallo, Pound Papers (Y).

68. Ezra Pound to E. E. Cummings, Rapallo, 8 Giugn, 1940, Pound Papers (H).

69. Ezra Pound to James Angleton, 7 June [1940], Rapallo, Pound Papers (Y).

70. Unless otherwise cited, Pound's wartime radio broadcasts are taken from *"Ezra Pound Speaking" Radio Speeches of World War II*, ed. Leonard W. Doob (Westport, Conn., 1978).

71. Heymann, *The Last Rower*, p. 99.

72. *"Ezra Pound Speaking,"* p. xi.

73. Heymann, *The Last Rower*, p. 102.

74. For a quantitative analysis of the various themes of the broadcasts, see *"Ezra Pound Speaking,"* Appendix 2, pp. 417–25.

75. Julien Cornell, *The Trial of Ezra Pound* (New York, 1966), p. 22.

76. Eustace Mullins, *This Difficult Individual, Ezra Pound* (New York, 1961), p. 246. Page has written an autobiographical account of his experiences, *L'Americano di Roma* (Milano, 1950).

77. Charles Norman in *Pound*, pp. 383–84, has examined the incident in depth and has found nothing to substantiate precisely what happened. On the other hand, Richard Rovere, *The American Establishment* (New York, 1962), p. 220, categorically states that Pound was refused permission to board the last diplomatic train that Americans took from Rome to Lisbon. Mary de Rachewiltz, *Discretions*, pp. 145–46, mentions the fact that officials at the American Consulate were "nasty," but offers no further clarification. Finally, Heymann, *Last Rower*, p. 109, believes that Pound may have brought the trouble on himself by giving the fascist salute when entering and leaving the Consulate.

78. *"Ezra Pound Speaking,"* p. xi.

79. Mary de Rachewiltz, *Discretions*, pp. 173–74.

80. Heymann, *Last Rower*, p. 75. See Chace, *The Political Identities of Ezra Pound and T. S. Eliot*, pp. 39–43, 71–85, for a discussion of both the personal and intellectual sides of Pound's anti-Semitism. A somewhat different approach is that of Michael Reck, *Ezra Pound: A Close Up*, pp. 58–59, who argues that Pound's anti-Semitism increased as Mussolini introduced anti-Jewish laws into Italy from 1938 to 1940.

81. "Yankee Accents in the Axis," *Newsweek*, XVII (March 17, 1941), p. 64.

82. New York *Times*, August 1, 1943.

83. Eunice Tietjens, "The End of Ezra Pound," *Poetry*, LX (April 1942), p. 39; Malcolm Cowley, "Books and People," *New Republic*, CIX (November 15, 1943), p. 689.

84. Paul Rosenfeld, "The Case of Ezra Pound," *American Mercury*, LVIII (January 1944), p. 98.

85. Heymann, *Last Rower*, pp. 99–102.

86. William Carlos Williams, *Autobiography* (New York, 1948), pp. 316–18.

87. Quoted in Reck, *Ezra Pound: A Close Up*, pp. 60–62.

88. Heymann, *Last Rower*, pp. 147–51.

89. *"Ezra Pound Speaking,"* p. xi.

90. The testimony of the four psychiatrists is found in Norman, *Case of Ezra Pound*, pp. 106–77.

91. Wyndam Lewis, "The Rock Drill," in Stock, *Perspectives*, p. 201.

92. Norman, *Pound*, p. 387, and Reck, *Ezra Pound: A Close Up*, p. 130, believe that much of Pound's wartime behavior is to be explained primarily as the result of mental disorders. Noel Stock (*The Life of Ezra Pound*, 460) also believes that Pound was on the brink of madness during the 1930s whereas Earle Davis, (*Vision Fugitive*, 113,) more or less skirts the issue by describing Pound as a "flawed idealist." On the other hand, two of his more recent biographers tend to agree with Pound's daughter, (*Discretions*, 173) that her father had lost his grip on reality by the time of the broadcasts: Heymann, *Last Rower*, p. 115, and Chase, *The Political Identities of Ezra Pound and T. S. Eliot*, p. 85.

93. Ezra Pound, *ABC of Reading* (New York, 1960), p. 32.

94. Pound, *ABC of Economics*, p. 67.

95. Stephen Spender, "Writers and Politics," *Partisan Review*, XXXIV (Summer 1967), p. 377.

96. William Carlos Williams, "Ezra Pound: Lord Ga Ga," *Decision* (September 19, 1941), pp. 16–24.

97. Williams, *Autobiography*, pp. 56–57. William Butler Yeats likewise confirmed Pound's lack of musical ability. See Stock, *The Life of Ezra Pound*, p. 72.

98. In the course of his May 9, 1942, broadcast, Pound announced that he was no longer a follower of Major Douglas's social credit theory: "No, I am not a social creditor. I passed by that alley away. I am a national money man." One may assume that Pound considered Mussolini and Hitler to be national money men as well.

99. Norman, *Pound*, p. 396.

100. Pound, *What Is Money For?*, p. 7.

101. Ezra Pound to George Santayana, January 16, 1940, *Letters*, p. 333.

CHAPTER 9: RETROSPECT AND PROSPECT

1. Personal interview with Malcolm Cowley, August 31, 1968, Sherman, Connecticut.

2. Stanley Weintraub, *Last Great Cause*, p. 262, describes how Errol Flynn dashed into Republican Spain during the Civil War with the obvious intention of enhancing his already substantial swashbucklng reputation rather than making any significant contribution to the Loyalists. Flynn was

but one of a number of American celebrities who crossed the Pyrenees, believing that their presence near the front was service enough to the Republican cause.

3. Russell Lynes, "The Artist as Uneconomic Man," *Saturday Review*, LIII (February 28, 1970), p. 79.

4. I am indebted to Harold W. Cruse for information pertaining to Gibson's activities in Algeria. Harold W. Cruse to Author, April 14, 1971, Ann Arbor, Michigan.

5. Arnold Toynbee, *America and the World Revolution* (London, 1962), pp. 92–93.

6. *Ibid.*, p. 101.

Index